Contents

Right parenting

New Age Parenting and Child-Health Handbook

DR. MANDAR V. BICHU
M.D., D.C.H.

Popular Prakashan
www.popularprakashan.com

Published by Harsha Bhatkal
for Popular Prakashan Pvt. Ltd.
301, Mahalaxmi Chambers
22, Bhulabhai Desai Road
Mumbai 400026
www.popularprakashan.com

First Published 2015

(4415)
ISBN 978-81-7991-856-2

Printed by
Saurabh Printers Pvt. Ltd.
A-16, Sector 4, Noida

Foreword

It is not easy to be a parent in today's world. The pressures of the nuclear family, the problems of working parents and the exposure a child gets in this era of technology require special skills to bring up a child. The future of your child balances on two pivots—Nature, which works through inherited genes over which we do not have much control and nurture, which includes parenting, the school environment, friends and peers and, of course, the cyber world . The most important aspect is parenting because it influences the child's attitude to the other aspects of nurture. Unfortunately, we are never taught parenting in school and college and are often influenced by how our parents brought us up. This could be good or not so good. (They did just the right thing, or I never will bring up my child the way my parents did.)

Dr. Mandar V. Bichu's book on parenting fills this gap. In simple language, he covers normal aspects of child care, starting with advice for parents to be. There is a much needed chapter on breastfeeding and other aspects of growth and advice on prevention of diseases and accidents as well as common illnesses in childhood. Travel tips will be a boon to parents who take regular vacations. The chapter on the cyberworld is of special significance, and I advise parents to pay particular attention to it.

This book is a simple and useful guide to parents and will benefit them and their children.

Dr. Armida Fernandez
Former Dean of LTM General Hospital, Mumbai
and Founder of N.G.O. SNEHA

(After completing her medical education with multiple medals and honours, Dr. Armida Fernandez joined the LTMG Hospital and LTM Medical College, one of the premier medical colleges in Mumbai. She spent almost three decades in that institution as professor of paediatrics and neonatology and retired as dean of that institution. She pioneered the cause of neonatology in the country and started the first NICU in Mumbai. She also set up the first human milk bank in the country. After retirement, she started the non-government organisation SNEHA (Society for Nutrition, Education and Health Action) that works on replicable, sustainable health projects for women and children in the slums of Mumbai. For her exceptional work, she has received many awards from various government and private bodies. In 2007, she was selected as one of the 50 most powerful women in India by the magazine *Femina*.)

Preface

What has changed in the twenty-plus years that I have spent as a qualified paediatrician and freelance writer-journalist? I guess many things—socio-cultural trends, media proliferation and technology invasion being the foremost outside the sphere of medicine. In these years, medical science has made great strides in developing newer treatments and technologies but has suffered in one basic area.

I sincerely feel that doctor-patient communication has deteriorated in modern medical practice. Most patients and parents must have experienced that, when they visit their doctors, there is hardly any interaction. The patient comes into the doctor's room, tells his symptoms, gets a quick check-up and then leaves with a prescription and sometimes an investigation form. Patient education, which ideally should be a major part of medical practice, is hardly given any consideration.

The confused patients and parents then seek solace in guidance from family and friends and also turn to that all-encompassing knowledge tool called the Internet! Wrong information from these sources presents its own dangers, but even when correct, it is mostly just raw data without any interpretation based on experience and training. This kind of information leads to further confusion. The difference between information and knowledge—and that between knowledge and wisdom—these subtleties are lost in this era of excessive reliance on search engine results and online encyclopaedias.

The result of this confused parental attitude is apparent in the family's poor lifestyle choices, the parents' panic in handling common health problems and the children's poor discipline and behaviour. For this situation to improve, the medical fraternity has to come forward and engage in a meaningful dialogue with the patient and parent community, using all possible platforms.

With this goal in mind, over the past two decades, I have been writing articles in major newspapers and magazines in the United Arab Emirates (where I have been residing since 1993). The first version of *Right Parenting* was published in 2008, exactly a year after my web portal www.rightparenting.com was launched.

The basic idea behind these initiatives was the same, to give scientifically correct and timely guidance about basic parenting and child health concepts, using jargon-free, everyday language. I feel that this is important to do because if the basic concepts are not clear, the execution is bound to be faulty. The same theme continues in this book.

This totally revised, updated and expanded new version bears the title *Right Parenting: New-Age Handbook of Parenting and Child Health*. It is specifically written for parents in the age of the web. Contemporary issues such as the effect of media, advertisements and technology.

The medical information has been referenced from authoritative textbooks and authentic websites. But more importantly, I have tried to give a personal touch to the proceedings by including things such as real life scenarios, myth versus reality sections and plain thinking aloud articles.

In this era of globalisation, the western (American or European) parenting perspective is freely available through many well-written books and comprehensive websites. Unfortunately, the Indian (or rather the Indian sub-continental) parenting perspective has not found that wide an expression through print and online media. This book is an effort in that direction, too. My own Indian upbringing and thought process have definitely come through in many discussions. Hopefully, that will resonate with the Indian sub-continental parent, who sometimes feels alienated from the commonly available parenting information.

The most important ingredient in this writing endeavour is not my medical expertise but rather my own parenting experience. I still remember that our examiner for the M.D. (paediatrics) exam, Dr. Mrs. Puri (a lovely lady sadly no longer with us), had said that we would understand real paediatrics only when we ourselves become parents. I understood the wisdom of her statement only gradually as I first became a father and later watched my two daughters grow up.

This journey taught me so many things. My wife Dr. Shubhada's immeasurable value in bringing up our daughters reinforced my belief that mothers are the true backbones of any family. My two daughters—Pallavi and Apoorvaa—made me realise that even extensive paediatric training cannot make you a perfect parent. In fact, there is no such thing as perfect parenting. Every day, every week, every year—in fact, every moment—is a new challenge that needs to be dealt with practicality, sensibility and sensitivity.

The moment a baby arrives in this world, parents are presented with a unique opportunity to shape a new life and take it in the right direction. This journey is not straightforward; there are many bridges to cross and many pitfalls to avoid. Parents will often stumble, lose their way and even feel frustrated. But ultimately it is a rewarding and enriching experience.

No book can prepare parents fully for this challenging journey, but a concise handbook is useful as a handy companion and guide. If this book serves that purpose, I may have done my duty as a writer.

I sincerely thank the *Khaleej Time*s and *Gulf News* editorial teams. It was because of their encouragement that I could give free expression to my thoughts. I reserve special thanks for Mr. Sudhir Shetty, Mr. Sudhesh Giriyan and Dr. B. R. Shetty for supporting my website www.rightparenting.com and providing me with an opportunity to engage in regular Right Parenting community health training sessions.

I am grateful to my friend, reputed dentist- maxillofacial surgeon Dr. Sanjay Kalvani for his guidance and inputs in writing the chapter on Dental Care. A lot of credit for this revised, reader-friendly new edition goes to Popular Prakashan's Mr. Satyajit Bhatkal, Mr. Harsha Bhatkal, Mrs. Swapna Pandit-Shinde, Ms. Armaity and the entire team for their constant encouragement and my editor Ms. Aparna Tulpule for her excellent editing skills.

And the biggest thanks are to all my medical college teachers, particularly two great personalities, Dr. Armida Fernandez and Dr. M. R. Lokeshwar, without whose blessings I would not have had the opportunity to practice the socially and emotionally fulfilling medical profession in the field of paediatrics.

Dr. Mandar V. Bichu

M.D., D.C.H.

(Founder, Right Parenting Lifestyle

Guidance Program and www.rightparenting.com.

You can reach me at drmandarvb@yahoo.com.)

I

New Baby Blues: The First Challenges

1

Ten Commandments for Parents-to-Be!

Scenario

9 am

Suresh and Seema are over the moon. Their doctor has confirmed that Seema is pregnant. They even see the baby inside her on the ultrasound monitor! Wow, it's so cool!

9:15 am

They come out of the doctor's room. The elation on their faces is slowly giving way to tension and apprehension.

Seema is remembering the problems her friend faced during pregnancy. She is also thinking of her mother's hundred suggestions to prepare her for motherhood!

Suresh is already worrying about how his happy married life is soon going to change into an endless circus of sleepless nights, nappy changes and feeding schedules! He is secretly making a budget so that his salary can cover future expenditure demands!

The worst thing of all? They still have 9 months to go through!

Discussion

What is the most tedious part of becoming new parents? Take my word for it, it is the waiting period of 9 months that seems unending—a period in which countless pundits(!) offer 'wise' words to the already anxious would-be parents, confusing them out of their wits.

The do's and don'ts of pregnancy and the effects and after-effects of the baby are described in such exaggerated fashion that, come D-day—I mean the delivery—most parents wait for the bundle of joy with a sense of trepidation, and not a few with downright terror!

But things are not so difficult if you plan this event properly.

Here are 10 Golden rules for new parents-to-be:

1. **Don't give a damn what anybody says (except, of course, your family doctor).**

   No, I am not telling you to show the concerned (and usually ill-informed) kith and kin the door. Just listen to them as you do to forgettable songs!

   Remember one thing: Being parents or grandparents of one, two or even a dozen children does not make a person knowledgeable about the intricacies of pregnancy or parenting. Just do the 'ignoring' tactfully and take care not to offend the well-wishers by telling them that they are out of tune with changing times. They are only trying to help and you would need all their emotional support before and after the birth of your baby.

2. **Be well informed.**

   Find books on topics such as pregnancy and parenting written by real experts and not by self-proclaimed gurus. Before buying a book, check the author's credentials. Make sure that he or she has the requisite medical degree to offer you good advice. Also check the style of writing to see whether it interests you. Medical facts, if told in a dry manner, can be a real drag to read.

   The Internet has become a great source of information. Parenting sites, notice boards, discussion groups give a wealth of interesting information. Again, you will have to sieve that information because there is no shortage of 'quack' websites. Websites of international health organisations, medical professional's associations and reputed hospitals are usually safe as sources of reliable information.

3. **Be positive in your outlook.**

   Having a baby is, indeed, one of the greatest joys of life. The caring and sharing of parenting are among the most emotionally enriching facets of human life. Embrace this event with joy enthusiasm.

4. **Be prepared for changes in your lifestyle.**

   Yes, the baby is going to make you change a lot. But isn't change a rule of nature? Don't be over-anxious about those sleepless nights, changing of nappies and feeding problems associated with babies. You will manage to cross those bridges when you come to them. It's not as difficult as it seems!

5. **Take care of health.**

   The care for the mother and the baby inside her is the prime concern during the pregnancy. Regular antenatal check-ups, proper nutrition, necessary nutritional supplements (iron, folic acid) and timely vaccination (against tetanus and hepatitis B) are easily ensured by selecting a reliable healthcare provider.

6. **Select a doctor and devise a plan for pregnancy and delivery.**

   Choose a doctor who not only has a good reputation but has enough time for you and is sympathetic and sensitive. Give the doctor full cooperation. Do not hesitate to discuss your concerns, fears and even minor worries bothering you. Let these discussions involve both the husband and the wife.

   If the prospective mother has any chronic illness such as diabetes, high blood pressure, asthma or thyroid problems, give the details of previous investigations and treatments. This way, the doctor can anticipate likely complications and devise a plan to counter them.

   Strictly follow all medical instructions.

7. **Be friendly with the doctor.**

   Instead of just maintaining a strict professional relationship with your doctor, try and be friendly with him or her. This almost always helps build trust and confidence.

8. **Be open-minded.**

   Don't have fixed ideas about the nature of delivery such as natural or 'normal' delivery versus medically assisted delivery such as caesarean. Don't have fixed ideas about having a baby of a particular sex.

   In spite of the great advances in medical technology, no one can predict every case with certainty.

9. **Develop your concept of the family.**

   Both of you—the husband and the wife—should be clear about the size and type of family you are planning, keeping in mind your present and future plans. It is most important that both parents support each other emotionally.

   Pregnancy and parenting are emotionally demanding states for the mother as well as the father. So, work like a team.

10. Relax and enjoy!

Being relaxed and happy is the most essential condition of parenting. Being grumpy and uptight about issues won't help.

These are the ten golden rules for would-be parents. Follow these ten commandments, and you will be happy and confident parents when your bundle of joy arrives on the D-day!

2

Routine Baby Care

Scenario

The wait is finally over. Seema and Suresh are now proud new parents!

The delivery was normal and the adorable baby girl came into this world with a loud, lusty cry. Today is the second day of her life. The doctor has examined mother and child and found them to be ready to be discharged.

The new mother and father are once again facing the familiar blues: How are we going to manage this bundle of joy at home, on our own?

Discussion

Taking care of a normal newborn baby up to her first birthday is not at all difficult if you follow these simple guidelines.

Parents' mood

- Don't burden yourself with worry and anxiety.
- Everything is new, and you may get worried by many things about your baby's physical appearance or breathing, crying, feeding or sleeping pattern. Rest assured that most of what you observe does not indicate that there is something wrong with her.

  'When Abnormal is Normal!' has more about this point.

Warmth

Your baby is going to need plenty of warmth, both physically and emotionally. Your loving presence is enough to provide her with emotional warmth. For keeping her physically warm, these are some guidelines.

- **Room temperature**

  ♦ If you have an air-conditioner, keep the room temperature between 20°C and 22°C.

- **Layered clothing**

  In the early months, the baby will need multiple layers of clothing, such as undershirt, nappy, pyjamas and a wrap-around blanket, to keep her warm. But in hot climates (above 24°C), single-layered clothing may be enough.

  ♦ If the room feels too cold to you, add a cap, gloves and socks to the baby's clothing.

  ♦ A simple rule is that, at any temperature, add one layer for the baby to what you are comfortable wearing. If you are wearing two layers of clothing, the baby needs three.

  ♦ If your baby's skin is hot to the touch, you are probably overclothing her.

  ♦ Do not overclothe the baby as it may lead to overheating, excessive sweating and dehydration.

Skin care

- **Bath**

  ♦ Until the baby's umbilical cord falls off by the 7th to the 10th day, give your baby sponge baths. Later, you can start bathing her daily. If you live in a cold climate, you may bathe her on alternate days.

  ♦ Use comfortably warm water for the baby's baths and make sure that it is not too hot.

  ♦ Use a mild baby soap.

  ♦ In the early months, keep the baths short (5–10 minutes) and, pat dry the baby with a towel immediately after the bath, making sure that she is not exposed too long to outside temperatures.

- **Applications and massage**

  ♦ Apply fragrance-free moisturizing baby lotion immediately after towelling dry the skin.

  ♦ Do not use baby talcum powder as its small particles may be inhaled, entering the baby's lungs and causing problems.

♦ Do not use skin care products that are not specifically made for babies.

♦ Do not apply *besan* (chick-pea flour) to make the baby fairer! It neither makes the skin lighter nor removes the facial or body hair.

♦ Do not apply *kaajal* or *surma* (kohl) in or around the baby's eyes. They may contain harmful chemicals.

♦ Do not put oil in the baby's nose or ears to clean them. These practices can sometimes cause serious medical problems. Remember, babies are naturally clean and beautiful. We must not do these needless things just because they are popular customs.

♦ Body massage using oil is another popular, long-standing Indian custom and is okay to do provided there is no skin reaction such as redness or a rash. Olive, almond or coconut oil is as good for the baby's massage as any expensive baby oil.

♦ Beware of the person giving the massage, though! The masseurs, who are usually old women with a repertoire of massaging tales, often give needless and potentially harmful baby care suggestions and have harmful practices such as milking baby breasts.

♦ It is better that the mother gives the baby a massage herself. The baby will enjoy it much more, and it will help mother-baby bonding.

- **Hair and nails**

♦ If you want to apply oil to the baby's scalp, do it half an hour before the bath. Once again, plain olive, almond or coconut oil is as effective as any expensive baby oil.

♦ Use a mild baby shampoo for washing hair and make sure to wash off the oil.

♦ Dry the washed hair immediately and then gently comb it to keep it tangle-free.

♦ Shaving off hair completely in infancy is a popular Indian custom, sometimes for religious reasons and sometimes with the hope of stimulating better hair growth. This custom has no effect on hair growth but can cause scalp or hair infection from unhygienic razors. In fact, the shaving may damage the hair roots and cause future hair problems!

♦ Carefully trim the baby's nails with baby nail clippers or blunt nail scissors. Baby's fingernails grow fast and may need to be cut once a week or even twice a week. Her toenails grow slowly and usually need a monthly trimming.

Umbilical care

- Properly clean the umbilicus with a spirit swab until the cord falls off and the area becomes dry.
- If there is any redness, discharge or foul smell, take the baby to the doctor, who will probably prescribe an antibiotic ointment for external application.

Eye care

- If there is any eye discharge, wipe it off with lukewarm water.
- If the discharge continues or increases, use eye drops or ointment according to your doctor's advice.

Feeding

- Breast feeding is the best feeding and should be the first and only type of feeding whenever possible. In the first 2–3 days, the mother usually has yellow, thick milk in small quantities. This early milk is called 'colostrum' and is enough to take care of the baby's needs. So, the small quantity is a reason to start outside milk feeds. Plus, this milk provides your baby with protective antibodies.
- Bottle feeding is a compromise, and its pitfalls must be understood before starting it. Never start bottle feeding, or any additional or replacement feeding, without discussing it with your doctor.
- The feeding schedule should be a semi-demand schedule. That means regular feeds every 2–3 hours when the baby is awake and additional feeds if the baby demands them between the regular scheduled feeds.

Stools

- The first baby stools, called meconium, are thick and dark black or dark green. The baby will pass meconium within the first 24 hours after birth.
- The next few stools are yellow-green.

- Breast-fed babies' stools are yellowish with runny, curd-like consistency. They are sometimes also described as light mustard in colour with seed-like particles.
- Formula-fed babies' stools are slightly firmer and look tan or yellow.
- Once the baby is weaned off breast milk and is on other foods, the stools may become more firm and look light yellow or brownish. They may sometimes show undigested food particles.
- There may be some day-to-day variations in colour, consistency, smell and number of stools. If the baby is otherwise active, feeding normally and growing well, such changes shouldn't worry you.
- A milk-fed baby, particularly a breast-fed baby, may pass stools only once in 4–7 days. This is considered normal if the stool consistency is soft and the baby is not showing any discomfort, vomiting or abdominal distension (swollen stomach). Check with the doctor if any of these associated symptoms are present.
- Seek immediate medical attention if the stool has blood, looks like currant-jelly, is colourless or white or if there are frequent, watery motions.

Urination

- A well-fed baby passes urine 6–8 times in a day.
- The colour of urine derives from the body's chemical waste products and depends on how dilute or concentrated the urine is.
- The usual colour of urine is light to dark yellow.
- When the baby is passing urine after a long time or in situations such as hot weather or fever, the urine may be concentrated (less dilute) and appear dark yellow.
- Highly concentrated urine may leave a pinkish or red-orange (brick-coloured) spot on the nappy. This colour comes from the crystals formed by the chemicals, urates and calcium in the urine and not because of blood.
- The symptoms that need medical attention are presence of blood in the urine, dark cola-coloured urine, seemingly painful urination, foul smelling urine, poor urine flow, double urine stream or not passing urine for many hours.

Sleep

- The average sleeping time of a newborn baby is around 18–20 hours a day but varies from baby to baby. Expect that the baby may stay awake during nights and sleep throughout days.
- Be prepared for some sleepless nights, but don't worry; it would just be a passing phase!
- More sleep-related information is in "Go to sleep my baby!"

Clothes

- Use cotton clothes that are pulled over the body and have no beads, buttons or knots.
- Wrapping the baby in a sheet is a popular Indian custom, and babies usually enjoy that. But in warm weather, wrapping can lead to excessive sweating and dehydration.
- When the baby soils itself, clean the soiled nappy area with water. Apply a protective barrier cream every time a soiled nappy is changed.
- Change the baby's nappies regularly, at least 5–6 times in a day.
- Using a cotton cloth diaper or a disposable diaper as a nappy is entirely a matter of individual choice.
- Do not use wet-wipes on a regular basis as they often cause skin irritation and allergy. Use them only occasionally, such as when you are away from home and do not have access to a washroom.

Consulting a doctor

- Among harmless symptoms in infants are occasional spitting or bringing up milk, noisy breathing (because of the small size of airways) and warm forehead. Occasional coughing and sneezing are normal physiologic reflexes.
- Immediately seek medical opinion when there are persisting or severe symptoms such as lethargy, refusal to feed, poor sucking, fever, excessive cough, breathing difficulty, bluish discoloration of tongue or lips, discharge from eyes, ears or the umbilicus, vomiting, abnormal jerky body movements or excessive loose motions.

Regular 'well-baby' visits

- Adults go to doctors only when they fall ill. For babies, regular visits even when the baby is well—or 'well-baby' visits—are necessary.

The earliest well-baby visit is for the neonatal screening tests on the second or third day after birth. During this visit, the baby's blood sample is taken by pricking her heel. This sample is examined in the laboratory to rule out important congenital (by birth) problems such as hypothyroidism, G6PD enzyme deficiency, galactosemia, phenylketonuria, congenital adrenal hyperplasia or cystic fibrosis. Diagnosing these problems early allows doctors to treat them immediately and prevent harm the baby.

Even when your baby is perfectly fine, you should schedule monthly visits to your doctor for the first 6 months and every 2 months for the next 6 months. These visits help check your baby's growth and development, screen for potential health problems, carry out necessary vaccinations, understand the weaning process and allow you to discuss any concerns.

3

When 'Abnormal' is 'Normal'!

Scenario

The baby is sleeping. It's her first day at home! Suresh and Seema keep looking at her. No, they are not looking at her very fondly. They are just nervously examining her from every possible angle.

Neither wants to admit it to the other, but many things about the baby are looking … hmm … quite different! Her head looks oddly shaped. Her feet look bowed. There are some rashes and spots on her skin. Her breathing keeps changing its rhythm.

What is all this? Is everything normal?

Discussion

In nature, there is rarely a sharp demarcation between the normal and the abnormal. Life in its countless variations defies rules and challenges norms. This is true of a newborn human baby, especially the way it looks!

Looks can kill! Looks are deceptive! Combine these oft-repeated statements with our natural curiosity and anxiety and you will easily understand why some 'abnormal' things seen in a newborn cause undue worry to the parents. But let me assure you that in most cases these so-called 'abnormal' observations are perfectly natural and normal.

So let's take a head-to-toe look at the new baby and understand some unusual observations.

Head

A newborn baby's head may have an odd shape and look swollen if there is moulding, which is a temporary displacement of soft skull bones; caput, which is circular swelling of the back of the head with mild bruising or cephalohaematoma, which is a localised collection of blood on one of the skull bones. These conditions occur due to increased pressures and minor injuries sustained during the delivery. They are temporary and settle by themselves within a few days or weeks of birth.

The two soft skull-spots (fontanelles)—one in the front and one at the back—are normal. The small spot at the back (posterior fontanelle) closes within the first few months and the larger diamond-shaped spot in the front (anterior fontanelle) fills up by one and a half years.

Face

- Because of delivery-related pressures, the new baby's face may look puffy and misshapen. It will 'normalise' after few days.
- Nose-block and noisy breathing are common in the early months.
- The newborn baby is hypersensitive to light and keeps her eyes tightly shut most of the time.
- There may be a bloody spot (subconjuctival haemorrhage) in the whites of one or both eyes. It is caused by minor injury during birth and subsides within a few weeks of birth.
- Up to 6 months, the baby's eyes can look crossed as the baby has not yet learned to focus them on things.
- The baby's outer ears may show skin-tags or pits.

Abdomen

- The umbilical cord is cut and clamped with a plastic clip at birth. Over the next 7–10 days, it shrivels, darkens and finally falls off.
- A balloon-like, boggy belly-button swelling of umbilical hernia often causes parental anxiety. It gurgles on touching and increases in size on crying. This is why abdominal pain is often wrongly attributed to it. Many parents keep it tightly wrapped, with a coin placed over it, but actually no treatment is necessary in most cases. Usually it corrects itself in a year.

Skin

The newborn baby's skin often gets under the parental skin with its confusing array of 'birthmarks' or temporary rashes.

- Mongolian spots are slate-grey or bluish spots on the buttocks and back (occasionally elsewhere). These are caused by the deposition of normal body pigment under the skin. They are harmless and disappear by the age of 7 years at the latest.

- Strawberry haemangioma is a small, ripe strawberry-like soft swelling that is sometimes present on the face or on other body parts. Stork bites or port wine stains are reddish stains mainly seen on the neck, forehead and eyelids. All these conditions are caused by excessive proliferation of the blood vessels just under the skin and are mostly harmless. In most cases, they disappear with time and rarely require treatment.
- Erythema toxicum is a transient rash on the chest with small whitish spots on a red base. It is harmless and needs no treatment.
- Miliaria (prickly heat) is a sweat-rash that appears as multiple, tiny, colourless blisters or as a reddish rash on the face and neck. It only needs the baby to be shifted to cool surroundings and dressed in loose clothes.
- Milia are pinhead-like, multiple, tiny, whitish swellings on the nose or cheek and Epstein's pearls are tiny pearl-like white spots on the roof of the mouth. Both are harmless, need no treatment and are caused by the proliferation of particular type of glands.
- The baby's body has immature heat regulation and blood circulation, causing the baby's hands and feet to become blue on exposure to cold (acrocyanosis). Exposure to cold may also cause bluish, blotchy marble skin (cutis marmoratus). Both conditions clear up and the baby is back to normal on providing warmth.

Various other body systems

- The female hormonal surge in the first few days of life leads to vaginal discharge or even vaginal bleeding in female babies. These are transient and without any significance. Similar hormonal changes can lead to genital and breast enlargement and even lactation in both female as well as male babies.

  Overzealous women massagers often try to 'milk' these 'baby breasts', which results in an infection and abscess of the breast. Please don't do such a thing; in fact, don't do anything to the enlarged baby breasts!
- The babies yawn. They sneeze. They cough. They are startled. They stretch themselves. These are all perfectly normal actions for babies.

- Periodic breathing is a pattern of breathing where the baby breathes very rapidly for a few seconds, then pauses and then resumes normal rhythmic breathing. Again, it is just a normal variation.
- Skin tags, ear tags, extra digits on hands or feet, mild curving of the foot (talipes) are physical anomalies that can be easily corrected and are usually much clinical importance.

Final word of advice

So, my dear fellow parents, it is unnecessary to peer suspiciously at each and every part of the baby, looking for a sign of abnormality when there is none! When you look at your bundle of joy, don't think of the abnormal before the normal. Whenever you are in doubt, consult your doctor. Most of the times, you will find that you were just making a mountain out of a molehill!

4

Jaundice in the Newborn

Scenario

Geeta delivered a baby girl just two days ago. She now notices that her baby's skin is looking yellowish. The nurse on duty takes one look at the baby and says, "Don't worry. Your baby has got mild jaundice."

Geeta remembers when she herself had suffered from jaundice a few years ago. The doctor had told her then that it was a virus infection affecting her liver! She is worried that her baby is suffering from a similar condition. So she calls up her husband and asks him to consult the doctor.

Discussion

Yellow-looking skin and eyes—that is the simple definition of jaundice for most people. In a newborn baby, it is certainly a worrisome sight for the new parents. Most of the parental concern is centred round one question: "Is it dangerous?" Thankfully, the answer is a big 'No' (at least in a majority of cases).

Jaundice by itself is not a disease. The word just means increased blood-level of a yellow pigment called bilirubin. Bilirubin is routinely produced after breakdown of old red blood cells, metabolised in the body and finally excreted through urine and stools. Abnormality in the production, metabolism or excretion of bilirubin can lead to its high level in blood, which is called jaundice. These abnormalities have many causes, which can be broadly divided into two major categories, physiologic or 'normal' and pathologic or 'abnormal'.

Physiologic jaundice in the newborn

The commonest variety of jaundice encountered in the first week of life is physiologic or 'normal' jaundice.

It is seen in more than 90% of newborns. It is physiologic because it happens as a result of the baby's immature body systems.

It is normal because there is no underlying disease and the condition is temporary, self-limiting and harmless.

Typically this type of jaundice starts on the second day after birth, reaches a peak after 3–4 days and disappears in 7–10 days. In premature babies, the onset and peak of jaundice are earlier, and the duration is up to 2 weeks.

Treatment of physiologic newborn jaundice

The treatment for mild cases of physiologic jaundice is just to expose the baby to mild sunlight and to give frequent feeds.

The glucose water prescribed by many is not a cure for jaundice and it is not necessary. Just ensure that the milk-feeding (by breast or bottle) is adequate.

Phototherapy is used to treat some cases of physiologic jaundice depending on the baby's bilirubin level, weight, maturity and associated problems. The baby is hospitalised and placed under blue or white tube lights that emit light of particular wavelengths.

Both sunlight and the phototherapy break down bilirubin into harmless water-soluble compounds which can be easily excreted. The side-effects of phototherapy, such as rash or diarrhoea, are temporary, minor and self-limited.

Indications and tests of 'abnormal' jaundice in newborns

Abnormal or pathologic jaundice is suspected in the following situations:

- Jaundice within the first 24 hours of life
- Very deep or rapidly deepening jaundice
- Sick looking or dehydrated baby
- Associated symptoms such as poor feeding, vomiting, constipation, abdominal distension or excessive crying
- Certain differences in mother's and baby's blood-group (for example, mother Rh-negative and baby Rh-positive, or mother O and baby A or B)
- Deficiency of certain enzymes (for example, G6PD)
- Jaundice persisting beyond 14 days

When the doctor suspects abnormal jaundice while checking the newborn, the diagnosis is usually confirmed through investigations such as specific blood tests and abdominal ultrasound scans.

Newborn jaundice and the brain

In rare cases of newborn jaundice caused by certain infections, metabolic diseases or blood-group incompatibility, excessively high unconjugated ('free' or un-metabolised) bilirubin in the blood can reach the brain and cause damage. This serious condition is called 'kernicterus'. Here, emergency treatments like 'exchange transfusion' may be needed.

Note that physiologic jaundice never causes kernicterus or brain damage.

Breast milk jaundice

Breast-milk jaundice develops in 1–2% of all newborn babies. In these cases, some chemicals in the mother's breast-milk interfere with the baby's bilirubin metabolism, leading to jaundice. It usually starts 3–5 days after birth and can last 1–3 months. Despite high bilirubin levels, babies remain healthy and without any complications.

The treatment of breast milk jaundice is to temporarily stop breastfeeding for 1–2 days and then resume it again. The raised bilirubin levels immediately drop following the stoppage. The mother can safely resume breast-feeding after a gap, and bilirubin won't rise to previous levels. There is no need to permanently stop breastfeeding in such cases.

Take-home wisdom

- Most cases of newborn jaundice are physiologic and harmless. They are temporary and correct by themselves over a period.
- Frequent milk-feeds and exposure to mild sunlight suffice for treating most cases.
- Phototherapy (exposure to special lights), a safe, simple and effective treatment, is used in some cases.
- In breast milk jaundice, the treatment is to temporarily stop breastfeeding for 1–2 days. There is no need to permanently stop breastfeeding in such cases.
- Certain cases of abnormal, severe or prolonged jaundice (beyond 2 weeks) merit investigations and expert management.
- Don't dress the baby in yellow clothes when going to the doctor for the jaundice check-up. That sometimes makes it difficult for the doctor to judge the skin's yellowness.

- Don't lose sleep over the bilirubin level as the doctor will consider other factors to decide its significance. Bilirubin level is expressed in different measurement systems and your unfamiliarity with them can cause needless worry. So leave it to the expert!

5

Colic? Cool it!

Scenario

It is midnight; their newborn baby is wailing and the first-time parents Naseem and Hanif are worried. Their baby, who was fine in the first month, has been showing a peculiar tendency for the last few days. He seems to be fine the whole day, but as night approaches, he becomes cranky and then goes into a prolonged cycle of loud cries followed by quiet intervals. His crying pattern is distressing to watch. He usually refuses feeds at that time and no amount of cuddling, patting or rocking seems to help! But once the crying cycle passes, he goes to sleep and is normal the next day.

Hanif decides to call their doctor. The doctor asks him a few questions and declares in a reassuring voice, “Oh, don’t worry. It just seems to be infantile colic!”

Discussion

A frown on the face, a prayer on the lips and a crying baby in the lap! These are the tell-tale signs of a colicky baby in the family.

Infantile colic is one of the commonest yet most troublesome problems of early infancy, which causes periodic stomach aches in babies … and headaches in the parents and a tough time for the doctors!

Some call this condition ‘evening colic’ for its post-evening pattern while others term it ‘3-month colic’ for its tendency to improve by the age of 3 months. It usually starts at the age of 1 month.

In the classical scenario, a previously perfectly well baby suddenly starts to cry loudly and continuously in the late evening. With the face flushed, legs curled up, hands tightly clenched, feet cold and lips sometimes pale, the baby presents a distressing picture. The abdomen is mildly distended and gurgling sounds can be heard or even felt over it. There is usually no relief from cuddling or feeding.

The crying goes on in bouts lasting 15–30 minutes for the next 4–5 hours. Then, after passing either gas or stools, the baby gets some relief and goes off to sleep exhausted. In milder cases, we just see a normal baby turn into an irritable one with a grumpy face in the evenings.

Causes of colic

What causes colic is still a mystery. Overfeeding, underfeeding, the baby's personality, parental interaction, maternal food (especially cow milk), sensitive intestines because of chemical or hormonal imbalance—practically everything under the sun has been blamed for colic.

Not every crying baby is suffering from colic. Feeling wet, cold, hot, hungry or lonely are also expressed in the only language babies know—crying! Faulty feeding technique, which causes the baby to swallow excessive air, coupled with poor burping technique is one of the most common culprits in cases of cry-babies.

Warning signals

Excessive crying may have serious causes. Do not let the description below make you panic. But you should watch out for the following symptoms:

1. Abnormal body temperature (high or low)
2. Prolonged refusal to feed
3. Associated problems such as vomiting, constipation or increasing abdominal distension
4. No relief from crying for long hours

If you have any doubt, it is wise to let an expert have a look.

Managing evening colic

Over-the-counter gripe water or herbal tea prescriptions are certainly not my cup of tea. Such medicines can have unnecessary sedatives and toxic chemicals. Instead, try the following simple measures:

- Keep the baby in a face-down position in your lap and gently thump the middle of the back.
- Gently rub the baby's stomach with your hand.

- Roll a warm towel or a warm water bag on the stomach. (Make sure that the temperature of the towel or the water-bag is warm and not scalding hot!)
- Snugly wrapping the baby and gently rocking her sometimes work wonders.
- If there is no response to such efforts, you can use over-the-counter anti-colic drops under your doctor's guidance.

I believe the primary task of the doctor is to explain to the parents the transient and harmless nature of this condition. Many a times, just a reassuring pat on the back is what it takes to take the frown off the parents' faces and put the smile back on the baby's face!

6

Premature Babies: A Primer

Scenario

Rajesh is frantically calling his doctor friend Suhas. Rajesh's wife has delivered 6 weeks before her due date. The doctors told him that the baby is premature and small. They have kept her in an incubator in the NICU (neonatal intensive care unit) equipped with various monitors and alarms. She is being fed from a tube passed through her nose. She is also undergoing frequent blood tests. The doctors say that she may be kept in the hospital for a few weeks.

Rajesh is worried. He wants to know more about premature babies and the management of their health.

Discussion

Prematurity and related problems are becoming more common and more visible with the advances in medical technology, which are improving the survival rates for prematurely born babies. Such babies require specialised care and that too for a prolonged period. Parents of such babies have many unanswered questions about their 'preemies'. Here is an attempt to explain this condition and its management.

Prematurity

A premature or pre-term (PT) baby is one born before completing 37 weeks inside the womb. (A full term baby is born 38 to 42 weeks after the conception.) A very premature baby is born before 32 weeks and an extremely premature baby is born before 25 weeks of gestation. Almost all PT babies have low birth weight (500–2500 gm).

The PT baby has a smaller body with a disproportionately large head, sharper facial features, thin translucent skin, fine body hair (lanugo) and some difficulties in the breathing, sucking and swallowing processes.

Causes of prematurity

The exact cause and mechanism of prematurity are unknown. Some factors in the mother or the foetus cause increased risk of prematurity.

Factors in the mother include past history of premature delivery; age less than 18 years or more than 35 years; poor nutrition; physical stress; addictions such as to tobacco, alcohol or drugs; any serious disease or problems of uterus and placenta.

Factors in the foetus include multiple pregnancy, foetal distress or intrauterine growth retardation.

Common risks

Because PT babies are out in the world before completing their full preparation for it, they run the risk of some important health problems, which may occur immediately after birth or in the long term. Very premature and extreme premature babies are at higher risk.

Immediate risks include certain respiratory, heart, gastrointestinal and brain problems; hypothermia; anaemia; jaundice; serious infections and disturbances in blood chemistry.

Long-term risks include cerebral palsy, developmental delays, vision problems, hearing problems, psychological and behaviour problems and chronic respiratory illnesses.

Use of incubators or warmers

Warmth is a prime need of any newborn baby, much more so of a pre-term baby. The PT baby lacks the insulating pad of body fat, and its body temperature regulation mechanisms are not fully functional.

Hypothermia or a reduced body temperature is dangerous because it slows down metabolism. The glucose stores in the body are consumed to maintain body-heat, which causes fall in blood glucose levels (hypoglycaemia).

To prevent all this, PT babies are kept in incubators or radiant warmers. Incubators are transparent plastic boxes in which the temperature can be accurately adjusted to keep the baby warm. Radiant warmers are electrically warmed beds that are open to air. This means that the air around the baby is warm in the closed incubators but at room temperature on warmers. The open warmers are used when there is need to frequently access the baby for medical reasons.

Special feeding

In the first few weeks, PT babies do need special feeding schedules. In very PT babies, milk feeds are postponed for the first few days and IV (intra-venous) fluids are given. This is done to prevent a serious gastro-intestinal infection called NEC (necrotising enterocolitis).

As PT babies (before 32 weeks gestation) do not have coordinated sucking and swallowing reflexes, breast milk or formula milk has to be given through tube-feeding. This feeding tube is passed through the nose into the stomach.

PT babies require more calories, proteins, minerals and vitamins. So they need supplements and sometimes a special PT-specific milk formula.

RDS

PT babies born before 34 weeks suffer deficiency of surfactant protein in their lungs. This protein keeps the lungs' air-sacs open during respiration and its deficiency leads to the collapse of the lungs. This causes RDS (respiratory distress syndrome) with breathing difficulty.

Oxygen, assisted mechanical ventilation and administration of artificial surfactant are the measures to treat RDS. Administration of corticosteroid injection to the mother before the anticipated PT delivery is one way of reducing risk of RDS.

Apnoea alarms

Apnoea is stoppage of breathing for more than 15–20 seconds with associated fall in heart rate (below 100/min.) or bluish discoloration of skin and mucous membranes (cyanosis) or both. Because of the immaturity of the brain's centre regulating respiration and other physiologic abnormalities, apnoea is a common occurrence in PT babies.

To alert the medical team to problems, special alarms are connected to PT babies, which sound a warning for apnoea. Physical stimulation often aborts such spells. Sometimes medicines (such as theophylline or caffeine) or assisted ventilation are needed to control the condition.

Frequent blood tests

The internal biochemical balance in the blood is very delicate in PT babies. Metabolic disturbances such as changes in blood levels of glucose, calcium, magnesium, bilirubin and electrolytes are observed very commonly and need immediate attention.

In ventilated PT babies, arterial blood gas levels (oxygen and carbon dioxide) need to be checked to adjust the ventilator settings.

When an infection is suspected, blood counts and cultures are done to treat the infective organism.

Discharge

When a PT baby is otherwise healthy, growing well, feeding from bottle or breast without any difficulty and able to maintain body temperature in an open crib, it is ready for discharge.

Most health facilities prefer to discharge the baby when it weighs at least 1.8 kg or 4 lbs. Parental readiness to accept the caretaker role is also an important deciding factor.

Family problems

When a PT baby comes home after winning the initial battle in NICU, different problems are waiting for it there.

Parents who are initially elated at the baby's homecoming soon get exhausted and start to feel lonely and abandoned in their efforts to attend to the special needs of a PT baby. They may have negative feelings such as denial, dejection, defeatism, blame, guilt or ambivalent attitude towards baby.

Sometimes even when a PT baby is perfectly normal, parents continue to have an over-protective attitude.

Siblings may display hostility towards the PT baby as they sense that more attention is given to the new entrant.

All these problems should be discussed in detail with the family throughout the hospitalisation so that they can cope with it better when they go home.

Management at home

The following are the basic principles of caring for a PT baby at home.

- Maintain a positive parental attitude.
- Prevent infections. Follow practices such as:
  - Hand-washing before handling the baby
  - Minimum handling of the baby by family members
  - No handling by casual visitors
  - Avoiding crowded places for outings
  - Face mask or protective gear for anybody near the baby who has an infection
- Prevent low body temperatures (hypothermia).

Maintain an ambient room temperature of around 27–28°C (80°F) and cover the baby in adequate clothing. A practical guideline is:

  - At 28°C (80°F), put on a single vest and a diaper.
  - At 24–28°C (75–80°F), add one more layer of clothing.
  - At 21–24°C (70–75° F), add two more layers of clothing.
  - Below 21°C (70°F), add two more layers of clothing and put on a cap and blanket.
- **Ensure proper feeding**

Feeding PT babies depends on their weight and ability to suck from the breast or a bottle. Until they attain adequate weight (2 kg or more), maintain a strict 2-hourly feeding schedule.

Expressed breast milk or sometimes a prescribed premature milk formula is used as the feed. The simple way of giving such feeds is through a spoon, a bondla (a snouted spoon) or a syringe. Take care to burp the baby well after any feed.

Supplements such as multivitamins, iron and calcium are usually needed and can be added to the milk feeds.

- **Adhere to regular follow-ups.**

  Regularly visit a doctor to monitor the PT baby's growth, development, vaccination and any other related conditions.

Danger signals

A doctor's opinion should be immediately sought in case of the following:

- Extremes of temperature (fever or hypothermia)
- Refusal to feed, poor sucking or reduced feeding

- Lethargy, irritability, excessive sleepiness or jerky body movements
- Severe, prolonged and frequent breath-holding spells
- Breathing difficulty
- Bluish discoloration of lips or mouth
- Diarrhoea, vomiting, constipation, abdominal distension, dark black or bloody stools
- Less urination
- Ear or eye discharge
- Redness around umbilicus, foul smell or discharge from umbilicus

Vaccination for PT babies

Usually, there is no difference in the vaccination schedule for a stable PT baby and any other normal newborn. There is no need to postpone the vaccines in the belief that PT babies are too fragile. In fact, that is the reason they need the vaccine to protect them from various illnesses even more.

If you have any specific concern in this regard, please discuss that with your paediatrician.

Final word of advice

Although the overall survival and health outlook for PT babies has improved greatly, there are many battles still to be won, especially in long-term effects. But don't worry about these issues as each case is different. With good medical care and positive, informed parenting, most prematurity-related problems can be controlled or cured.

When it comes to prematurity, parents have to be truly mature to handle all its consequences!

II

Child Nutrition

1

Best Feeding: Breastfeeding

Scenario

"Name the two most important ways of reducing infections in newborn babies." This used to be the examiners' favourite question in my days of paediatric residency. As a budding child-specialist, you were supposed to promptly respond: "Hand washing before handling the baby and breastfeeding." The importance of breastfeeding was thus emphasized right during the formative years as a resident doctor. Later on in my medical practice, I heard many queries and doubts from parents regarding breastfeeding. I will try and clear up some of those.

Discussion

Reasons for breastfeeding

Breastfeeding is the most natural way to feed the baby. It is free, safe, convenient and healthy. Breast milk is readily available and is always fresh, uncontaminated and at the right temperature. It offers many health advantages to the baby and the mother.

Breast milk contains cells, antibodies, enzymes and other chemicals that protect the baby against many types of infections. It contains specific growth factors promoting the development of the brain and the retina. Breast-fed children are less likely to get diarrhoea, middle ear infections, chest infections, and serious life-threatening infections like meningitis. Frequency of colic and allergic eczema is also lower in breast-fed children.

For the mother, breast milk offers some protection against serious diseases like cancer of the breasts and the ovaries. It helps her regain her normal figure faster. Frequent breastfeeding is one (but not certain) method to delay conception.

Psychologically, breastfeeding plays an important role in the emotional bonding of the baby and the mother.

Breastfeeding basics

When should one start breastfeeding? The earlier the better. Preferably, the mother should be encouraged to breastfeed immediately after delivery as it promotes the production of prolactin and oxytocin hormones that facilitate milk production and milk release respectively.

Taking practical considerations into accounting, breastfeeding should start within an hour after normal delivery and within 4 hours after a caesarean.

Colostrum

For the first 3–4 days after delivery, the mother secretes yellowish, thick milk in small amounts, which is called colostrum. In many cultures there is a mistaken belief that the colostrum is not good for the baby and that's why the mother is often wrongly advised to discard colostrum. This practice of not giving colostrum to the baby should be strongly discouraged. Also, there is no need to give water, glucose water, honey or artificial milk in those days when the milk hasn't 'come in' the breasts and only colostrum is secreted.

Colostrum is sufficient to satisfy the nutritional and fluid requirements of the new baby. More importantly, it provides a rich supplement of vitamins and antibodies. IgA antibodies from colostrum coat the baby's intestinal lining to protect against infections and also prevent harmful proteins from entering the bloodstream from the intestine and causing allergy.

Breastfeeding technique

A quiet comfortable setting and a mentally relaxed mother are the pre-requisites for breastfeeding. With the baby held closely and facing the mother's breast, the nipple of the feeding breast should be touched gently to baby's cheek or upper lip. Reflexively, the baby opens its mouth wide, seeks the nipple and starts sucking. Take care that not only the nipple but most of areola (dark skin around the nipple) is in the baby's mouth as more than two-thirds of the milk-making system is within 3 cm of the base of the nipple.

Right position of feeding, nipple and areola are in baby's mouth

Wrong position, only nipple in the baby's mouth

Breastfeeding positions

Indian method

Cradle position

Modified cradle position

Football hold

Side-lying position
(Reproduced from Training Manual on Breastfeeding Management by Dr. Armida Fernandez)

Burping the baby

While sucking milk from the breast or a bottle, the baby also sucks in air, particularly if the feeding position is incorrect. That sucked air can cause abdominal discomfort, colic or vomiting. That is why burping or removing air after every milk feed (whether breastfed or bottle-fed) is an important part of the feeding and baby care routine.

The best way of burping is to hold the baby against your shoulder and pat (or mildly thump) the middle of the back. The direction of the thumps should be upwards to facilitate the upward movement of air.

Frequency of breastfeeding

The ideal techniques are demand feeding, which means feeding the baby as often as she demands, or semi-demand feeding, which means feeding the baby at scheduled intervals and whenever she demands.

Initially, the feeding pattern may be irregular, but it soon settles down so that a feed every 2–3 hours is sufficient. The more the baby suckles, the greater is the milk output.

Alternate the side with each feed so that both breasts get the same amount of stimulation and continue producing milk.

Duration of one feed

Babies differ in their feeding habits. Some might take 5 minutes to feed at a time and others might spend 30–45 minutes. It is better to allow the baby to suckle until it leaves the breast on its own. The other breast should be offered if the baby seems still interested in feeding after finishing with one breast.

Fore-milk and hind-milk

At the beginning of a feed, breast milk is greyish, thin and watery and is called fore-milk. It is rich in sugar (lactose), proteins, vitamins and minerals. Hind-milk appears at the end of feeding and is thick, white and rich in fats.

Hind-milk gives satiety (a feeling of fullness), and so it is better to let the slow feeder finish with one breast rather than switching sides.

If the baby gets only the fore-milk, its high water and sugar content may cause passage of frequent, loose stools. Although this is not pathological, it can be avoided by allowing the baby to get both fore-milk as well as hind-milk.

Breast milk adequacy and supplements

Regular, adequate weight-gain and frequent passage (6–8 times in a day) of pale yellow or colourless urine are indicators that the breast milk intake is adequate for the baby. A well-fed baby is usually happy, playful and sleeps well.

For the first 3 months, there is no need to give the baby any food except breast milk. Even in dry, hot climates, breast-milk is usually sufficient to satisfy the baby's water requirements.

Giving water or gripe-water or any other fluid such as juice or a soup before the 4th month is undesirable as it serves no purpose excepting increasing the risk of infection.

From the 4th month onwards, breastfeeding should be supplemented with fruit juices, soups, mashed fruits and cereals. This process of weaning is important and gradually prepares the baby for normal food. Many authorities recommend starting semisolids only after 6 months of exclusive breastfeeding.

Expressing breast milk

Expressed breast milk (EBM) is the next best alternative to actual breastfeeding for working or sick mothers. Breast milk can be expressed either manually or with a mechanical or electrical pump.

To manually express breast milk, the mother should first massage the breasts from the sides to the centre. Then, holding a clean cup near the breast, she should push back, press and release the central upper and lower edges of the areola between her thumb and index finger. At first there might be no milk, but soon it will spurt in small jet streams. Next, the mother should press the edges of the areola on the sides in the same way to make sure that all the milk from the breast empties out. Do not pull, press or squeeze the nipple.

Before using a mechanical or electrical pump for expressing breast milk, the mother should learn the proper technique from a doctor.

At room temperature, EBM can be used within 8 hours after expression. When kept in a refrigerator, it can be used within 24 hours. In a deep freezer, it can be stored for up to 3 months. Heating or boiling EBM is not necessary before using it, but it can be brought to room temperature by just keeping it outside the refrigerator for some time.

Using a cup and a spoon or a *bondla* (snouted feeding spoon), EBM can be fed to the baby.

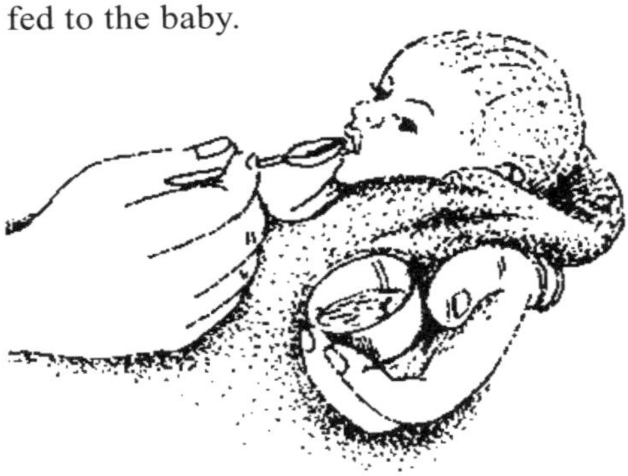

Katori (cup) and spoon feeding

Use special spoon feeding spoon

(Reproduced from Training Manual on Breastfeeding Management by Dr. Armida Fernandez)

Common problems in breastfeeding

Problem	Common Causes	Solution
Insufficient milk	Anxiety, family pressure, wrong ideas about breastfeeding, poor motivation	Be confident. Motivate yourself. Take professional advice and guidance.
Sore or cracked nipples	Wrong feeding position, occasionally fungal infection	Correct and comfortable feeding position, antifungal cream if necessary
Retracted or flat nipples	Physiological or anatomical	Regularly massaging nipples, suction pump, nipple shield
Engorged breasts	Physiological	Frequent feeding or warm compress, massage, expression of breast milk
Mastitis	Engorged breasts, blocked duct	Frequent feeding or warm compress, massage, expression of breast milk
Breast abscess	Infection	Warm compresses, antibiotics, incision and drainage if necessary

Duration of breastfeeding

One can very well continue breastfeeding until the baby is 2 years old. But nutritionally, breast milk cannot completely satisfy the demands of a growing baby beyond 6 months of age and has to be supplemented with other foods.

Exclusively relying on breastfeeding for nutrition beyond 6 months may lead to nutritional deficiencies, particularly iron and vitamin D deficiencies causing anaemia and rickets.

In fact, as the baby enters the 2nd year, breastfeeding is more important to satisfy the baby's emotional need to be close to mother than for nutrition.

Final word of advice

Though it is the natural way of feeding, breastfeeding still needs to be taught to every new mother. Explaining the great benefits of this practice, teaching its correct technique and offering regular encouragement go a long way in motivating mothers to successfully continue breastfeeding. Doctors, nurses and elder female family members all have a role to play in this respect. It is our social responsibility.

2

Bottle-Feeding: Boon or Bane?

Scenario

Neha is a working woman. She is about to resume work after maternity leave. So far, she has been breastfeeding her baby but now wants to begin bottle-feeding in addition. While she is at work, a domestic help is going to be looking after her baby. Neha is feeling guilty that she won't be at home to continue breastfeeding her baby and that she is exposing the baby to the dangers of bottle-feeding.

The doctor reassures Neha that she should not feel guilty about her decision. She just has to understand that bottle-feeding needs extra care and it is a temporary phase which should be over by the baby's first birthday. He also encourages her to continue breastfeeding whenever she can.

Discussion

Even while pleading 'no contest' to the fact that breast feeding is best feeding, we must understand one sometimes has to settle for the alternative of bottle-feeding. Let's take a look at the rights and wrongs of bottle-feeding.

Disadvantages of bottle-feeding

It helps to know the pitfalls before starting bottle-feeding. The following disadvantages are commonly associated with bottle-feeding.

- Infection through contamination is a common danger. Gastro-intestinal, respiratory and ear infections are more common in bottle-fed children.
- Nutritional problems like not gaining adequate weight may result from too dilute a formula. Too concentrated formula may cause high sodium level and even fits. Using cow's milk can lead to iron deficiency and goat's milk can cause folate deficiency. Obesity is more common in bottle-fed children.

- Risk of illnesses is higher because bottle-fed children lose out on the natural protection provided by breast-milk. Apart from infections, many other illnesses like colic, eczema, asthma and dental caries are more commonly seen in bottle-fed children.
- Wrong eating habits develop so that many bottle-fed babies show a reluctance to eat semisolid and solid foods. They are also prone to constipation.

Beside health reasons, there are practical difficulties in bottle-feeding. Preparing the formula, sterilising the bottles and nipples add to the daily domestic chores. Economics, too, is against bottle-feeding. Buying fresh or formula milk is expensive, isn't it?

Advantages of bottle-feeding

Despite all the arguments against it, bottle-feeding does offer some advantages, all of which could be grouped under one heading—convenience.

- As anyone in the home can feed the baby with a bottle, it frees the mother to pursue her career and social activities without feeling tied down. There need not be any restrictions on her diet drinking or medicines.
- It is a convenient mode of feeding while travelling or in public places.
- Bottle-fed babies need a fewer number of feeds as it takes longer to digest animal milk.
- When bottle-feeding, the mother knows exactly how much milk the baby is taking, which often gives a sense of security and satisfaction about the adequacy of intake.
- It is the only method of feeding available when breast-feeding is not possible because the mother suffers from a severe illness or is on certain medicines harmful to the baby such as lithium, radioactive iodine, anti-thyroid medicines and anti-cancer drugs.

Types of milk in bottle-feeding

Cow's milk, buffalo's milk and milk formulas are the popular choices for bottle-feeding. In some regions, people use the milk of goats, camels and donkeys. Raw animal milk is fed to babies in some tribes, but it is a dangerous practice with a very high risk of transmission of infection and difficulty in digestion.

Evaporated cow's milk—with water removed from natural milk—available in tetra-packs has the advantage of prolonged storage and is easier to digest than whole milk. Condensed milk (with water removed but sugar added) and skimmed milk (with too much of proteins and minerals and too little fats and calories) are not advisable for babies.

Milk formulas (formula milk)

Formula milks, or milk formulas, have a base of cow's milk and are chemically modified to match human milk as closely as possible. Vitamins and minerals are added to improve their nutritional value. Formulas are available as powder and liquid (ready-to-feed).

Special milk formulas are sometimes used for premature babies and for babies with certain metabolic, digestive or allergic problems. They should only be used on a doctor's prescription.

Fresh milk or formula milk

The adjective 'fresh' gives a sense of something superior to a layman, as in fresh fruits, fresh vegetables, fresh meat. But understand that fresh milk is only some animal's milk and designed for the young of that particular species.

Formula milk is prepared by chemically converting cow's milk to characteristics that closely match human milk. That is why, if one can afford it, formula milk is a nutritionally superior choice.

Choosing the milk formula

Despite tall claims and counter-claims by different brands of formula milk, there is practically no difference between them and one can safely choose any reputed brand according to one's budget and preferences. If the baby is feeding comfortably and gaining weight normally, it doesn't make any sense to change from one brand to another.

Nowadays, most leading brands have come up with No. 1 (from 0–6 months), No. 2 (from 6–12 months) and No. 3 (from 1–4 years) formulae, which are supposed to cater to the particular growth patterns and nutritional needs at these ages.

Bowl and spoon or bottle

Sterilization of a bowl and a spoon is easier and more likely to be foolproof. But spoon-feeding is time-consuming and requires a high degree of motivation in the parent or care-giver. So, even though bowl and spoon feeding is more hygienic, the bottle remains the most popular way of milk feeding.

Still, it is always preferable to do away with the bottle and switch over to a cup as soon as the baby is ready to drink from it. You can do it by the time baby turns 9 months or older.

Preparing fresh milk

As compared to human milk, cow's milk has a higher concentration of heavy protein (casein) and a lower concentration of sugar (lactose). Buffalo's milk, in addition to these differences, also has more fat. These animal milks need preparation or 'humanisation' before they are given to babies.

To prepare whole (full cream) cow's milk for feeds, boil it for 10 minutes, which breaks down casein into softer curds, and add sugar, about 1 teaspoonful for every 2½ oz or 75 ml.

To prepare whole buffalo's milk, follow the same steps as for cow's milk and remove the cream to reduce the fat.

After preparing (or humanising), cow's and buffalo's whole milk can be given to babies undiluted.

Preparing formula milk

Formula milk usually comes with a measure. One measure, filled flat to the top, added to 1 oz or 30 ml of boiled water makes 1 oz of formula milk. Check the formula container or leaflet for exact instructions.

Cleaning and sterilising bottles and nipples is the most important precaution to avoid infections from bottle-feeding. Follow these steps.

1. Wash the used bottles, caps and nipples thoroughly with mild detergent in warm water.
2. Clean the sticky interior of used bottles with detergent and brush.
3. Thoroughly rinse the bottles, caps and nipples in running water to remove all traces of soap.
4. Place the cleaned feeding equipment in a wide container of water. Cover the container. Boil for at least 5 minutes, but preferably for 10 minutes.
5. Remove the sterilised equipment using tongs and keep aside to air-dry.

6. Prepare the feed in the bottle just before the feeding time.

The commonest mistake is drying the bottle and nipple inside out with cloth after taking them out of the boiling container. This 'cleaning' only serves to introduce germs from the cloth and wastes the earlier sterilisation process!

Duration of bottle-feeding

By around 9 months, the baby is ready to hold a cup for feeding and that is the cue to stop the bottle for good! Don't let the habit of bottle-feeding go on and on for the sake of convenience. The risks involved in this feeding practice are much higher than the benefits. The longer you continue the bottle-feeding habit, the more difficult it will be to stop and the more harmful it will be to your baby's overall health and nutritional habits.

Is there a strategy to stop bottle-feeding? Start the process by 9 months and keep a strict deadline of stopping bottle-feeds by the first birthday. Here are some suggestions:

- At breakfast and main meals, offer milk and other liquids (juices and water) in a cup, which can be a normal cup or a closed, snouted 'sipper' cup.
- First stop the morning bottle, then the afternoon and evening ones, and finally the night bottle. The night bottle is often used as a soothing or sleeping bottle!
- Progressively dilute the milk feeds with extra water in the bottle you plan to stop, finally giving only water in the last feeds.
- Stopping daytime bottles becomes easier if you make the meals and meal-times interesting. Remember, the baby demands the bottle not only to satisfy hunger but often as a substitute for comfort or company.
- Offer the baby encouragement at every step.
- Once you have stopped bottle-feeding, either throw away the bottles or hide them. Out of sight, out of mind!

General tips for bottle-feeding

- Whenever possible, the mother should do the bottle-feeding, holding the baby in the crook of her arm. This promotes emotional bonding.
- Don't bottle-feed a baby who is lying on her back as there is a risk of choking and ear infection.

- Burp the baby well after feeding.
- Choose good quality feeding equipment from reputed manufacturers.
- Check the temperature of the milk by releasing a drop on the inside of your wrist or the back of your hand. The milk should be fed at body temperature.
- If the milk seems too cold, warm it by placing bottle in warm water. Do not warm the milk-bottle in a microwave oven.
- Check nipple-hole size by making sure that milk flows out in slow drops. Too small a nipple-hole causes underfeeding and tires the baby. You can enlarge the size by piercing with a red-hot needle. Too large a hole can lead to overfeeding, obesity and even choking.
- Check the milk level in the bottle while feeding. Holding the bottle in a slanted position often leads to excessive air-sucking. To prevent that, always make sure that there is no air in the bottle while feeding.
- Check the integrity of the formula pack and its expiry date.
- Stop bottle-feeding once the baby is 9 months and learns to hold a feeding cup in its hands! No bottle-feeding beyond first birthday!

Word of advice

Bottle-feeding has been portrayed as a big bad wolf by paediatricians all over the world and not without justification, but it is a well-established tradition and is here to stay. Educating the mother about its dangers and its correct techniques is the only way of taming this wolf!

3

Weaning

Scenario

Mr. and Mrs. Srinivasan are in their forties and became parents for the first time 3 months ago. They have been very careful about everything that concerns their precious baby. Now they are wondering if they should start weaning their baby and introduce her to semisolid foods. Their friends and family members have been giving them conflicting advice about when to start weaning and what foods to introduce. The Srinivasans are sure about just one thing—they want to do what is best for their baby. So they make the right decision: they decide to visit their doctor and discuss the weaning process in detail!

Discussion

Any important transition involves a process of adaptation or adjustment. Weaning is one such important transitional phase in the baby's feeding pattern. Parents should not only know the answers to the questions of 'what', 'when' and 'why' about weaning but also understand the logic behind them.

What is weaning?

Weaning is the process of introducing the baby to foods other than milk. Excessive reliance on milk feeds (either breastfeeds or artificial milk feeds) and delayed weaning are perhaps the most important causes of feeding difficulties and nutritional deficiencies later in life.

When should we start weaning?

Most Indian experts advise parents to start weaning by the baby's 4th month of life. But most Western experts advise weaning only after 6 months of exclusive milk feeding (either breastfeeding or artificial milk feeding). I concur with the Indian recommendation of starting weaning by the 4th month.

Before the 4th month, the baby is physically and physiologically not ready for semisolid feeds. Her digestion process is still immature, her stomach capacity is low and her swallowing mechanism is not yet developed for semisolids. By the 4th month, these developments occur and she can be introduced to semisolid foods.

After the 6th or 7th month, the baby shows increasing resistance to any attempt to change her set feeding pattern. It is increasingly difficult to start weaning after this age.

Why is weaning necessary?

Beyond 6 months of age, milk alone cannot meet the increasing energy and nutrient demands of a rapidly growing baby, making addition of other food items necessary.

The process of weaning teaches babies to swallow semisolids and solids and makes them ready to accept different tastes, textures and types of food. This paves the way for making them ready to accept food in its traditional, 'normal' form.

Weaning is not only about providing adequate nutrition or filling up your baby's stomach. It is more about teaching the baby how and what to eat and to establish good eating habits.

General principles of weaning

- Weaning develops the baby's diet in terms of consistency from liquids (other than milk) to semisolids to solids.
- As far as possible concentrate on using fresh, natural or home-cooked food items rather than relying on readymade baby foods.
- Introduce the first new food in the morning when the baby is awake, alert and active. It also gives you the whole day to observe if anything goes wrong.
- Start one item at a time and allow around 4–5 days for the baby to adapt to it.
- If the baby initially spits out any new food, it does not mean that the food is unsuitable or that the baby does not like it. Spitting is a passing phase in the process of adaptation. Continue to give that food.
- Give new food in small (half teaspoonful) measures. Initially, give only one or two teaspoonful of a new food item per day. Increase the quantity gradually once the baby adapts to that particular food item.

- Introduce a new food item every week instead of just giving the same things again and again.
- The aim is to make the baby adapt in such a fashion that, by 1 year, she should be able to eat almost every item from the normal food cooked in her home.

Timetable for weaning

Regardless of cultural and national differences, the basic schedule of weaning remains pretty much the same. The following are the common guidelines for introducing major food items in a baby's diet in addition to breast milk or artificial milk feeds.

- 4–6 months: Pureed or mashed fruits and vegetables, rice and lentil gruels, vegetable soups
- 6–7 months: Wheat preparations, meat, chicken, cheese and yoghurt
- 8–9 months: Egg yolk followed by egg white
- 9–10 months: Fish
- 11 months onwards: Continued introduction of a variety of tastes, textures and types of food

These are just rough guidelines and not absolute rules. Every parent would need to modify these to suit the family's food preferences and the baby's attitude, aptitude and appetite.

Specific food-items

- Fruits like banana, apple, pear and *chikoo* are tolerated well from the beginning. Later, introduce other fruits such as orange, sweet lime, papaya, mango, berries, grapes and melons.
- Choose a ripe fruit.
- Remove the peel and any seeds or stringy parts.
- If the fruit is soft, just mash it lightly. If it seems too hard, first soften it by boiling in a little water and then mash it.
- Later, fruits can be given in tiny slices.
- Vegetables like potato, carrot, pumpkin, bottle-gourd (*doodhi* or *lauki*) and green leafy vegetables like spinach (*paalak*) and fenugreek (*methi*) are good choices and should be given well-cooked and mashed. Pressure cooking or stewing are the best cooking methods for vegetables.

- Lentils and beans are good vegetable sources of proteins. Yellow lentils such as *tur dal* or *moong dal* can be given from the very first phase of weaning. They should be initially pressure cooked and given as standalone gruels. Later, they can be given as rice and lentil mixed gruel (*khichri*).

  Green *moong dal*, green peas, red *masoor dal*, red kidney beans or French beans are usually started after 6 months.
- Meat, chicken and fish should be thoroughly cooked, soft and trimmed of fat and skin. All bones should be carefully removed. Initially, these foods should be given minced and later as small, soft pieces. Pressure cooking, stewing or grilling are the preferred cooking methods for non-vegetarian items.
- Egg should be completely cooked (boiled for at least 3–4 minutes). Raw egg is often thought to be nutritionally very rich but is not. In fact, it could be contaminated with bacteria like salmonella that cause diarrhoea. It also tends to destroy vitamins in the body.
- From 8–12 months, gradually start introducing the home-cooked foods that the rest of the family eats, which means food containing salt, spices and condiments.
- Avoid food that is too salty, spicy, or sugary as well as deep fried food, fruit squashes and fizzy drinks.
- Don't even think about introducing foods such as chocolates, cakes, chips and ice-creams. Many parents are surprisingly eager to do this as they feel it is fun to see their baby enjoy these treats! There is no benefit in introducing such fun foods so early, and they will hamper the development of your baby's healthy food preferences.

Home-made cereals

There is no need to use mixer-grinder to make a very smooth paste of home-made cereals. This practice denies the baby the opportunity to understand and adapt to the granularity of normal food. Just mash the soft foods well with spoon or fingers and introduce such foods right from the beginning.

Weaning for allergic baby

In a baby with a strong family history of allergic disorders like eczema or asthma, it is preferable to delay weaning and rely exclusively on breast-feeding until the baby completes 6 months.

Strongly allergenic foods like cow's milk, citrus fruits, wheat preparations, fish, eggs, nuts and chocolates are deferred as long as possible, preferably until 1 year of age. But before making any such dietary changes, take proper medical and nutritional advice from experts.

Readymade baby foods

Dry cereals, biscuits, pureed fruits, vegetables, chicken, and meat preparations—the sheer variety of baby foods in market is amazing. The main advantage of such baby foods is that they are either readymade or can be conveniently prepared within minutes. Another advantage is that most of them are fortified with vitamins and minerals to make them nutritionally more balanced.

On the flip side, they are more expensive and the additives or preservatives used in them could be troublesome. Some of them may even contain harmful chemicals in small amounts.

A general observation is that babies tend to accept commercially available baby foods faster and in larger quantities. This is perhaps because they have been made more 'palatable' through certain processes! That is why babies weaned on such readymade baby foods often show resistance to accepting normal home-cooked food. Babies who are weaned mainly on home-cooked foods adapt to 'normal' foods much faster.

How much food and how often

The minds of many mothers seem to be occupied with one question: 'How much should my baby eat?' If you want to successfully wean your baby and introduce good food habits, the most important step is to do away with this fixation with the quantity of food.

Remember that the capacity of the baby's stomach is not big. You should start with a very small quantity (1–2 teaspoons per day) of semisolids. Keep each mouthful to half-teaspoonful. This amount gives the baby a chance to easily swallow the food and develops confidence in his ability to ingest semisolids without choking.

Giving large portions can make your baby choke, vomit or altogether refuse the food. Even if you succeed in force-feeding those large mouthfuls of food, you will just end up making the baby obese.

Increase the quantity of food in small portions (additional 1–2 teaspoons) only when you think that your baby is enjoying the food and seems to be ready for more. Even a seemingly small quantity of 7–8 teaspoons of semisolids per feed by the age of 1 year is quite sufficient.

As regards the number of semisolid feeds, this is what I advise. Start with 1 such feed per day in the first 2 weeks of weaning. Then increase it to 2 feeds per day for the next 2 weeks, then 3 feeds per day for the next 2–3 months and a maximum of 4 feeds by 1 year.

Note that the baby's milk feeds are not included in this number. As the baby adjusts to semisolid feeds, the number of milk feeds should come down.

Final word of advice

Weaning is the most important stepping stone for the development of good and healthy eating habits that will last in later life. This is a gradual process requiring patience, persistence and imaginative work from parents.

Remember these golden rules.

- Take medical advice before starting the weaning process. Do not rely on family and friends. Your learning the correct weaning principles will go a long way in establishing good food habits in your baby.
- Natural foods and home-cooked foods are much better choices, and readymade baby foods are not really necessary.
- Quantity is the least important thing when you are feeding the baby new foods. Do not worry about how much your baby is eating.
- Variety is the key to successful and healthy weaning. Choose the correct food options.

4

Balanced Diet

Scenario

Sheela Dixit is not happy with her 4-year-old son's diet. He just wants to eat junk food like cakes, chocolates, candies and chips. He doesn't want to eat home-cooked food and always wants her to order a pizza or a burger from outside! She desperately asks her doctor, "What should I do to make him eat a balanced diet?"

Discussion

If you want to avoid having to ask such a question of your doctor, you have to understand and follow a few basic principles about food and feeding.

What is a balanced diet?

Food consists of 6 main groups—grains; fruits; vegetables and legumes; milk and dairy products; meat, poultry, and seafood; and oils and Fat. Balanced diet is one which has the right amounts of foods from each of these groups. A balanced diet helps to meet nutritional needs, prevents diseases, provides energy and manages weight.

Do we have to totally avoid foods like crisps, chocolates, cookies, candies, cakes, colas, biscuits and ice-creams? Many children and even adults are hooked on such foods. These foods are called 'extra foods' or 'non-essential foods'. They do not fit into the main food groups. They are not essential to provide nutrients and may contain too much added fat, salt and sugars. However, extra foods do play a major role in the 'enjoyment' of food and it is not necessary to totally banish them from the diet. But they should be eaten only occasionally, say, once a week, and in small portions.

Regular and excessive consumption of extra foods hampers eating the necessary healthy food groups in right amounts. Extra foods also supply a lot of excess calories, sugar, fats and salt, which may lead to major health problems such as obesity, diabetes and high blood pressure in the long run.

General principles of balanced diet

- Every day, choose different varieties from the main food groups in adequate recommended serving sizes.
- Eat larger quantities of plant-based foods (grains, cereals, legumes, vegetables and fruits) but moderate quantities of animal-sourced foods (meat, poultry, fish and dairy products).
- Choose unrefined whole-grain products rather than refined grain products. Brown or wholemeal bread, brown rice and unrefined flour (*chakki aata*) are better nutritional choices than white bread, white rice and refined flour (*maida*).
- Eat a variety of legumes and beans. Choose vegetables of different colours (green and yellow as well as red and orange) as each colour group offers different nutrients.
- Eat a variety of fruits. Eating a fruit is a better choice than having a fruit juice. While choosing the fruit juices from supermarket shelves, choose 100% natural fruit juices with no added sugar or preservatives.
- White meats (poultry, turkey, fish) are better choices. Red meats (mutton, beef) should be used sparingly. Choose lean cuts of meat, rather than fatty prime cuts.
- For everyone over 2 years of age, low fat milk and dairy products are better nutritional choices.
- Use oils and fats sparingly. Choose plant oils such as olive, canola, sunflower, safflower or peanut (groundnut) oil. They are rich in healthy fats. Butter, ghee (clarified butter) and lard are loaded with unhealthy fats, and their consumption should be kept to minimum use.
- Nuts are rich in proteins and minerals but also in fats, so eat them sparingly. Walnuts and almonds are rich in good fats. Peanuts, hazelnuts and pistachios are also good nuts.
- Eat extra foods only occasionally and in minimal quantities. Extra foods are non-essentials such as biscuits, cakes, desserts, pastries, soft drinks; high fat snack items such as crisps, pies, sausage rolls and other takeaways; lollypops and chocolates.

- Drink plenty of water. Keep your intake of sugary or carbonated drinks to a minimum.
- Regular physical activity is considered a part of balanced nutrition.

Visual charts to plan balanced nutrition

Nutritional concepts have been evolving and changing over the years. But the basic principles have remained largely the same. Experts have prepared some visual charts about balanced diet guidelines for the general public.

Food Pyramid: In 1992, the United States department of agriculture (USDA) devised a simple guideline called the 'food pyramid' to highlight the importance of eating the right amount of food from different food groups. The figure shows the food groups and dietary recommendations.

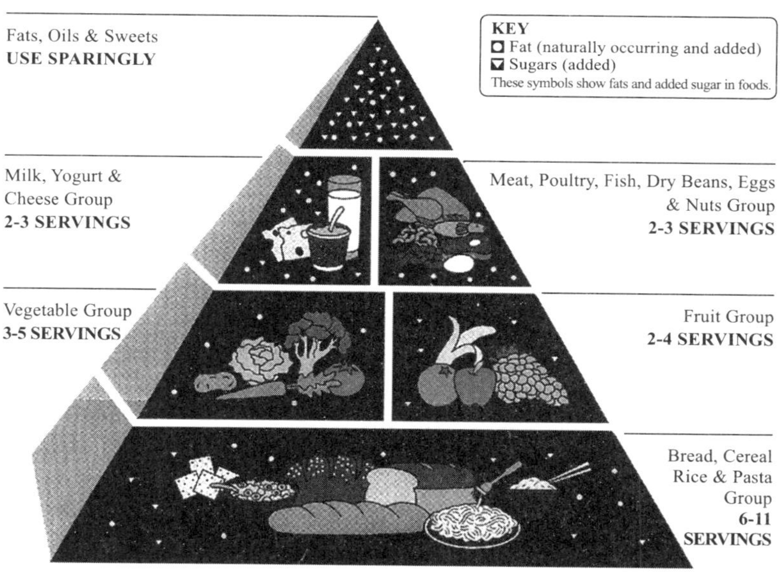

Image courtesy the USDA

MyPyramid: In 2005, the food pyramid guidelines were modified into a program called MyPyramid. This was done because experts felt that the original food pyramid did not include all food categories and did not show physical activity and discretionary calories.

Image courtesy the USDA

MyPlate (2011)

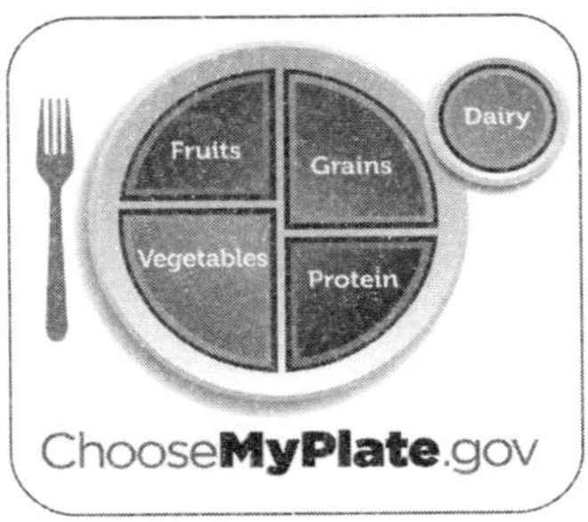

Image courtesy the USDA

In 2011, USDA made further changes to its visual guide and created the simpler MyPlate. Here half the plate is filled up with fruits and vegetables, with vegetables occupying the larger part of that half. The other half of the plate is occupied by grains and proteins, with grains occupying the larger part of that half. A side dish represents dairy products, which are smaller than all others.

Some other recommendations of the MyPlate program are:

- Use half of the grains as whole grains.
- Use low fat dairy.
- Choose different sources of proteins, mixing animal sources (meat, poultry, fish) with vegetable sources (beans, lentils, nuts).
- Cut back on foods high in solid fat or with added sugar and salt.
- Enjoy your food but eat less.
- Cook more often at home so that you can control what you are eating.

- While eating out, choose lower calorie menu options.
- Be physically active in your way. Start with any activity that suits you and do it at least for 10 minutes at a time.
- Parents are the role models for their children and should set a good example with healthy food habits.

Basic Food Groups Chart (for age 4 years and above)

No	Food group	Contains	Number and size of serving
1	Grains	Carbohydrates, protein, fiber, vitamins, minerals For grain-based foods such as bread, cereals, pasta, rice and noodles, wholemeal or wholegrain varieties have more fiber, vitamins and minerals.	3–12 servings Serving size • 2 slices of bread • 1 *chapati* or *roti* • 1 cup cooked rice, pasta, noodles, porridge • 1⅓ cup (150–200 gm) breakfast cereal flakes
2	Vegetable and legumes	Vitamins, minerals, dietary fiber, carbohydrate Capsicum, broccoli, cauliflower, cabbage and tomatoes are high in vitamin C. Dark green and orange vegetables like spinach, broccoli, carrots and pumpkin are high in vitamin A. Green vegetables, dried peas, beans and lentils are a good source of folate.	2–9 servings Serving size • ½ cup (75 gm) cooked vegetable, dried beans, peas or lentils (dal) • 1 cup raw (salad) vegetables • 1 medium sized potato or sweet potato

3	Fruits	Vitamins, carbohydrates, natural sugars, fiber	1–5 servings Serving size • 1 medium sized fruit (apple, banana, orange, pear, mango) • 2 small pieces (kiwi, plum) 2 small pieces (kiwi, plum) • 1 cup diced or canned fruit • 1 cup grapes • ½ cup fruit juice
4	Dairy products	Calcium, protein, riboflavin, vitamin B12	2–5 servings Serving size • 1 cup (250 ml) fresh milk, reconstituted powder milk, yoghurt, custard) • ½ cup evaporated milk • 2 slices of cheese
5	Protein sources	Protein, iron, niacin, vitamin B12	0.5–2 servings Serving size • 1 large egg • 100 gm cooked meat, chicken, fish equivalent in volume to a deck of playing cards • ½ cup of cooked beans, lentils, peas, chickpeas • ⅓ cup peanuts or almonds

6	Extra foods	Sugar, salt, fats (mainly saturated fats)	0–3 servings Serving size = amount giving 150 calories • 1 (40 gm) doughnut • 4 (35 gm) plain sweet biscuits • 1 slice (40 gm) plain cake • ½ small bar (25 gm) chocolate • 1 ½ scoop (50 gm scoop) ice cream • 1 can of soft drink 1 oz potato chips (about 15 chips) • 2 tablespoon (40 gm) cream, mayonnaise • 1 tablespoon (20 gm) butter, margarine, oil

(This chart uses information from the Department of Health and Ageing, Australian Guide to Healthy Eating.)

General strategies for balanced diet for a child

- Start early. Breastfeed the baby, limit bottle-feeding, avoid commercially available baby foods and properly wean to home-cooked and natural foods.
- Keep food portions small and do not force the child to eat more.
- Educate yourself and your child about good nutritional concepts.
- Become a good role model by adopting healthy food habits yourself.
- Cook and eat at home more often.
- In restaurants and fast-food outlets, try to choose healthier, low-calorie food items from the menu.
- Use fresh foods and avoid processed and packaged foods.
- Make mealtimes enjoyable family times with no distractions.
- Involve your child in buying and preparing healthy foods.
- Keep healthy snacks (like fruits and nuts) at an easily accessible and visible place in your house.

- Do not stack the house with potentially unhealthy snacks such as chocolates, chips, candies, cakes, biscuits and soft drinks.
- Make sure your child drinks plenty of water.
- Make physical activity a regular part of every family member's routine.

Five Food–Feeding Fixations

If parents are asked about what worries them the most about their children, most will say, "Their eating habits!" Food and feeding seem to occupy centre stage in most parents' minds, sometimes even at the cost of neglecting other important areas of parenting. They suffer from typical food and feeding fixations, which should be avoided to ensure good nutritional habits in children.

1. Bottle and milk fixation

It has become a routine practice in many modern families to start bottle-feeding the baby at the earliest and on the slightest pretext. Once started, this unhealthy habit is often continued until the pre-school years. In such families, giving a milk-bottle at night becomes a favourite method of putting the baby or child to sleep.

Understand one thing clearly: Bottle-feeding is an unhealthy habit and should only be used as a transient, stop-gap compromise. It should stop the moment the baby becomes ready to hold a cup and drink fluids from it. This stage usually comes by the baby's 9th month of life. So, even by allowing some margin, the first birthday is the right time to say good-bye to the bottle.

The longer you continue with the bottle, the longer you expose your child to the risk of infections (like gastrointestinal and ear-nose-throat infections) and tooth decay. Problems like reluctance to eat solid foods and constipation are also common in bottle-fed children.

Bottle fixation invariably results in overdependence on milk as the main primary source of nutrition until the pre-school years. This deprives the children of normal home-cooked, 'non-milk' foods.

Mixing milk in various weaning foods to improve their palatability and acceptability is a common parenting ploy. But this defeats the main purpose of weaning, which is to make a transition from milk to non-milk semisolid foods.

That is why in my practice, I always advise parents to not add milk to weaning foods like rice or bread, *roti* or *chapati*. If these items need to be softened, they can be soaked in non-milk food like *dal* (lentil soup) or curry. This way, babies who are already partial to the taste of milk learn to accept and appreciate the tastes of non-milk items.

2. Baby food fixation

Aren't all those attractively packaged baby foods so enticing and so convenient? But don't just go for the convenience and certainly don't fall for their 'healthier, more nourishing' advertising slogans. Babies weaned on baby foods often get accustomed to their tastes and refuse to accept home-cooked foods. Again, most baby foods have a base of cow's milk, and so babies weaned on them often don't readily accept non-milk weaning food items.

To speak out the bitter truth, your babies don't really need special baby foods. What they need are the normal home-cooked family foods, but just modified a little in taste and texture to make them easier for consumption.

3. Mixer–grinder fixation

To mash semisolid foods like rice gruel or *khichri*, we just need our fingers or at the most a spoon! To use a mixer-grinder to ground the semisolids into a smooth paste is a practice best avoided from the beginning.

Hand-mashed or spoon-mashed food retains some of its granularity, which is an important part of the texture of normal food. Babies fed on such foods adapt to normal food textures earlier and easier. Babies who get used to the too-smooth, pasty foods ground in a mixer sometimes show a choking tendency with normal foods even after they have grown older.

4. Hearsay fixation

In most cultures, various foods are labelled with attributes like 'hot', 'cold', 'gassy' and what not. Parents hear a lot about it from family and friends. This hearsay evidence—these prejudices, really—often prevent many nutritious food items from being used regularly in children's diet.

Every human body has a different system and reacts differently to different foods. So don't generalise these hearsay food tips.

Give every nutritious item without any prejudice in your mind. On repeated observations, if you feel that a particular item is causing a disturbance in your baby's health, consult your doctor before deciding to stop giving that food item.

5. Quantity fixation

Though listed last, this is the most important fixation. A parent must learn that how much a child eats is not as important as they might think.

From the very beginning of infancy starts the parental fixation about the quantity of milk or food consumed by the baby. Unless the baby is showing unsatisfactory weight gain, there is no need to be unduly worried about the question of quantity. The baby's portions are measured in a few teaspoonfuls while most parents think in terms of bowls and plates!

Learn to respect your baby's judgment about when he or she wants to stop feeding. Babies are better judges of their own system than you are. Your forced overfeeding might succeed for some time but, in most cases, it will lead to unpleasant food battles with your child in later years.

5

Anorexia, the 'No Appetite' Problem

Scenario

Geeta Subramaniam is a smart, young working mother. But she is exasperated. Her 6-year-old son Vijay is not eating well, or at least that's what she believes.

She states her problem, "Doctor, I am not just saying that my kid doesn't eat enough. He doesn't eat at all. I really feel that he practically lives on thin air!"

She then goes on to tell the whole story. "All this started towards the end of his 1st year. Earlier, he used to be a hungry baby, gulping down milk and cereals without needing much persuasion. But then he slowly started avoiding it. This pattern gradually worsened over the years. Now, he mostly avoids solid foods, vegetables in particular. The food remains on his plate, but he makes little effort to eat it himself. He takes an awful lot of a time to finish it and often refuses it altogether."

The doctor takes a quick look. The child looks active, playful and happy. Even his weight and height are falling within the normal range of values.

The doctor chuckles inside, while maintaining a serious demeanour on the outside. He just says to himself, "Yet another one!" It is yet another case of 'No appetite in my kid' that is going to need some major explanation to the mother!

Discussion

Why does a baby, once readily consuming whatever food-items were given to him, suddenly start refusing food and gradually become uninterested in it? There are many reasons for this transition and the 'no appetite' (anorexia) problem.

Natural factors

The decreased appetite that develops towards the end of the 1st year is due to a number of natural reasons. It may happen temporarily in the painful teething stage. More commonly it happens because of babies' increasing mobility. This gives them increasing freedom and with it, an increasing number of attractions that become distractions when it comes the routine and mundane milk and cereals.

By 1 year, the baby also starts developing individual likes and dislikes for foods. Bafflingly to parents, these likes and dislikes keep changing. At the same time, the baby's rapid initial growth now slows down and the caloric requirement starts decreasing.

All these perfectly natural things combine to create an impression in the parent's mind that 'my sweet little baby has suddenly lost his appetite!'

Parental factors

Parental attitude usually makes the situation worse. Most parents seem to take the natural slump in the baby's appetite as some sort of a personal failure and a great risk to the baby's health. This leads to overzealous attempts to feed the baby, who naturally responds by rebelling against the 'enemy' that food has become. Over-reliance on milk feeding, late introduction of semisolid foods and refusal to allow the baby to self-feed are other important factors in this regard.

The nutritional importance of milk is often over-emphasized. Watching the kid take large quantities of milk might be warming the cockles of many a parent's heart, but in fact it just serves to make it difficult for solid food to find its proper place on the daily diet chart. Drinking is certainly a much simpler process than eating and becomes the baby's preferred mode of ingestion. This preference is even more firmly fixed in the baby's mind if semisolid foods are introduced later than the recommended 4–6 months of age.

By the 9th month, the baby can hold things like a biscuit for eating or a cup for drinking. By 1 year, the ability to hold spoon and eat from the bowl develops to a reasonable degree. But many parents do not let the babies self-feed for fear of messiness. This is wrong as it gives the baby no opportunity to learn self-feeding and be self-reliant in that respect.

Parents often have some arbitrary ideas about which foods the baby should eat and how much. To attain these usually unrealistic goals, they put pressure on themselves and the baby, often making feeding time into battle time. The negative experiences about food and feeding at this early age are likely to leave deep imprints on the baby's growing mind and result in a long-standing problem.

Food factors

Food that has great taste, texture and appearance is bound to catch the fancy of the young, or for that matter adults. Making that kind of food is, again, the responsibility of parents. Do not try to force food items that your child dislikes but are 'healthy' in your mind (e. g., milk, spinach, broccoli). Try to find suitable alternatives or special recipes! For example, if your child dislikes milk, try to compensate by offering other milk products like curds, yogurt or cheese or try giving a milkshake.

Babies learn to eat a balanced and nutritious diet as a family tradition. So see to it that your own diet is in order!

Appetisers

The expectation that magic medicines would correct the problem of poor eating and the 'starving' child would suddenly start devouring the family's food stores is a mirage. Commonly prescribed appetite stimulant medicines have side-effects like drowsiness and are not recommended for such cases.

Giving a daily supplement of a vitamin and mineral preparation is all right as it would ward off any possibility of nutritional deficiency developing in fussy eaters. But that would not change the child's appetite dramatically.

Health factors

Practically any acute or chronic illness affects the appetite for the worse. This effect is more pronounced at younger ages. Even a simple cold can dampen the appetite for many days. Anorexia that is pathological should be suspected when there are associated symptoms like nausea, vomiting, diarrhoea, jaundice, cough, fever or a gross fall in growth in terms of weight and height.

Anorexia nervosa is a specific illness that deserves a special mention. This condition, with an unknown and probably genetic cause, is seen commonly in young, adolescent girls. The sufferers show an irrational fear of obesity, an obsession with 'perfect body figure' and an absolute avoidance of food. They are severely underweight and have irregular or even absent menses after puberty. This condition needs specialised care in a hospital set-up.

Final word of advice

Most of the times, a 'no appetite' problem is not really a medical problem. It is often caused by normal age-related changes and wrong parental concepts about foods and feeding methods.

Establish good eating habits in your child at a very early age and always take a qualified doctor's opinion before formulating your 'food and feeding policy'!

6

Food Allergy

Scenario

As 6-year-old Javed walks into the room, his mother almost screams. His face is looking bloated and his lips are swollen. He also says that he has slight breathing difficulty. He was perfectly fine before lunch. What has happened?

The mother immediately takes him to the nearby clinic. The doctor takes one look at Javed and says, "This looks like an allergic reaction. Anything new in his routine? Like a new cream, soap, clothes or food? Or was he bitten by some insect?"

The mother is unsure. Then she recalls that Javed had eaten soya curry with his lunch and that he had had soya for the first time.

The doctor says, "So it looks like food allergy."

Discussion

"To feed or not to feed, that is the question." If Hamlet had had a child with a food allergy, he would have asked this question in despair.

Food allergy and food intolerance are quite common problems in childhood and are susceptible to both under-diagnosis and over-diagnosis by parents and medical practitioners. This section will clear some common doubts.

What is food allergy?

In food allergy, the body's immune system reacts in an exaggerated manner to otherwise harmless proteins in food, which leads to adverse symptoms or signs following ingestion of that food. Such adverse reactions to food can also happen without the immune system's involvement.

Food intolerance is a broader term used to describe all such conditions when some food consistently and repeatedly causes adverse signs and symptoms.

Food allergy affects 2% of the general population and 6–8% of children. The first 6 years of life (especially infancy) is the most common period of occurrence, but food allergy can occur at any age. Family history of allergies and the presence of other allergic problems (e. g., eczema or asthma) add to the risk that a child will develop food allergy.

Offending foods and additives

Here are eight foods that most commonly cause allergy—the Big 8 of food allergy. Cow's milk is the most common offender, with 2–4% of infants allergic to it.

- Cow's milk
- Fish
- Shellfish
- Eggs
- Peanuts
- Tree nuts (e. g., almonds, walnuts, cashews, pistachios, hazelnut, macadamia)
- Wheat
- Soya

Food additives like tartrazine (E102) and benzoic acid (E210) can cause food intolerance in the form of exacerbations of asthma and eczema. Others like sodium nitrate or monosodium glutamate (*ajinomoto*) can cause headache and flushing. Sorbitol, an additive in soft drinks, can lead to diarrhoea.

Manifestations

The symptoms of food allergy often manifest within minutes of ingestion of the offending food. But sometimes they may appear after a few hours or days.

Commonly, the allergy to foods manifests in the form of symptoms related to the skin (hives, itchy rashes, swelling); the respiratory system (cough, wheezing, sneezing, nasal congestion) or the gastrointestinal system (nausea, vomiting, diarrhoea or abdominal pain).

Worsening of asthma, eczema or migraine might be observed in some cases. In infants, colic, vomiting or growth failure might be pointers to food allergy.

Anaphylactic shock is the most severe and life-threatening allergic event that can occur within minutes of ingestion of the offending food. It is fortunately a rare complication. It is particularly liable to occur with peanuts, fish, shellfish or eggs.

Sudden choking feeling, breathlessness, itching or burning sensation, swelling of face and mouth (angioedema), vomiting and collapse with fall in blood pressure are symptoms that mark anaphylactic shock, which can occur with even a single morsel of the offending food. Immediate resuscitation, with administration of adrenaline, oxygen and bronchodilators, is required to treat this condition.

Diagnosis

In spite of technological advances, the diagnosis of food allergy is still mainly clinical. Careful observation by parents and a detailed medical history is the key to diagnosis. Notice what kind of food induces an adverse reaction in your child and whether it is repetitive. Note the quantity of food eaten by the child, the cooking pattern and the timing of symptoms. Maintain a food diary to make a note of these details. Review the diary when you take your child to the doctor.

Food challenge is the most important diagnostic test where the offending food is eliminated from the child's diet for 2 weeks. If any improvement is seen after this, the food is reintroduced in small, increasing quantities while noting its effects to confirm or reject the diagnosis of allergy.

This 'open' type of food challenge is simple to conduct but may be marred by the personal biases of patients, parents or doctors. The 'blind' challenge offers food extracts in gelatinized capsules so that the child and parents do not know what food is given and their biases cannot influence the effects. This is a more expensive method but not necessarily a more accurate one. Any food challenge should be carried out in a medically supervised set-up where emergency resuscitation is available.

Allergy tests like skin-prick tests or measurement of antibody levels are expensive, often inconclusive due to the possibility of false positive or negative results, and are more useful only for immediate allergic reactions. Such tests should be done under the guidance of a doctor specialised in handling such cases.

Lactose intolerance and gluten sensitivity

In lactose intolerance and gluten sensitivity, the affected individual shows troublesome signs and symptoms after eating foods containing these substances. These signs and symptoms are not food allergies in the strict sense but intolerances to food components.

Lactose intolerant patients cannot digest the milk sugar lactose. They have either total or partial deficiency of the intestinal enzyme lactase, which is necessary to digest lactose. This deficiency may be hereditary or acquired following a gastrointestinal infection or surgery. Whenever such individuals drink milk or eat milk products, they experience nausea, abdominal pain, bloating, gas formation and/or loose motions. The condition can be diagnosed by a simple stool test. The only treatment needed is to avoid milk and milk products. Replacement of regular milk with lactose-free milk or soya milk can be considered after consulting the doctor and the nutritionist. The hereditary type of lactose intolerance can be lifelong but its severity usually decreases over the years. The lactose intolerance following an infection is usually transient.

Gluten sensitivity is most commonly seen in an autoimmune condition called celiac disease, where affected individuals cannot tolerate foods containing wheat, rye or barley. On eating such foods, they show symptoms such as bloating, nausea, abdominal pain, vomiting, diarrhoea and constipation. In children, growth failure is a common result and some may also show anxiety, depression or hyperactivity. The diagnosis is confirmed by a blood test that shows the presence of specific antibodies and a small intestinal biopsy. The treatment is avoidance of gluten-containing foods.

Tackling food allergy

There are no medicines or injections to cure food allergy. Avoidance of the offending food is the only way to manage it. In many instances, slow reintroduction of a food item is tolerated after prolonged discontinuation.

Think carefully about the nutritional and psychological implications of avoidance of foods and seek a dietician's opinion.

Carefully check nutrient labels while buying foods. Discuss food components with the waiter or chef before placing an order in a restaurant.

For cow's milk intolerance, some hypoallergenic milk substitutes can be tried. Exclusive breast-feeding until 6 months and avoidance of strong allergenic foods until the end of 1 year is sometimes recommended for children with strong history or family history of allergic disorders.

Prognosis

Allergies to cow's milk, eggs, soya and wheat usually subside by the age of 10 years, often by the age of 5 years. This applies to 85% cases of cow's milk and egg allergies and 100% cases of soya and wheat allergies.

The anaphylactic type of allergy to peanuts, tree nuts, fish and shellfish can often be lifelong. Such patients should wear alert bracelets and should learn to recognise the symptoms and self-administer the emergency drug-adrenaline.

7

Vitamins and Minerals

Scenario

Scene 1: Aarti's son is 4 years old. She is worried about his poor appetite. She asks her doctor to suggest a tonic supplying vitamins and minerals.

Scene 2: Zubair is a teenager who is studying for his final exams. He sometimes feels tired and listless. He requests his doctor to prescribe a vitamins and minerals supplement.

Discussion

Vitamins and minerals are perhaps the most eagerly demanded, most easily prescribed and most happily sold medicines! Pharmaceutical companies are making billions by selling them.

Agreed, vitamins and minerals are very important parts of a balanced diet. But is it really necessary to give them as special daily supplements? Let's find out the truth.

What are vitamins and minerals?

Vitamins and minerals are considered essential micro-nutrients. They are 'essential' because of two reasons. One, they play an important role in the body's functioning. Two, they are not synthesized—or produced—in the body, at least not in adequate amounts. That is why they need to be supplied through food or supplements. They are 'micro-nutrients' because they are required in small quantities measurable in micrograms or milligrams.

Vitamins are organic compounds present naturally in various plant and animal-sourced foods, and they are also produced synthetically in laboratory. Minerals are inorganic compounds which are naturally present in soil as well as in plant and animal-sourced foods.

Fat-soluble vitamins dissolve in fat, and water-soluble ones dissolve in water. Vitamins A, D, E and K are fat-soluble whereas

Vitamin C and vitamins belonging to the B-complex group are water-soluble. During the cooking processes, water-soluble vitamins are much more likely to be destroyed by heat or by dissolving in water.

Functions and problems of deficiency

Vitamin	Importance in the human body	Problems caused by deficiency
A	Growth, immunity, vision, integrity of skin and mucus membranes	Dryness of skin (xerosis), dryness of eyes (xerophthalmia), night blindness
D	Strengthening of bones and teeth	Rickets (weak bones and teeth)
E	Anti-oxidant, which prevents tissue damage	Haemolytic anaemia
K	Essential in the blood clotting system	Haemorrhagic disease of newborns (bleeding tendency)
C	Wound healing, tissue repair, general immunity, improved iron absorption	Scurvy (painful bones, bleeding gums, easy bruising)
Folic acid	Red cell formation, normal development of embryo	Megaloblastic anaemia, congenital problems in embryo
B12	Red blood cell formation, nervous system function	Megaloblastic anaemia, nerve affection
Other B-complex vitamins (B1, B2, B3, B5, B6 and biotin)	Various metabolic processes ensuring energy production and storage, healthy functioning of nervous system	B1—Beriberi (affects nerves and heart) B3— Pellagra (affects gastrointestinal system, skin, brain)

Food sources of vitamins

Fat-soluble vitamins (A, D, E and K) are usually found in fatty foods such as animal fats like butter and lard, fatty fish, dairy products, liver, and vegetable oils. The human body can synthesize vitamin D on exposure to mild sunlight.

Water-soluble vitamins (C, folic acid and B-complex) are usually found in fruits, vegetables, grains and dairy products.

Vitamin B12 is present only in dairy products, eggs, meat and fish. It is not found in vegetable sources.

Excess vitamins

Hypervitaminosis is a state arising out of excessive consumption of vitamins. It usually does not happen in case of water-soluble vitamins. If taken in excess amounts, they are simply washed out of the body through urine.

Excess fat soluble vitamins—vitamins A and D—can accumulate in body and cause problems. Hypervitaminosis A can be acute or chronic. In the acute state, severe headache, nausea, vomiting and double vision occur because of increased intra-cranial pressure (a condition called pseudotumour cerebri). In the chronic state, poor appetite, weight loss, hair loss and bone changes can take place.

Hypervitaminosis D can cause increased calcium levels leading to harmful effects on the heart, kidneys and eyes. It also can cause pseudotumour cerebri.

Mega-dose vitamin therapy

Taking large doses of vitamins–especially of vitamins C and E—is believed to prevent many conditions like cancer, heart disease and aging. But these theories have not been conclusively proved.

Megadoses of vitamin A in measles and of vitamin D in Vitamin D deficiency rickets are found to be useful, if used under medical supervision.

Important minerals

Minerals in the diet can be macro minerals (required in higher amounts) or trace minerals (required in very small amounts). Calcium, phosphorus, sodium and potassium are some important macro-minerals. Iron, zinc, fluoride and iodine are some important trace minerals.

Mineral	Importance	Dietary sources
Calcium	Strengthens bones and teeth; important in blood clotting, muscle contraction, nerve transmission	Dairy products (milk, yoghurt, cheese), fortified cereals, spinach

Phosphorus	Cell function, energy utilisation, bone growth	Dairy products, peas, meat, eggs
Sodium	Body's fluid balance	Dietary salt, table salt, packed and processed foods
Potassium	Body's fluid balance, blood pressure control	Banana, sweet potato (yam), soybean, yoghurt
Iron	Part of haemoglobin (a red cell oxygen-carrying pigment), nervous system function, immunity	Meat (especially red meat), seafood, green leafy vegetables
Zinc	Immunity, nerve function, reproduction	Red meats, seafoods, fortified cereals
Fluoride	Prevention of dental cavities, bone growth	Fluoridated water, fluoride toothpastes, some sea fish
Iodine	Formation of thyroid hormones	Iodized salt, processed foods

Vitamins and mineral supplements

Many people believe vitamins and minerals improve appetite and energy. No, they don't! Although vitamin-mineral combinations are the favourite prescriptions that parents like to ask and doctors like to write for the treatment of reduced appetite or energy levels, they do not really play any role in that condition.

So, when are vitamin and mineral supplements necessary? The body's vitamin and mineral requirements are met if one takes a balanced, varied diet. Only when the diet is inadequate or faulty, are these supplements useful. If you take such supplements, make sure that the quantities of vitamins or minerals are not above their RDA (recommended daily allowance) levels.

How do we ensure that we get adequate vitamins and minerals from our daily diet? Follow these simple guidelines.

- Choose fruits and vegetables of different colours.
- Use whole grains instead of refined grains.

- Use fortified dairy products and oils. (Fortification is a process where certain vitamins and minerals are added to food products.)
- If you are a non-vegetarian, try to eat a healthy variety of meat, poultry and seafood.

Besides choosing the right food, you must also cook it right.

Follow these cooking tips to preserve vitamins.

- Pressure-cooking, microwave cooking, grilling, roasting or stir-frying, are preferred methods of cooking.
- Deep frying, boiling and baking destroy vitamins.
- Cut vegetables and fruits close to cooking or serving time.
- Do not soak or wash vegetables for too long.
- Do not throw away the cooking water for vegetables. Use it to make gravies and soups.
- Do not rinse rice before cooking or, if you do, use the rinsing water for cooking.

8

Iron Deficiency

Scenario

Swati is 3 years old. She looks chubby and fair. Her mother is shocked when the doctor tells her that Swati is pale and is probably suffering from iron deficiency.

The mother exclaims, "How could that happen? We never noticed that she was pale. In fact, Swati is the heaviest child among all her cousins. Yes, there is one thing, though. She hardly eats solid foods. Throughout the day, she just keeps drinking milk from her bottle!"

Discussion

In the discussion on minerals, we have seen the importance of iron. Let's take a closer look at its deficiency, which causes many problems, usually in a slow and silent manner. It is a very common and easily preventable health problem affecting not only children but adults as well.

Importance of iron

Iron is important for haemoglobin production in the body. Haemoglobin is a pigment in the red blood cells, which carries the all-essential oxygen to tissues and carries away the harmful carbon dioxide produced during metabolism. In a case of iron deficiency, the haemoglobin in red blood cells starts decreasing and as a result, the oxygen carrying capacity of blood decreases, leading to problems in different body systems.

Iron is needed for an important enzyme needed for proper functioning of the nervous system. It also plays a role in immunity against infections.

The total body iron content in a newborn baby is 0.5 gm whereas that in an adult is 5gm. To make up this difference, the body needs around 10–15 mg of iron per day during the growing years. Adults require around 30 mg of iron per day—females needing slightly more than males as they regularly lose iron during menstruation.

Iron-rich foods

Iron in the diet is available in two forms—haem and non-haem. Haem iron is available through animal sources whereas non-haem iron is available through plant sources.

Meat (especially red meat), fish, green leafy vegetables (e. g., spinach, fenugreek), dried dates and pulses are rich dietary sources of iron. *Raagi* and *baajra* are the cereals with high iron content. Jaggery (molasses), a sugar substitute commonly used in the Indian subcontinent, is another excellent source as it is prepared in iron vessels.

Iron deficiency

Inadequate intake through food is the most common cause of iron deficiency. Among children, this happens in case of:

- Over-reliance on milk feeding
- Poor weaning pattern (inadequate solid foods)
- Fussy eating habits
- Poor dietary selection ('junk' foods)

Deficiency can occur in spite of adequate intake if there is decreased absorption of iron, which can happen when certain food items like tea (containing tannin) and cheese interfere with iron absorption. It can also happen in some malabsorption disorders.

The intake and absorption may prove inadequate if there is chronic blood loss, or long-standing loss of blood, which could be through worm infestation (hookworms), peptic ulcer, piles or heavy menstruation (in adolescent and adult females).

For the first 6 months, babies usually do not develop iron deficiency as iron stores passed on to them from the mother prevent it. From around the 8th month to 3 years of age, the risk of iron deficiency is the greatest as the stores are progressively depleted to satisfy the growing body's increasing iron needs.

In adolescent girls, after the onset of menstruation, the iron requirements go up but intake may not. They are at an increased risk for iron deficiency. Later in life, pregnancy and lactation places females in the at-risk category.

Milk feeding and iron deficiency

Breast milk contains iron not in large quantities but in a form that is absorbed easily and thus helps to prevent iron deficiency in the early months. After 6 months, breast milk alone is not sufficient to supply the baby's iron requirement.

Cow's milk contains less iron and that iron is more difficult to absorb. Sometimes, cow's milk can also cause chronic occult (hidden) blood loss through stools in many babies.

Exclusive or predominant milk feeding (whether breastfeeding, formula or cow's milk) beyond the age of 6 months deprives babies of iron-rich semisolid and solid foods. Such 'milk babies' may look chubby but usually suffer from iron deficiency.

Iron deficiency manifestation

Iron deficiency is manifested by anaemia (decrease in the oxygen carrying capacity of blood), which is seen as decreased blood haemoglobin level. (Note that iron deficiency is just one of many causes of anaemia.)

Pallor or paleness of skin, conjunctiva and nail-beds is the most important sign of iron deficiency. The deficiency develops gradually, so a person seeing the child after a long time is more likely to notice it rather than family members.

Not eating well, pica (eating unusual things like mud on the floor or paint on the wall), irritability, tiredness, lethargy, palpitations and shortness of breath are other warning signals. In severe cases, heart failure can also occur.

A number of studies have pointed out that even when not causing anaemia, iron deficiency can have significant negative effects on intellectual development. Decreased alertness, shorter attention span, delayed speech and learning defects have been observed in iron deficient toddlers, and these effects often persist into later years, sometimes even after treatment.

Diagnostics

Blood tests to check haemoglobin and microscopic blood picture are usually sufficient to diagnose the iron deficiency. Specialised blood check-ups are sometimes needed to rule out similar problems. Stool examination to rule out worm infestation or hidden blood loss is also important to detect the cause of deficiency.

Treatment and prevention

Most cases of iron deficiency are managed by giving oral iron supplements in proper doses. Vitamin C, which improves iron absorption, is often given as an adjuvant, or supporting element. The therapy is continued for a minimum of 3 months and preferably for 6 months to ensure adequate build-up of body stores.

Iron supplements cause gastric irritation in some patients. In other cases, it is not certain that the patient will take the supplements as prescribed. Only is such cases, when oral therapy is not possible, are intravenous or intramuscular iron injections necessary. These injections do not correct the deficiency more rapidly than oral preparations.

In very severe cases of anaemia, blood transfusions are necessary in the form of packed red blood cells.

Awareness, a balanced diet with less reliance on milk feeds, proper introduction of iron-rich semisolid and solid foods and regular deworming (on medical advice) are the means to prevent this important health problem.

III

Child Growth and Development

1

Growth and Development

People often use growth and development as interchangeable words to describe their child's progress, but that is wrong. These two processes are different, even though they happen simultaneously. In simple words, growth is about gaining in physical size and development is about gaining various individual abilities.

Growth

From a tiny tot sleeping peacefully near the mother's bed on the first day of life, your baby is going to grow larger, heavier and longer day by day. This multidimensional increase in the baby's physical size is called growth. Weight, length (height) and head size (head circumference) are the major parameters to assess growth. The following average values are intended to give you a rough idea of what to expect. They are not absolute norms.

Age	Weight	Weight gain
At birth	2.5–3.5 kg	
0–3 months		1 kg/month
4–6 months	2 × birth-weight	Doubles the birth-weight
4–6 months		0.50 kg/month
6–9 months		0.33 kg/month
9–12 months		0.25 kg/month
At 12 months	3 × birth weight	Triples the birth-weight
1 year to puberty		2 kg/year
During puberty		5 kg/year

Age	Length (Height)	Height gain
At birth	50 cm (20 inches)	
0–1 year		25 cm (10 inches)

At 1 year	75 cm (30 inches)	
1–2 years		12.5 cm (5 inches)
2–3 years to puberty		5–6 cm (2 inches)/year
During puberty		10–12.5 cm (4–5 inches)/year

Age	Head size	Gain in head size
At birth	35 cm (+ or – 2.5 cm)	
0–3 months		2 cm/month
4–6 months		1 cm/month
7–12 months		0.5 cm/month
At 1 year	47 cm (+ or – 2.5 cm)	

Development

Development is the fascinating, continuous journey from immaturity to maturity, in which the baby acquires new physical and mental skills with progressing age.

The development starts from the head, with the baby learning to hold it steady, and proceeds towards the feet, with the baby learning to stand and walk.

There are important milestones along the baby's development in various areas, such as physical activities (general and skilled), vision, speech and language, emotions, social interaction and overall understanding of others, learning, thinking and problem solving.

Generally, in physical development, a baby starts to hold the head steady on the neck by 4 months; rolls over from the stomach on to the back and from the back on to the stomach by 5–6 months; sits with support by 6 months and without support by 7 months; creeps, crawls and stands with support by 9 months and starts walking with or without support by 1 year. In cognitive and social development, a baby starts to smile in response to people by 6 weeks and starts speaking monosyllables like 'ma' and 'ba' by the 7th month and bi-syllables like 'mama' and 'baba' by 8 months.

This timetable of developmental milestones is not exact or absolute. It is just a general guideline, and different babies may show different pace of achieving these milestones. A baby lagging behind in just one milestone (such as sitting, walking or speaking late) is most likely to be normal if the overall developmental milestones are progressing on expected lines. But if there is an overall delay in multiple milestones, there may be a cause for concern.

Developmental Milestones up to 5 years

Some important developmental milestones up to the age of 5 years are listed below. Once again, a gentle reminder that this is a general guideline of what to expect. The ages mentioned here are the average ages at which most babies achieve certain milestones. But there are significant individual variations. Some babies achieve some milestones earlier and some later.

2 months

- Smiles responsively (social smile)
- Fixes eyes on an object and follows it to 90 degrees
- Starts cooing
- Startles on hearing a sound
- Quietens on hearing a sound, especially the mother's voice

4 months

- Starts holding the head steady on the neck (head holding)
- Looks at own hands and plays with them (hand regard)
- Follows object that moves from side to side through 180 degrees
- Turns head towards the source of sound
- Laughs and squeals
- Begins to babble, at first generally and then expressively (trying to imitate the sound it hears)

5 months

- Rolls over from the stomach on to the back (prone to supine)
- Puts fingers, toes and any handheld object in mouth (mouthing)
- Looks at own feet and plays with them (foot regard)
- Reaches for objects

6–7 months

- Sits with support
- Rolls over from the back on to the stomach (supine to prone)

- Transfers an object from one hand to the other
- Holds object in palm, first touching it with the fingers (palmar grasp)
- Can follow an object that moves all around (in 360° circle) by turning the head and eyes.
- Babbles monosyllabic sounds like 'ma', 'da' and 'ba'
- Cries on seeing a stranger (stranger anxiety)

9 months

- Sits without support
- Stands with support
- Crawls on the stomach , progresses to creeping on four limbs
- Roughly holds a small object between thumb and index finger (inferior pincer grip)
- Holds a bigger object in the palm in a scissor-like grasp.
- Says two-syllable sounds (mama, dada and baba), but without knowing the meaning
- Understands the meaning of 'no'
- Looks for fallen objects (object permanence)
- Play 'pat-a-cake' or 'peek-a-boo'

1 year

- Walks without support, only a few steps at first and slowly becoming better
- Neatly holds a small object between thumb and index finger (neat pincer grip)
- Bangs two things together
- Speaks with meaning at least one complete word, besides two-syllable words (mama, baba and dada)

1½ years

- Walks up or down the stairs with support
- Sits on a chair
- Starts to scribble
- Drinks from a cup and eats with a spoon
- Has a 15–20-word vocabulary
- Follows simple single-step commands (Stand up. Sit down.)
- Builds a tower of three cubes

2 years

- Begins to run, kicks a ball, throws a ball overhand
- Stands on tiptoe
- Points to body parts
- Has a 50-word vocabulary
- Speaks two-three word sentences
- Copies or scribbles straight lines, vertical and horizontal
- Follows two-step commands (Go there and bring that ball.)
- Begins to sort shapes and colours
- Builds a tower of more than 4 cubes
- Puts on shoes, socks and pants

3 years

- Climbs and runs well
- Walks up the stairs, with one foot alternately on each step
- Walks down the stairs, with both feet on each step before going to the next
- Pedals a tricycle
- Has a vocabulary of 1000 words
- Speaks three–four word sentences; speech understandable even to strangers
- Counts up to 10
- Sings nursery rhymes
- Builds a tower of more than six cubes
- Copies a circle
- Dresses and undresses fully, needing little help

4 years

- Goes up and down the stairs, with one foot alternately on each step
- Hops or stands on one leg for 2 seconds
- Speaks fluently, engages in conversation with another person
- Copies the plus (+) sign
- Draws a person with two–four body parts
- Has a vocabulary of 1500 words

- Speaks sentences of four–five words
- Can button clothes fully

5 years

- Skips or does somersault
- Hops or stands on one leg for at least 10 seconds
- Draws a person with at least six body parts
- Copies a cross (X), a triangle and other geometric shapes
- Has a vocabulary of 2000 words
- Speaks sentences with five–six words
- Dresses and undresses independently
- Ties shoelaces

Warning signals at various stages of development

Infancy

- Generalised significant delay in many milestones (especially social smile and head-holding)
- A body that feels too stiff or too loose
- Lack of response to caregiver's speech or actions
- Not making sounds
- Not following objects

Later ages

- Generalised significant delay in many milestones
- Losing previously achieved milestones
- Absence of expressions of affection or emotions
- Delayed speech
- Not learning new things

The Trivandrum Developmental Screening Chart (TDSC) is a simple tool to assess early developmental delay and requires no training to use. TDSC uses major developmental milestones from birth to 2 years, which give a fair idea of whether a baby's physical and mental development is within the normal limits.

The chart shows 17 common developmental milestones with the age (in months) for each milestone. To use the chart, find your baby's age on the horizontal axis and hold a finger or a pencil straight up from the number. The milestones to the left of that vertical line

Trivandrum Child Development Screening Chart

Make sure your child sees, hears and listens

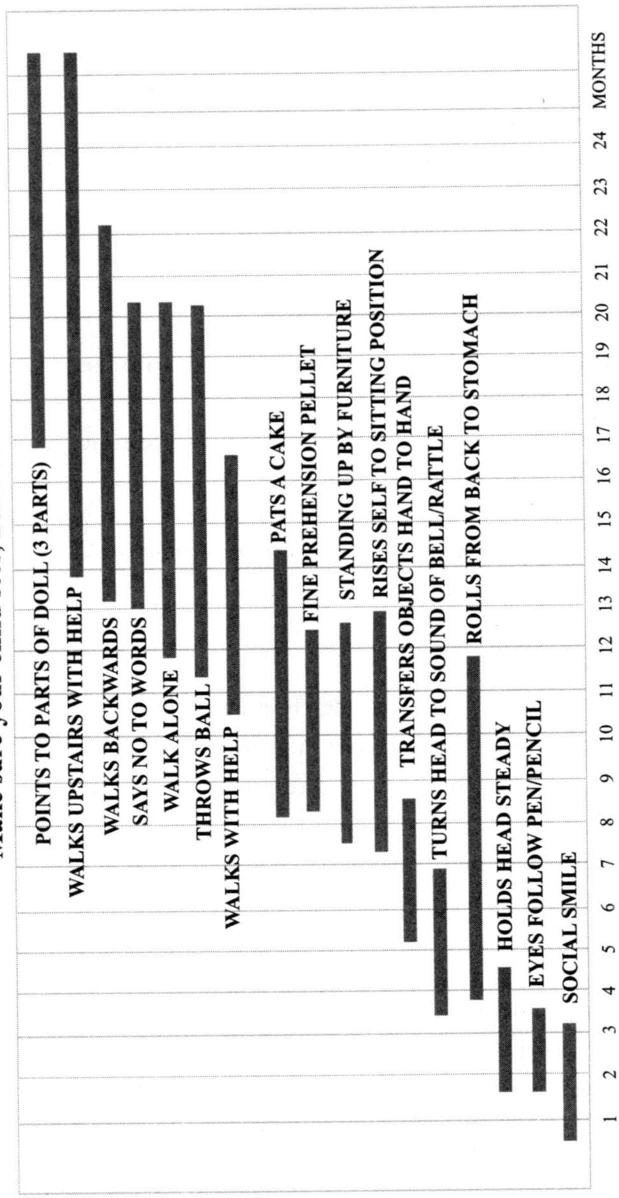

NOTE: To use this chart keep a pencil vertically on the age of the child. all miestones talling to the left of the pencil should have been achived by the child.
Based on BSID Baroda norms & Trivandrum Developmental Screening Chart (TDSC)

This represents normal range

made by the finger or pencil should have been achieved by now. The milestones to the right are still to be achieved.

If your baby is not achieving the milestones as per this chart, you should seek a specialist's opinion immediately.

General tips for parents

Growth-charts depict normal ranges for parameters like weight, length and head size (head circumference) for specific age and sex. If the periodic check-ups show that your baby's growth parameters are within the normal range and are showing an upward curve, the growth is normal. If the curve is downward or flattened, there is a need to evaluate. That's why it is important to maintain a regular growth chart, with a record of the baby's weight, length and head circumference. Make sure that these parameters are measured and plotted by a trained professional.

While keeping a record is useful, do not be too obsessed about these recorded numbers. No single number can be considered a 'normal' or 'perfect' growth parameter at any age. That is why you should never get caught up in this 'number' game when it comes to your baby's weight or height. Record each major developmental milestone by date. Mostly your child's development is likely to go on in an 'auto' mode, so you won't have to really worry.

A minor delay in individual milestone is usually acceptable. Only when there is a distinct generalized delay in most major physical and mental milestones, there is a need to investigate. Be aware of the warning signals. Have regular check-ups with a reliable paediatrician with whom you can freely discuss any doubts.

Health advice from elders and friends is welcome and well-meaning but it is not always correct. Always verify its correctness with your doctor.

Final word of advice

Never ever compare your baby with any other baby in any aspect. Don't be upset if your baby is not chubby like this neighbour's baby or not sleeping soundly like that relative's baby. Your baby is a unique individual who will show unique patterns of growth, development, personality, sleeping, teething and feeding. Nature does not create clones; it thrives on diversity and individuality.

Just follow the norms of nature with sensitivity, add a dash of sensibility and you should do fine as parents!

2

Growth and Development Charts

There are certain charts showing typical growth and development. You can use these to track your child's progress. These charts are prepared by Indian Academy of Paediatrics based on research on Indian children. In each type, there are separate charts for boys and girls. In some charts, multiple graphs are incorporated. Each chart or each graph is either depicting the range of one particular growth parameter at different ages or comparing one growth parameter against another growth parameter.

It is not very difficult to use such a chart. For example, in charts depicting stature, weight, head circumference or BMI for age, the value for that particular growth parameter is on the y (vertical) axis and the value for age is on x (horizontal) axis. The pairs of the two values are plotted to form the graph. The ranges are depicted by the percentile lines within the graph. A percentile is the percentage of population at or below the values on that graph. The 5th percentile, the 50th percentile and the 95th percentile represent the lowest, the median (average) and the highest value for that parameter.

These charts have been provided in this book as a ready reference for the ranges. Still, it is wise to understand how to plot and interpret these charts by consulting your paediatrician.

Growth charts from WHO and CDC (Center for Disease Control, US) are also used by many doctors. You can access these charts on the web.

The links are as follows;
http://www.who.int/childgrowth/standards/en/
http://www.cdc.gov/growthcharts/

Length for age, weight for age and head circumference for age, 0–36 months

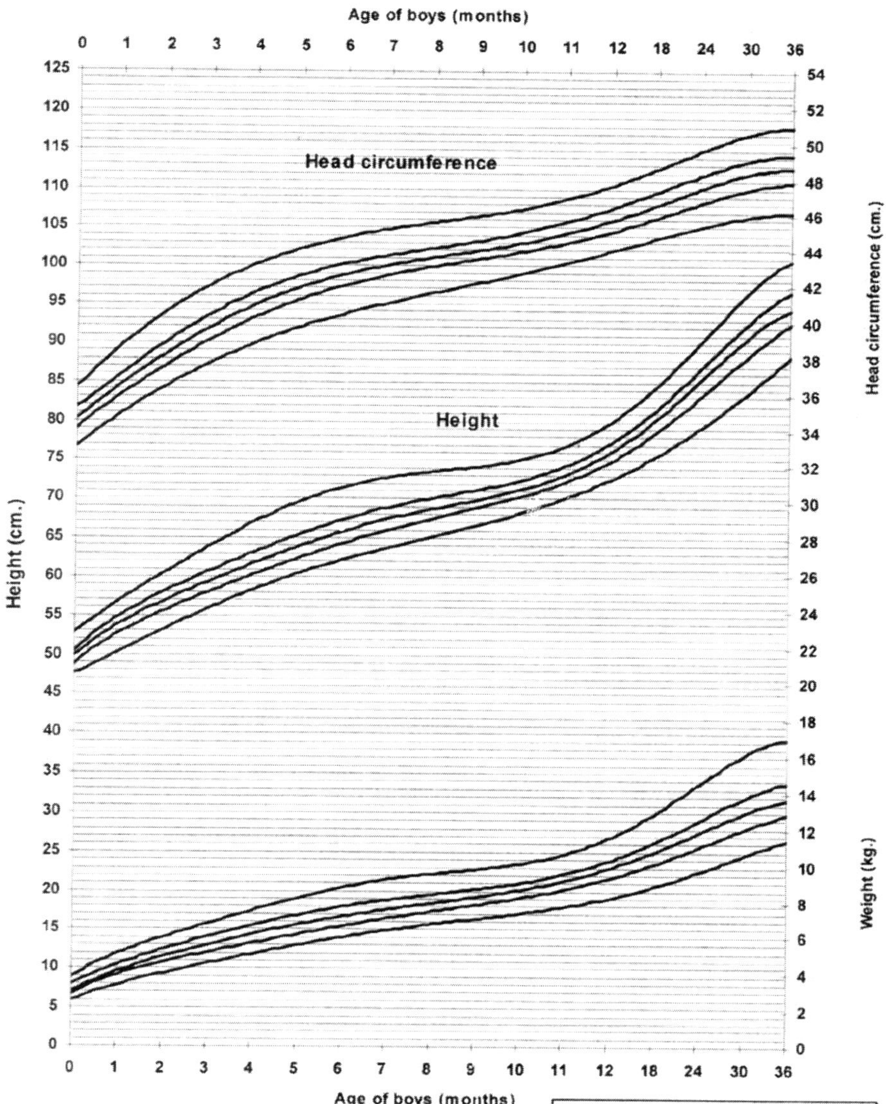

Centile Sequence: from top
97th, 75th, 50th, 25th, 3rd

Chart designed by Agarwal KN, Agarwal DK, Bansal AK for Indian Academy of Paediatrics.

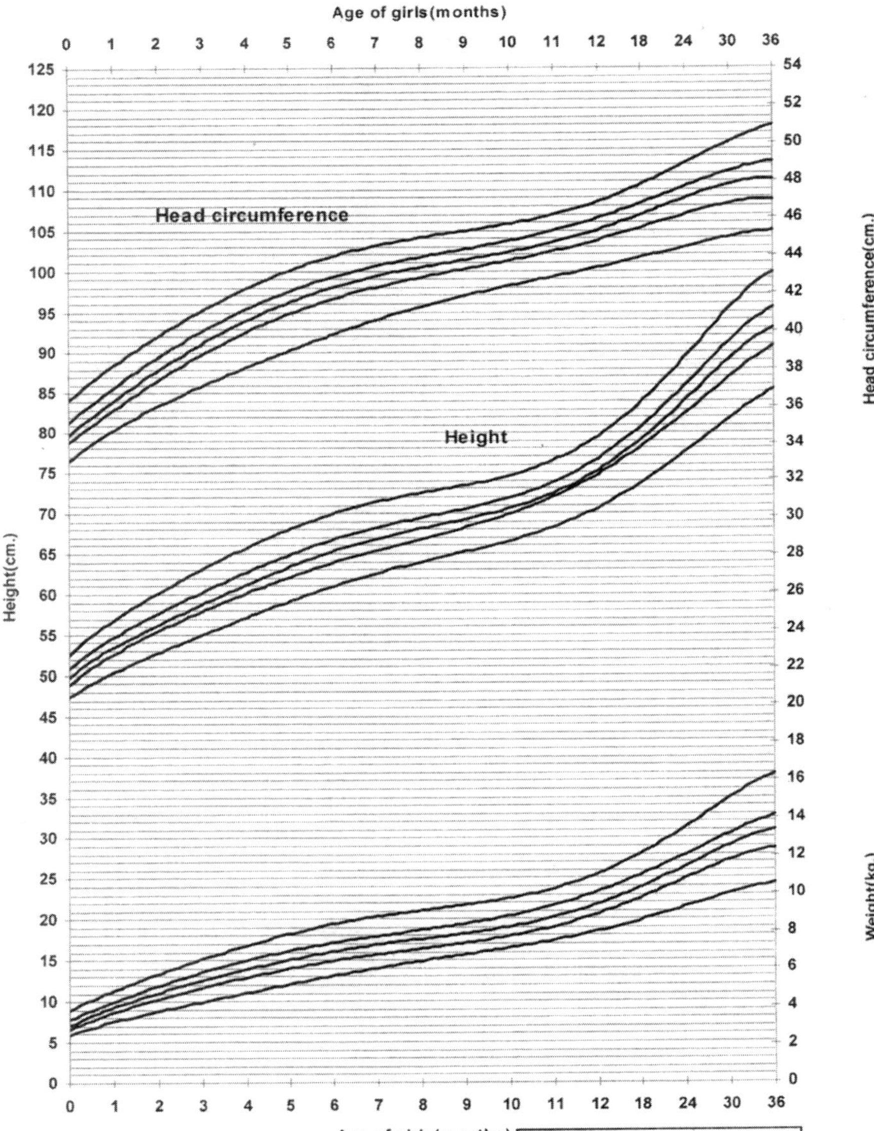

Centile Sequence: from top
97th, 75th, 50th, 25th, 3rd

Chart designed by Agarwal KN, Agarwal DK, Bansal AK for Indian Academy of Paediatrics.

Stature for age and weight for age, 2–18 years (for boys)

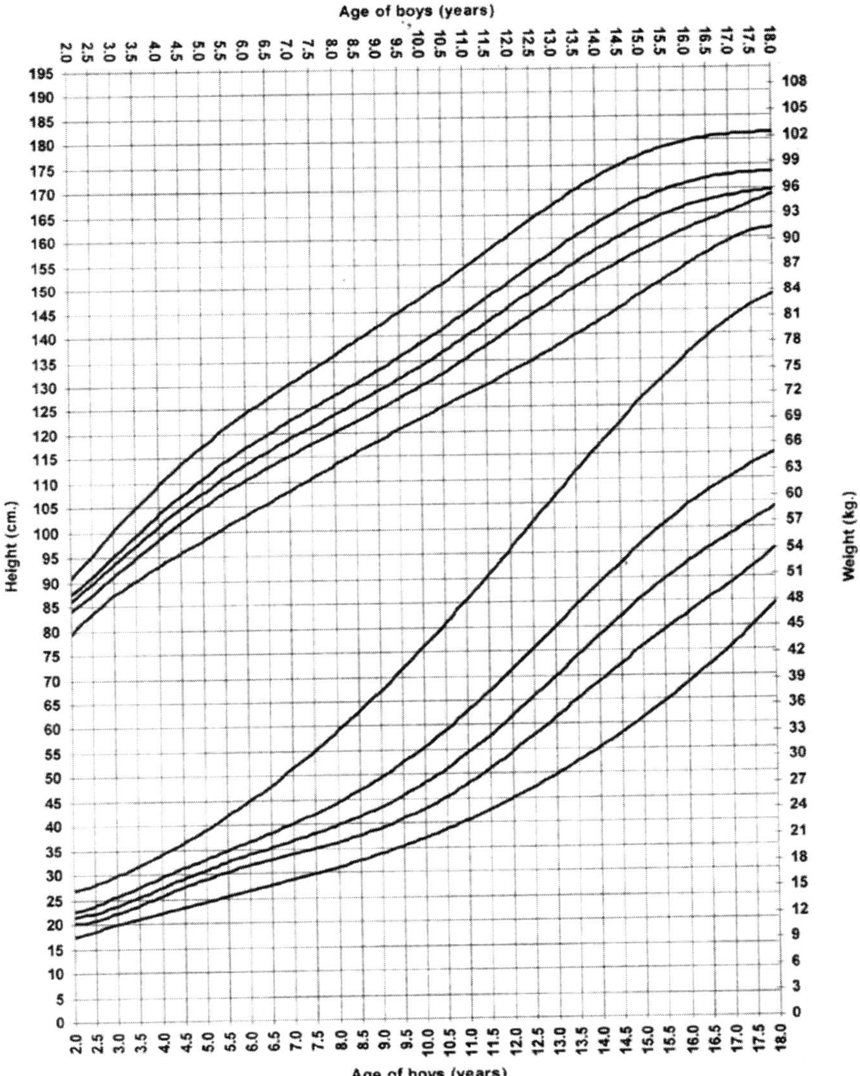

Centile Sequence: from top 97th, 75th, 50th, 25th, 3rd

Chart designed by Agarwal KN, Agarwal DK, Bansal AK for Indian Academy of Paediatrics.

Stature for age and weight for age, 2–17 years (for girls)

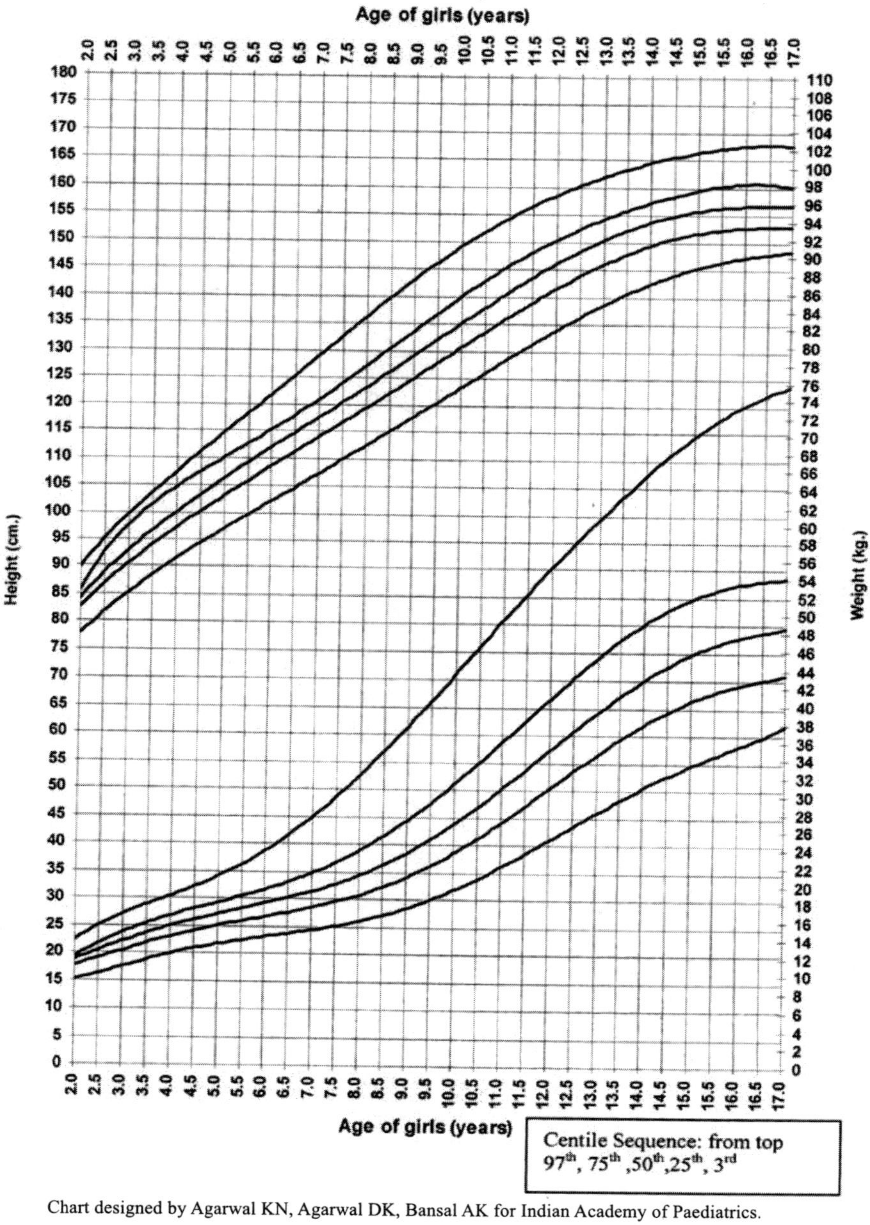

Chart designed by Agarwal KN, Agarwal DK, Bansal AK for Indian Academy of Paediatrics.

BMI, Weight for stature, 2–18 years

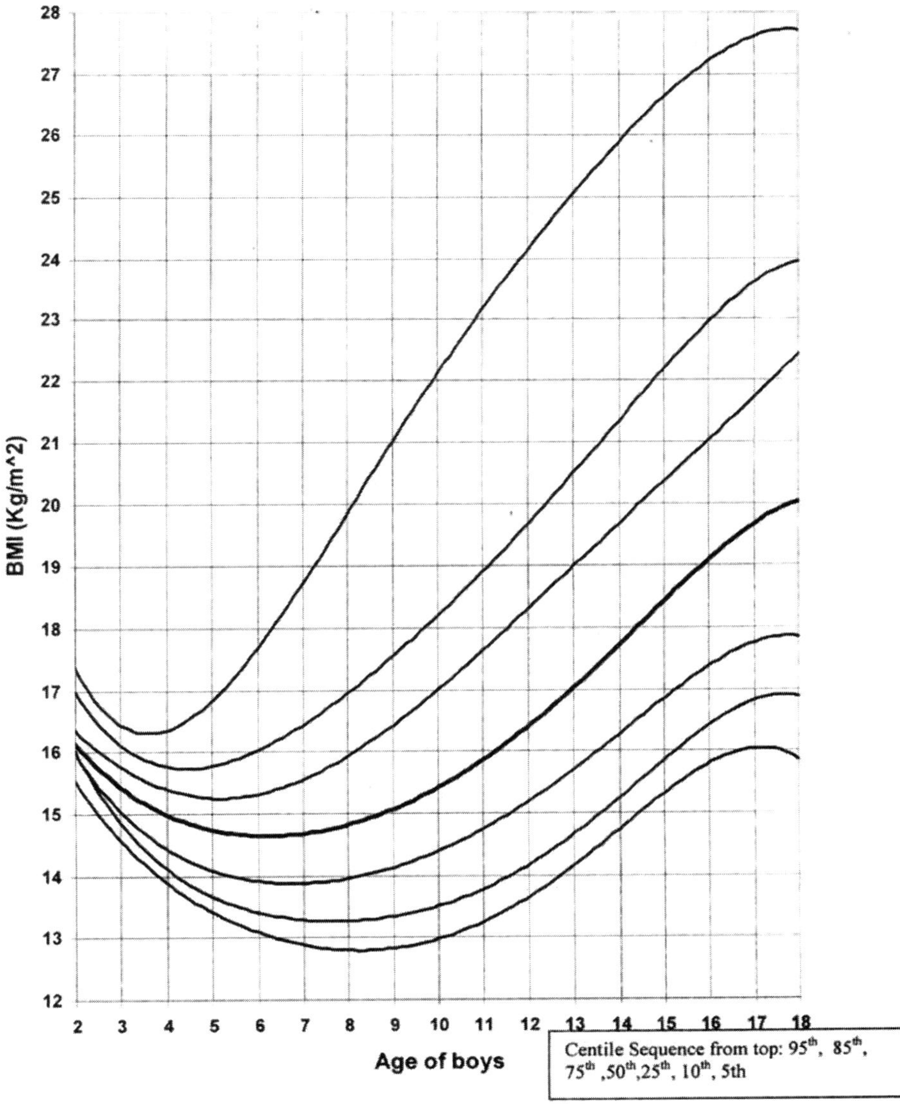

Chart designed by Agarwal KN, Agarwal DK, Bansal AK for Indian Academy of Paediatrics.

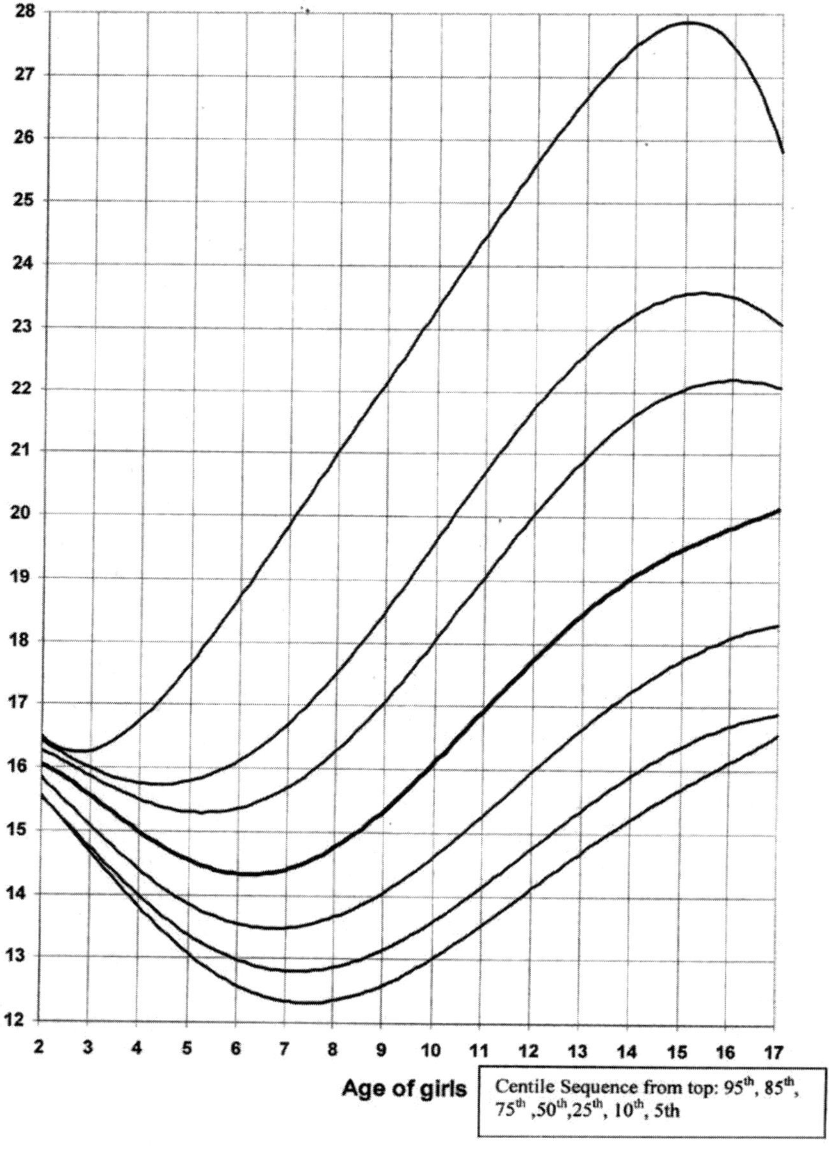

Chart designed by Agarwal KN, Agarwal DK, Bansal AK for Indian Academy of Paediatrics.

3

Failure to Thrive

Scenario

"My baby is not putting on weight. For the last 3 months, he has weighed the same," Asmita ruefully tells her friend Mamta.

Mamta is in the same boat and immediately says, "My Priya, too, looks so thin and small compared to other toddlers. It is as if she is not growing at all."

Together the friends visit their doctor, who tells them that their children are suffering from 'failure to thrive'.

Discussion

What is 'failure to thrive'? The term means that the child is lagging behind the normally expected weight gain and other growth norms without any apparent cause. It is not a single specific condition, and multiple causes may be responsible for such an abnormal pattern of growth.

Most commonly, this condition is found in children below 3 years of age. This is because growth and weight gain in infants and toddlers is rapid and obvious, and parents easily notice any unusual change. But the condition can and does occur even in older children.

Diagnosis

A simple method to diagnose this condition is to maintain a growth chart and look for any abnormal pattern. Two abnormal patterns would be a flat or downward-sloping curve instead of the steady upward-sloping curve that indicates normal growth. Weight for age is the most commonly used growth chart to diagnose 'failure to thrive'. There is no single normal or ideal weight for any age. But there is a normal range of values.

In the usual pattern, the weight gain is rapid in infancy. Usually, birth weight is doubled by 4–6 months and tripled by 12 months.

Thereafter, weight gain slows down until puberty, with a gain of around 2 kg every year considered normal. After puberty (12–18 years), the weight gain is again rapid at around 5 kg every year.

Failure to thrive is diagnosed under the following conditions:

- The child's weight is persistently below the normal range for the age.
- There is sudden major weight loss at any age.
- The weight remains unchanged for three consecutive months in infancy.

Causes

In many cases, failure to thrive may not be caused by any physical illness but due to parental neglect, which may be due to socioeconomic reasons (such as poverty, lack of education and awareness) or emotional reasons (such as unwanted child, parental conflicts, depressed mother). Parental ignorance about right foods and feeding methods is often the underlying cause.

Sometimes, the reason may be an underlying medical disease. Any serious congenital problem, systemic disease or chronic infection can lead to failure to thrive.

Investigation

Doctors do a thorough medical check-up of the patient and also get a detailed history of the family environment and dietary pattern. Complete blood count, routine urine and stool testing, serum electrolyte levels and chest X-ray are the basic lab tests in such cases. Depending on the suspected cause, the doctor may order more tests like hormonal, chromosomal, metabolic or radiologic screening.

Treatment

A case of failure to thrive caused by parental neglect needs counselling and community help for the parents. Health and dietary education for parents can solve the problems caused by parental ignorance.

If failure to thrive is caused by a medical condition, that underlying condition needs to be treated.

Hospitalisation is needed in severe cases. In such cases, a special feeding formula is given through a tube passed through the nose into the stomach. A weight gain of half a kilogram per week is taken as a good response to treatment.

Importance of diagnosis and treatment

As 'failure to thrive' happens in the early years, which is the prime growth period for the child, it can seriously affect long-term physical and mental development. To get an idea of how crucial this period is, consider the medical fact that as much as 50% of human brain development takes place in the baby's first year. Imagine the effect of any nutritional deficit in that crucial period.

Final word of advice

Maintain a positive family atmosphere and be aware of correct nutrition and growth patterns. Schedule regular well-baby visits to monitor your baby's growth. Get timely nutritional advice and identify any problems.

Remember that not all babies grow at the same rate or have same weight. Breastfed babies are often leaner than bottle-fed babies, which is normal. Babies of leaner parents tend to be normally leaner.

When the growth pattern suggests failure to thrive, get immediate medical advice.

4

Childhood Obesity

Scientists have come up with some interesting theories about why the human race is getting fatter. Evolutionary scientists say that, as early humans moved from warm areas to cold areas, they evolved a new set of genes for depositing brown fat in their bodies. This fat would be burned to keep them warm and see them through famines. But as humans developed farming and other technologies which assured a stable supply of food, the same once-protective fat-depositing genes began to play a villainous role and made the human race prone to obesity and diabetes!

Another popular science theory says that early humans had to walk and run long distances in order to hunt and gather food to survive. Strenuous physical activities were part of their daily routine. But as humans evolved and used their intelligence to develop farming and many labour-saving inventions and innovations, life became too easy. The human body systems, which were originally built for a daily physical grind and limited food, now get hardly any exercise but plentiful food. That is why the human race is becoming fatter day by day!

Whatever may be the reasons, one thing is sure that the world is suffering from a global epidemic of obesity. Overweight is weight higher than normal for a particular age or height. Obesity is excess body fat in addition to excess weight. According to some recent major studies by important bodies such as World Health Organization:

- Global overall obesity cases have increased by 82% over the last 20 years.
- There is 100% rise in obesity in West Asian countries over the last 20 years.
- Childhood obesity has doubled in children and tripled in adolescents in the last 30 years.

- In 2010, more than 40 million children under the age of 5 years were overweight and 35 million of them were from developing countries.
- Of the total global population, 65% is in countries where there is a greater risk of death from overweight and obesity than from underweight.

Reasons for childhood obesity

In some instances, hormonal disorders, genetic problems and medications may be associated with overweight or obesity. But more than anything else, obesity is considered to be a lifestyle disease.

Lifestyle factors

Faulty diet pattern

The parental craving for 'chubby' babies and error of equating 'heavy' babies to 'healthy' babies is often the first negative influence on the child's diet pattern. Unhealthy dietary habits like foregoing breast-feeding, excessive use of bottle-feeding and readymade baby-foods, and feeding large portions start in the early months of a baby's life.

Such poor dietary habits deteriorate. In later years, there is lack of fruits and vegetables in the diet and increasing intake of 'unessential' pleasure foods like cakes, chocolates, chips, colas, donuts and ice-creams. Instead of fresh, home-cooked food, children are often given fast foods, pre-packaged foods and restaurant foods. The portion sizes have increased drastically in the home and outside.

Decreased physical activity

Increasingly insecure social environment and increasing educational workload have ensured that children spend more time cooped up at home than actively playing outside. Playing with electronic devices (computers and gadgets) and watching television have become the main childhood activities.

More and more schools are cutting physical education programs altogether or reducing the time spent on fitness-building physical activities. This serious lack of physical activity is equally or perhaps even more important than wrong food habits in making today's children fat.

Dangers of childhood obesity

Overweight children are at risk of developing medical problems that affect their present and future health and have a direct impact on their quality of life.

Immediate dangers

Overweight and obese children are more prone to serious medical problems like high blood pressure, high cholesterol, Type 2 diabetes, liver and gall bladder diseases and bone and joints problems. They have an increased chance of developing asthma and stoppages in breathing while sleeping (sleep apnoea).

Overweight children may be taller and more sexually mature than their peers, creating expectations that they should behave as old as they look, not as old as they are.

These children often face isolation and ridicule from their peers. This can result in serious depression and low self-esteem. They can develop food-related psychological problems like anorexia nervosa and bulimia.

Future dangers

Obese children and adolescents are likely to be obese as adults and are more at risk for adult health problems such as heart disease, type 2 diabetes, stroke and osteoarthritis. Overweight and obesity are associated with increased risk for many types of cancer. Overweight girls may have irregular menstrual cycles and fertility problems in adulthood.

Body Mass Index (BMI)

Body mass index (BMI) is an easy-to-use tool to diagnose weight problems. BMI is defined as a person's body weight (in kg) divided by the square of height (in meters).

BMI = Weight (kilograms) / (height (metres))2

In adults, BMI under 18.5 is considered underweight; between 18.5 and 24.9 is normal; between 25 and 29.9 is overweight and above 30 is obese.

In children, BMI calculation takes age and sex into account. There are age- and sex-based percentile charts for BMI, which give a good idea about any weight problems.

American Academy of Paediatrics recommends using BMI charts to screen for obesity and overweight in children above the age of 2 years.

Parenting strategies to counter childhood obesity

Good food habits

- Breast-feed in infancy.
- Avoid or limit bottle-feeding.
- Give home-cooked, fresh foods rather than readymade processed foods.
- Give smaller portions of food. Don't be over-concerned about how much your child eats.
- Use recommended portions of varied fruits, vegetables, whole grain cereals, low fat dairy, lean meats and monounsaturated or polyunsaturated fats. Try to achieve a balanced diet.
- Avoid excess sugar, salt and saturated or trans fats.
- Limit fast foods and unessential 'pleasure' foods.
- While eating out in restaurants choose the right menu items (e.g., grilled or steamed dishes rather than fried dishes) and ask for smaller portions.

Physical activity

- Encourage sports activities like running, swimming, cycling, outdoor games (e. g., kho-kho, kabaddi, football, cricket, hockey) and indoor games (e. g., basketball, squash, badminton) which burn accumulated calories.
- Limit the idle time spent indoor in front of a computer, gadget or television.
- Make sure that the school's physical education program is adequate to keep your child active.
- Group physical activities (martial arts, yoga, exercise training, dance) are suitable for older children.

Parental role model

- Don't equate your child's weight with his health.
- Don't force food on a child who doesn't want to eat.
- Don't use food as reward or punishment.

- Make an extra effort to cultivate the good food habits and exercise routine yourself because children often pick up parent's habits, whether consciously or unconsciously.
- If you are managing an obese child's diet, make sure that the entire family participates as a unit in that diet plan. This doesn't mean that the healthy family members have to cut down their food intake but they all should follow the advised dietary changes such as avoiding the so-called 'pleasure foods' and fast foods at the dining table.

5

Understanding Short Stature

Scenario

Ajith and Shweta are both short. They see that their 5–year-old son, Ramesh, is the shortest in his class. "Is he going to be short just like us?" is their not unreasonable worry. So they decide to visit their doctor.

Sharmila is 10 years old and looks quite short compared to her classmates. Her father and mother are both tall and quite surprised that their child is so short. But they both remember that they too were quite short in their early school years and grew tall only after reaching puberty. Still, they do not want to leave anything to chance and seek medical opinion.

Discussion

Stature or height, apart from weight, is the aspect of child growth that worries parents the most. "He is the shortest student in his class" or "I hope she will grow tall—unlike me!" are comments one commonly hears from parents, and it is easy to feel their anxiety hidden under an apparently nonchalant exterior.

Factors determining height

The normal height of a child is determined by a number of factors.

- Height of parents, which shows the genetic potential and family trend
- Hormones such as growth hormone and thyroid hormone
- Good family environment with parental love and nurturing
- Balanced nutrition

Normal pattern of height gain

The height or rather the length of the newborn baby is approx. 50 cm or 20 inches. By 1 year, it usually increases by 25 cm

(10 inches) and reaches 75 cm (30 inches). During the 2nd year, the child gains 12.5 cm (5 inches) and during 3rd year, another 7.5–10 cm (3–4 inches).

Thereafter, until the age of 12 years, the yearly height gain is 5–7.5 cm (2–3 inches). After puberty, during the adolescent years, height gain is again faster. Girls gain around 8 cm (3 inches) per year and boys 10 cm (4 inches) per year.

Short stature

Short stature is defined as height that falls below the normal range when compared to others of the same age, sex and ethnic background and also taking into consideration the heights of other family members.

Causes of short stature

Many cases of short stature may be a result of normal natural variations. Constitutional delay in growth and familial short stature are two common conditions in this category.

Then there are cases where short stature is caused by an underlying problem. Malnutrition, parental neglect, hormonal disturbances, some bone disorders (e. g., achondroplasia), some specific syndromes (e. g., Turner syndrome) and any severe chronic illness can lead to short stature.

Constitutional delay versus familial short stature

Although children with both conditions show short heights and slow growth rates, there are certain important differences. In constitutional delay, the parents are of normal height and the child will grow up to normal height, only the growth will occur after puberty at a later age. In familial short stature, the parents are short and the child will grow up to be a short adult. The table shows the differences.

	Constitutional Delay in Growth	**Familial Short Stature**
Parental height	Normal	Short
Growth rate of height in childhood	Lagging behind normal	Lagging behind normal
Physical milestones (teething, puberty, sexual development)	Delayed	Normal

Bone age on x-rays	Delayed	Normal
Family history	Delayed puberty, pubertal growth spurt, normal adult height	Shortness, genetic
Treatment	Mostly not needed Explanation of the condition and reassurance	Not needed Explanation of the genetic nature of the condition
Adult height of child	Normal	Short

Hormonal problems causing short stature

Hypopituitarism is a condition in which the pituitary gland functions below its normal capacity. Pituitary is a small gland in the brain secreting the growth hormone and other important hormones. Hypothyroidism is a condition in which the thyroid gland in the neck is functioning below its normal capacity. Both these conditions cause significant short stature.

Apart from these hormonal conditions, untreated or uncontrolled diabetes, excessive steroids (either taken in medicines or caused by adrenal gland dysfunction) and severe vitamin D-resistant rickets can cause shortness.

Investigation

A detailed analysis of the home or family environment is done to make sure that the child is receiving good nutrition and nurturing. Parental heights and their growth histories are noted.

A thorough clinical examination and routine blood and urine analyses are done to check for any common underlying illness.

Specialized tests like x-rays to determine bone age, blood biochemistry, hormonal studies, chromosomal analysis and brain scans are sometimes necessary.

Treatment

The treatment for short stature depends on the cause of shortness. Correction of underlying systemic illness, malnutrition or psychosocial deprivation is necessary if these are the responsible factors.

Familial short stature does not need any treatment. Constitutional delay in growth mostly needs just reassurance. Occasionally, hormonal therapy for sexual development is needed.

Pituitary and thyroid hormone deficiency needs appropriate hormonal replacement. One important fact about these hormonal treatments, especially growth hormone, is that they are to be used only by expert advice and only when there is a proven deficiency of that hormone in the body.

Final word of advice

Tall stature is a social obsession. Regardless of several short people who have made it big in life, shortness is still looked down upon. For a short child, the emotional support of parents is essential. Short children should be made to realise that height is a minor part of the person they are and other positive attributes would help them overcome this relatively minor physical handicap.

Appendix: Predicting height

Adult height from childhood height

There are various statistical formulae to predict adult height from childhood height. As usual, they provide only a general indication and are not considered absolutes. Here are two formulas by Tanner. (Values are in centimetres.)

- Adult height = 2 × Child's height at 2 years
- Adult height = 1. 87 × Child's height at 3 years

Child's height from parents' heights

Statisticians have worked out formulae for this. Here are the steps, if you are keen to go through this exercise. (All values are in centimetres.)

Step 1: Measure parents' heights in centimetres.

Step 2: Calculate mid-parental height, which is the average of the parent's heights. If A = Father's height and B = Mother's height, mid-parental height = (A + B)/2.

Step 3: Calculate the corrected mid-parental height by adding 6.5 for boys and subtracting 6.5 for girls.

- Corrected mid-parental height for boys = Mid-parental height + 6.5
- Corrected mid-parental height for girls = Mid-parental height – 6.5

Step 4: Calculate the anticipated adult height of the child.

Anticipated adult height of the child = Corrected mid-parental height +/ – 8

Note that this is a range and not a single number.

IV

Immunisation

1

Understanding Vaccines

Scenario

Dr. Vyas smiles with pleasure when Mr. and Mrs. Bhatnagar and their 6-month-old son Arnav enter his consulting room. They make such a perfect, nice and happy family! Behind them walks in a grand old lady in her seventies. Almost bowing with deference, Mr. Bhatnagar introduces her, "She is my mother. She has come to visit us."

Dr. Vyas gives her his best smile, but she barely notices it. Acknowledging him with a brief, curt nod, she begins to talk in an officious tone, "I used to work as the chief secretary."

Dr. Vyas is duly impressed and asks, "At the state secretariat?"

She shakes her head and replies in an irritated tone, "No, not there, in our housing society's office."

Taking no notice of Dr. Vyas's disappointed face, she continues, "I was just going through Arnav's vaccination chart, and I must say I was shocked to see it. So many vaccines for such a small baby. We never had so many vaccines in our days and we did just fine. Then why are so many vaccines given today? Isn't it all an unnecessary expense? My friend told me that she read on a website that these vaccines are dangerous and often cause serious problems."

Dr. Vyas tries to speak, but the chief secretary goes on, "My grandson has a cold and still they brought him for his vaccines because, they said, you told them that it was okay. Then they tell me that it is okay to give the baby a bath after the vaccines. What is all this? I told my son that I must speak to the doctor and unless my doubts are cleared, I won't let them carry on with this nonsense."

Dr. Vyas takes a deep breath to calm himself. He is going to have to give his discourse on vaccines to convert yet another adamant vaccine-nonbeliever into a believer!

Discussion

In the history of medicine, vaccines occupy a pride of a place as one of the most successful advancements. Thanks to vaccines, millions of lives have been saved from many deadly diseases.

Vaccines prevent serious illnesses, and we all know that prevention is better than cure. Vaccines do not kill natural immunity—rather they stimulate immunity against various infections.

A vaccine is a modified product from an infective organism like a bacteria or a virus. Giving a vaccine is deliberately introducing a mild, insignificant infection in the body to stimulate and prepare the body's defences. When there is a real infection, the defence system is ready and able to combat that infection.

The immunity offered by most vaccines starts to wane after a few years. A booster dose is a repeat dose of a vaccine to 'boost' the decreasing immunity. A booster is not an extra-powerful vaccine. Some parents ask whether there are too many vaccines today. It is true that the recommended vaccination schedule has expanded over the decades. Compared to a handful of vaccines in the earlier programs, the number of vaccines given today has increased considerably. Thanks to continuing research and advancement in medical technology, now we have vaccines against illnesses against which we earlier had no helpful preventive measures.

Emerging trends suggest that we will have many more vaccines in the years to come. Rather than feeling worried by this phenomenon, we should be happy that the next generations are going to get much better prevention against many life-threatening illnesses.

Misconceptions about vaccines

There is a misbelief that vaccines are dangerous. Most vaccines have very mild and minimal side effects like some pain, redness or swelling at the injection site and fever. These side effects are occasional, transient and easily avoided with a few doses of analgesics. Serious side effects, though possible, are very rare.

Do not avoid vaccinating your child because you are afraid of the side effects. The benefits of vaccines far outweigh their minor side effects.

There are some dubious websites blaming everything wrong under the sun on vaccines. But understand that any vaccine is used in a public program only after multiple, rigorous trials of its safety and efficacy. Expert Indian and international bodies consisting of experienced doctors and scientists carefully evaluate all the research data and only then recommend a vaccine for general use.

Another common question from parents is whether a lot of precautions are needed after vaccination, like not feeding the baby for an hour or not giving a bath the next day. But these are misconceptions. For oral vaccines like the oral polio vaccine or rotavirus vaccine, feeding needs to be postponed for just 15 minutes after vaccine administration. This is done to avoid the child vomiting out the vaccine with the milk. As far as the bathing is concerned, it should go on as usual. There is no harm in bathing after vaccination.

Parents want to know whether they can we give vaccines when the child is ill. There is no need to avoid vaccination for minor illnesses like cold, cough or loose motions. Only when the child is running a high fever and looking really sick should the vaccination be postponed.

Basic vaccination

The vaccination schedules—the vaccines that are given to all babies—are decided according to a country's peculiar disease risk patterns and preventive needs. According to their environments, different countries have different disease risk patterns, different public health policies and therefore different vaccination schedules.

Certain vaccines are considered so important that they are universally included in the vaccination schedule starting at birth. They protect against a variety of the most common and potentially life-threatening diseases at the vulnerable age 0–2 years.

The basic vaccination programme includes OPV or IPV (oral or injectable/inactivated polio vaccine), DPT (diphtheria, pertussis, tetanus vaccine), Hib (haemophilus influenza type b vaccine), HBV (hepatitis B vaccine), measles vaccine and MMR (measles, mumps, rubella vaccine). In most developing countries, BCG (bacille calmette guerin) vaccine against tuberculosis is also included in the basic schedule.

All over the world, these basic vaccines are available free of cost in government hospitals and health centres. The inclusion and timing of individual vaccines and the duration between them may vary from country to country.

Many parents seem to think that once they complete the government-sponsored basic schedule of vaccination, the protection is complete. Unfortunately this is not true in the strict sense. The basic government vaccine schedule does not cover all the preventable diseases. This is mainly because it is economically not feasible for most governments to offer all the vaccines free of cost. Some vaccines are excluded because the diseases they protect against are not common in the relevant region. Most government schedules are intended for the infants up to 18 months, and older children are not covered.

That is why, even if you have completed the government vaccination schedule for your baby, you should always discuss with your doctor whether any other vaccines are necessary for your child.

Between 4½ to 6 years, doses of OPV, DPT (or DT for children over 6 years), MMR, chickenpox and typhoid vaccines are given as boosters. At 10–12 years of age, the Tdap (tetanus, low-dose diphtheria, acellular pertussis) or Td (Tetanus, low-dose diphtheria) booster is advisable.

Other vaccines

Apart from basic vaccines, there are quite a few vaccines available through private medical clinics and hospitals. These include vaccines against pneumococcal infections, rotavirus, influenza, hepatitis A (common infective jaundice), typhoid, human papilloma virus (HPV), meningococcal meningitis, cholera, chickenpox, influenza, Japanese encephalitis, yellow fever and rabies.

Of these, pneumococcal conjugate vaccine (PCV), rotavirus, hepatitis A, chickenpox, typhoid and human papilloma virus (HPV) vaccines are now already included in the ideal schedule recommended by the Indian Academy of Paediatrics.

The influenza vaccine is recommended by the American Academy of Pediatrics for everyone above 6 months who wants to avoid the flu. Indian Academy of Paediatrics recommends this vaccine for high-risk individuals.

Vaccines like meningococcal meningitis, cholera, Japanese encephalitis and yellow fever are necessary for persons travelling to endemic areas (areas where the risk of these specific diseases is higher) or when there is an epidemic.

The rabies vaccine is given after a dog-bite or animal bite.

Adherence to vaccination schedule

The dates in the vaccination schedule serve as guidelines, and a few days here or there do not make much difference. But do not delay too long because that would jumble up other timings and make the entire schedule go haywire.

Vaccination is all about bringing your child under protection against illnesses. Any delay from your side could leave your child unprotected during that period. That is why always try to adhere to the prescribed dates.

Expense

Unfortunately, the cost of the vaccinations sometimes forces parents to avoid them. Most parents try to explain it away by saying that, as they themselves have done well without all such 'new' vaccines, their children could certainly do without them. It is a silly argument, and it is dangerous, too.

Another factor that takes from the importance of vaccination is that it is for a normal and healthy child. Parents who would not mind spending much more on treatment when their child is sick balk at spending much less for preventive vaccines when the child is perfectly fine.

As a paediatrician, I am appalled by this casual attitude, which could cost a human life or impair it, when it is perfectly possible to prevent harm through awareness and planning. I welcome all the protection that a child gets and strongly recommend all the possible vaccines as per official recommendations. As a parent, I view the expenditure on this account as an investment in my child's healthy future!

Myth	Reality
Vaccines are needless.	Vaccines are essential to provide protection against deadly diseases.

Vaccines have serious side effects.	The side effects of vaccines are usually minimal and easily manageable. The benefits far outweigh the risks.
In the presence of symptoms like cough, cold or loose motions, we should avoid vaccination.	There is no need to avoid vaccination in minor illnesses. Only in case of severe symptoms and high fever should vaccination be postponed.
Vaccines are too expensive.	Many vaccines are offered free of cost through government programs. Even if bought privately, a preventive measure (against death or disability caused by a disease) is priceless.
The basic government vaccination program is enough, and there is no need for other vaccines.	Some important vaccines are not included in the basic government programs. It is wise to discuss their need with your doctor.

Vaccine	Protects against	Schedule	Comments
BCG	Tuberculosis, a bacterial infection that can affect practically every organ system	At birth	Given intradermally (into the skin layers) on the left arm. Protects against severe forms of tuberculosis. After about a month, a swelling develops at the injection site, which breaks with a discharge and forms an ulcer, which heals to form a permanent scar.

OPV (oral polio vaccine) or IPV (inactivated polio vaccine)	Poliomyelitis, a viral illness that can sometimes cause paralysis and even death	At birth, at 2, 4, 6, 18 months and at 4–6 years	Both, OPV (oral) and IPV (intramuscular injectable) polio vaccines are equally effective in protecting against paralytic form of polio. IPV is now favoured for its better safety profile, but OPV provides the easier administration route and community protection.
DPT (diphtheria, pertussis, tetanus)	Diphtheria, a bacterial membrane-forming throat infection with severe complications Pertussis, a bacterial respiratory infection with whooping-type of cough Tetanus, a bacterial infection affecting the central nervous system and causing muscular spasms	At 2, 4, 6, 18 months and at 4–6 years	Given as IM (intramuscular) injections. There are different versions: DPT with a whole cellular pertussis component and DTaP with an acellular pertussis component. The latter has less severe side-effects (pain, fever, local swelling) but is wrongly marketed as a 'painless' DPT vaccine.

Hib (H. influenza type b)	H. influenza Type b, a bacterial infection affecting the respiratory tract, ears and brain	At 2, 4, 6 and 18 months	Given as IM injections
Rotavirus	Rotavirus, a common viral infection causing severe vomiting and diarrhoea in young infants and children	2 doses given one month apart, between 2 and 8 months	Given orally
PCV (pneumococcal conjugated vaccine)	Pneumococcal infection, a bacterial infection affecting the lungs, brain and ears	At 2, 4, 6 and 12–15 months	Given as IM injections Different types are available according to the number of bacterial strains covered.
HBV (hepatitis B vaccine)	Hepatitis B, a viral infection affecting the liver	At birth, at 2, 4 and 6 months	Given as IM injections on the arm Boosters are generally not needed but may be advised in hemodialysis patients and those with immune deficiencies.
Measles	Measles, a viral infection with skin rash and complications of the respiratory, nervous and gastrointestinal systems	At 9 months	Given as IM injection Sometimes, after a week, fever and rash may develop, which are mild and transient.

MMR (measles, mumps, rubella vaccine)	Measles, a viral infection with skin rash and complications of the respiratory, nervous and gastrointestinal systems Mumps, a viral infection causing salivary glands swelling and sometimes multi-system complications Rubella, a viral infection causing skin rash and lymph gland swellings Maternal infection in early pregnancy can lead to multiple congenital abnormalities in the baby.	At 15 months and at 4–6 years	Given as subcutaneous (under the skin) injection Sometimes, after a week, fever, skin rash or salivary gland swellings may develop, which are mild and transient.
Chickenpox (varicella vaccine)	Chickenpox, a viral infection with skin rash and sometimes serious complications	At 12 months and at 4–6 years	Given as subcutaneous (under the skin) injection Two doses with a minimum 1-month gap are necessary to complete the protection.
Hepatitis A	Hepatitis A, a viral infection affecting the liver and causing jaundice	At 12 and 18 months	Given as IM injection on the arm

Influenza (flu vaccine)	Influenza, a viral infection mainly affecting the respiratory system and with many serious complications	Every year above the age of 6 months	Given as IM injection, preferably at the beginning of the flu season Every season, a new vaccine is prepared against that year's most probable seasonal influenza viral types.
Typhoid	Typhoid, a bacterial infection affecting the gastrointestinal system with many serious complications	At 2 years	IM injection Repeated every 3 years, preferably before travel to areas where the disease is common
Meningococcal meningitis	Meningococcal infection, a bacterial infection affecting the brain and its coverings, with serious life-threatening complications	At 2 years	IM injection, repeated every 3 years, preferably before travel to areas where the disease is common. Different vaccines are available with protection against different types of bacteria.
HPV (human papilloma virus vaccine)	Human papilloma virus infection, a viral infection that can lead to cervical and other types of cancers and to genital warts	3 doses in 6 months between 9–26 years, with the ideal age group of 11–12 years	IM injections The main health benefits are for females, but it is advised for males, too.

Rabies vaccine	Rabies, a serious viral infection transmitted through infected dog bites or other animal bites, which affects the central nervous system and classically causes hydrophobia or fear of water in patients.	5 doses on days 0, 3, 7, 14 and 28 after the dog or animal bite in unimmunised patients (post-exposure prevention)	IM injections Pre-exposure prevention needs fewer doses and is given to people at increased risk.

For most practical purposes, the information in this chart should be enough for most parents. More information follows for parents who want to know more about some of the important vaccines.

2

BCG

BCG (bacillus calmette guerin) is a live attenuated vaccine against tuberculosis. It uses bacteria that are systematically weakened in the lab so that they cannot cause disease but can provide immunity. The bacteria used in BCG usually infect cows but are closely related to the bacteria causing human tuberculosis.

TB or tuberculosis is a disease caused by the bacteria mycobacterium tuberculosis. It mainly affects the lungs but can involve every system in the body, most notably the brain, bones and joints and kidneys.

If left untreated, TB leads to multiple complications and even death. It is completely curable if treated in time, but the treatment is prolonged and needs multiple medicines.

The overall protection offered by BCG is about 50% , meaning that a vaccinated person has 50% less chance of acquiring tuberculosis as compared to an unvaccinated person.

It is less effective in preventing adult type of TB, which commonly affects the lungs, but is more effective (70–80% protection) against more severe forms such as TB meningitis and miliary TB.

The World Health Organisation (WHO) recommends routine BCG vaccination for all children in countries with high incidence of TB. In India, BCG is given to all newborns immediately after birth.

BCG is given intradermally, or into the skin layer, on the left arm. Immediately after vaccine administration, a papule (a raised spot) may form at the site, which may last about 2 days. After 2–4 weeks, a blister forms at that spot, which eventually breaks open, giving off some watery or pus-like discharge. It then dries up and forms a small scar.

Adverse effects

BCG has been in use since 1921 and has been given to over a billion people. It is a very safe vaccine and has a very small risk of adverse reactions. Here are some adverse reactions:

- Enlargement of nearby lymph-glands (in the armpit or over the collarbone on the same side as the vaccination) is the commonest side effect. It is called BCG lymphadenitis.
- If wrongly given subcutaneously (or sometimes even when correctly administered), it can lead to pus formation, called BCG abscess.
- Sometimes the BCG scar can become large and raised. Such a scar is called keloid.
- Rarely, it can lead to allergic reactions.
- Rarely, it can cause the disease.

BCG lymphadenitis is managed according to severity. If the lymph gland is small (less than 1 cm), does not show pus formation and does not increase in size, it is left alone. Multiple matted glands, a single large (over 1.5 cm) gland, a progressively growing gland or a gland with pus formation may need treatment. The treatment choices differ from case to case. Needle aspiration, surgical removal, antibiotics or anti-TB medicines are the usual options. The BCG abscess is treated on the same lines.

Contraindication

Because it is a live vaccine, BCG is contraindicated—should not be given—in individuals with weak immunity as a result of diseases (immune deficiency states or cancers) or immunity-lowering treatments (steroids, anti-cancer medicines or radiotherapy).

3

OPV versus IPV

Poliomyelitis or polio, a once rampant killer and debilitating disease, is almost eradicated from the world. A polio-free world is the aim of global health agencies, and the only way to achieve this objective is through an intensive and extensive vaccination program.

Polio is a viral infection that spreads through the ingestion of food and water that are contaminated by infected stools. In 95% of cases, polio virus infections are asymptomatic, that is, there are no symptoms. Some 4–8% patients get abortive polio, or a flu-like mild illness consisting of fever, malaise, diarrhoea, cough and cold. Of all cases, 1–5% are non-paralytic polio characterised by fever, headache, vomiting and neck stiffness. Paralytic polio, the dreaded variety that leads to paralysis of the limbs and respiratory muscles, is seen only in an unlucky few that form only about 0.5% of all cases. In this variety, the virus attacks and permanently destroys motor nerve cells, causing paralysis of the muscles controlled by those nerves.

Prevention

As there is no specific medicine available against the polio virus, vaccination is the only hope against the disease and luckily, this hope has come true.

Polio vaccines have made the global eradication of the disease almost a reality. These vaccines are of two types: inactivated polio vaccine (IPV) developed by Salk in 1955 and oral polio vaccine (OPV) developed by Sabin in 1964.

IPV

This vaccine uses a strain of polio virus that has been chemically killed and inactivated. Because of this, IPV cannot cause polio by itself. It is an injectable vaccine and requires 3 doses, one each at 2, 4 and 6 months, for primary vaccination. Booster injections are required after that, one at 18 months and another at 5–6 years. Almost 99% protection is achieved after completion of the primary schedule of three injections. Like any other injection, it can cause pain, redness or swelling at injection site.

OPV

This vaccine belongs to the category of live vaccines. The virus in live vaccines is not killed but is weakened so that it can replicate in the body, to prepare the immune systems against a real infection, but cannot cause the disease. It has advantages such as easy oral administration, cheap cost, better intestinal immunity (local protection against intestinal colonisation of polio viruses) and herd immunity (passing on immunity in a community).

Pulse polio immunisation is a public health drive in which OPV is administered on particular days to all children in a particular region, regardless of their polio vaccination status. This helps in ensuring immunity throughout the community.

The OPV schedule is similar to IPV. But the standard three doses (at 2, 4 and 6 months) give only about 80% protection, which is why five or sometimes six primary doses are necessary to achieve adequate (90–95%) protection. This is because other micro-organisms in the intestines often compete with the vaccine's polio virus to prevent its proper take-up.

Another downside of this vaccine is the very remote possibility of causing paralytic polio by itself, not only in the person receiving OPV but also in the persons who come in contact. Normal or immunised individuals only rarely suffer this complication, but the risk is greater in persons with reduced immunity.

Changes in vaccination policy

OPV has been the main weapon in the fight against polio. The complications associated with OPV use have been too few and statistically insignificant. Thanks to its use, naturally occurring ('wild') polio infection has almost disappeared from developed countries. The only possibility of contracting polio in these regions is through the live vaccine itself. This is why many such countries, where naturally occurring polio has disappeared, are shifting the focus to inactivated polio vaccine IPV.

In the US, the American Academy of Pediatrics now recommends an all-IPV schedule. In India, the Indian Academy of Paediatrics recommends a combined OPV-IPV schedule which is as follows:

- At birth—OPV
- At 6, 10 and 14–18 weeks—IPV
- At 6 and 9 months—OPV
- At 18 months—IPV

Do not be confused by these different schedule recommendations. An all-OPV schedule, an all-IPV schedule or a combined OPV-IPV schedule are all effective if followed as per medical advice. So, discuss with your doctor which polio vaccine your baby should be receiving and then follow that advice.

4

DPT and Hib Vaccines

DPT is a combined vaccine against three deadly diseases—diphtheria, pertussis and tetanus. More commonly, it is called the 'triple' vaccine.

Hib vaccine offers protection against infections of bacteria known as hemophilus influenzae type b. These bacteria can cause severe and at times life-threatening infections of the ear, nose, throat, sinuses and brain. Children below 6 years are the most likely targets of these infections.

Diphtheria is a contagious bacterial illness caused by the toxin of the bacteria corynebacterium diphtheriae (C. diphtheriae). It usually starts as a severe sore throat in which a grayish or blackish membrane covers the throat and causes difficulty in swallowing and breathing. In advanced cases, the heart, kidneys and nervous system are affected. Most cases occur in children under the age of five years and almost half the untreated patients may die.

Pertussis is another contagious bacterial disease and it is caused by bordetella pertussis (B. pertussis). It starts as a common cold-like illness but proceeds to a severe kind of cough called whooping cough, in which long bouts of coughing are interspersed with a gasping 'whooping' sound. The patient often goes blue in the face while coughing and vomits afterwards. Most of the cases are seen in infancy and, although it is not deadly, the illness has a long course of almost 2–3 months.

Tetanus is a life-threatening disease caused by the toxin of the bacteria called clostridium tetani. Contaminated wounds are the usual entry portals for these soil-residing bacteria. The toxin, known as tetanospasmin, affects nerve function and causes muscle spasms. The illness often starts as the spasm of the jaw muscles causing 'lock-jaw' and then becomes more generalised. It has a high mortality rate, especially in newborn babies; it can kill more than 95% of affected babies.

Treatment

Proper antibiotics, anti-toxins (in diphtheria and tetanus) and good supportive care are the mainstays of treatment of these diseases. But prevention through vaccination remains the best and most effective measure.

DPT vaccine offers about 85% protection against pertussis and almost 100% protection against diphtheria and tetanus. Hib vaccine offers almost 90–95% protection.

DPT and Hib schedule

DPT and Hib injections at 2, 4 and 6 months complete the primary series of these two vaccines. A booster should be given at 18 months.

In developing countries like India, Pakistan and Bangladesh, the primary series could be started earlier, at the age of 1½ months and the interval between the doses could be shorter at 4–6 weeks. This is because of the higher risk of these illnesses in these countries.

In developing countries, Hib vaccine is often—and unfortunately—avoided as an 'optional' vaccine. If a baby who missed out on the Hib vaccine and is less than 6 months old, requires all three Hib vaccine doses, spaced 1 month apart, followed by an 18-month booster. If such a baby is 6–12-month old, it requires two doses of the vaccine spaced 1 month apart, with the 18-month booster dose. If the baby is 1 year or older, a single dose of Hib suffices.

Side-effects

Mild post-vaccine fever is possible for a day or two in the case of these vaccines. As these vaccines are given as deep intra-muscular injections in the thigh, limping, pain, redness and swelling around the injection site can happen. Usually these side effects subside within 2–3 days. Most of these side effects are easily treated with an occasional dose or two of an analgesic or antipyretic medicine like paracetamol.

Sometimes a small lump is felt under the skin at the injection site, which can last a few months. It is harmless and self-limited.

Complications

Skin infection (cellulitis or abscess) can happen occasionally at injection site and should be suspected if swelling, redness and pain persist 3 days after injection.

Severe screaming or high-pitched crying episodes lasting for more than 4 hours, fits, shock, encephalopathy (harmful effect on the brain) and very high-grade fever (more than 105° F) are other and more serious complications of DPT vaccine. Fortunately, these severe complications are quite rare.

Contraindications

Progressive neurologic disease, uncontrolled convulsions or severe complications observed in a previous DPT dose are conditions in which DPT is contraindicated.

DT, Td and DaPT

As most of the complications associated with DPT are due to its pertussis component, the DT vaccine is often used successfully to prevent diphtheria and tetanus in cases where DPT use is not possible. After the age of six years, the risk of severe pertussis is much less, and the likelihood of associated vaccine-related complications is much higher. So DT is the preferred booster injection.

After the age of 10 years, the diphtheria component of the vaccine can give rise to severe reactions. Then, Td, a vaccine with the full amount of the tetanus vaccine but reduced amount of the diphtheria vaccine, is used.

The whole cellular version of the pertussis vaccine, routinely used in DPT vaccine, contains a troublesome antigen, LPF (lymphocyte promoting factor), which causes most of the complications. So, DaPT, a vaccine containing a purified 'acellular' version of pertussis, was developed. Many doctors wrongly promote this vaccine by calling it a painless vaccine. It is not so. Like any other injection, DaPT too would cause pain while being injected. It is not painless but it has less chance of causing post-injection side effects such as pain or swelling.

Tetra-, penta- and hexa- valent vaccines

To reduce the number of injections during the vaccination schedule and to improve convenience and compliance, scientists have come up with combinations of vaccines. The tetravalent vaccine combines diphtheria, pertussis, tetanus and H. influenzae b vaccines. The pentavalent vaccine adds the hepatitis B vaccine to these. Hexavalent vaccine further adds the inactivated polio vaccine.

Final word of advice

Do not dwell on the negatives of vaccination. They have been mentioned just to alert you, not to scare you away from vaccines. The minor risks associated with vaccines pale into insignificance when you consider the tremendous benefit they offer humankind in its fight against disease.

5

Measles and MMR Vaccines

In India, a standalone measles vaccine is recommended in the 9th month and a combined MMR vaccine in the 15th month. The MMR vaccine provides protection against three types of viral illnesses—measles, mumps and rubella—which are common in childhood. All of them are transmitted through tiny droplets released in the air by infected individuals while coughing, sneezing or breathing.

In most developed countries, measles risk is minimal before the age of 1 year and the vaccine is not recommended as a standalone in that age-group. There, the first dose of the MMR vaccine is given at the age of 1 year and the second dose at the school entry age of around 5 years.

Measles

Measles is a serious viral illness causing 1 million deaths all over the world every year. The incubation period (the period between exposure and development of symptoms) is around 2 weeks. Just before developing the full-fledged illness, there is a phase with cough, cold and conjunctivitis. Koplik spots, which are greyish white sand grain-sized dots inside the mouth, are often seen and are considered specific to the disease.

The actual illness starts with high-grade fever (104°F or more) and a characteristic rash. The rash in measles is made up of flat red spots that merge with each other giving an appearance of a red sheet enveloping the body. It starts at the top (back of the neck) and then spreads downwards to cover most of the body. Loose motions, hacking cough and ear discharge are often seen.

Measles has serious complications involving the heart, lungs and brain and can even cause death.

Mumps

The mumps virus leads to an illness with fever, bodyache, headache and painful enlargement of the salivary glands. The swollen glands often give a 'puffed cheek' appearance.

Inflammation of the brain, testes, pancreas, kidneys, thyroid and heart are the known complications of this illness.

Rubella

Rubella is a mild illness by itself. It leads to mild fever and enlarged lymph glands. Its rash is similar to measles but is much less prominent and short-lived. This is why it is also called '3-day measles' or 'German measles'.

Rubella is dangerous when it occurs in pregnant women. In those cases, it can lead to several severe abnormalities in the foetus, causing congenital rubella syndrome. Babies born with this syndrome have growth retardation, deafness, skin rashes, jaundice, enlarged liver and spleen and various defects in the heart, eyes and blood.

Treatment

As with most viral infections, the treatment of these infections is supportive and symptomatic like controlling fever, pains, aches and cough with analgesics and cough syrups. Soothing lotions like calamine can be applied on skin rashes. Antiviral medicines are used only rarely in very severe cases; these medicines are used in specialised health centres.

Measles and MMR vaccine schedule

In a country like India, measles is very common in infancy, and vaccine protection is very much needed at that age. For the first 6 months, the antibodies passed from the mother protect the baby against measles. But these antibodies also interfere with proper uptake of the vaccine. That is why, at around 9 months of age when the effect of these protective antibodies has waned, the measles vaccine is administered. The second dose (as MMR) at 15th month ensures complete protection against measles during childhood.

Because the vaccine's protection levels for measles start dropping over the years, another dose (as MMR) is added at school entry (4–6 years).

The measles infection provides lifelong immunity, making vaccination unnecessary after an attack. But you have to be sure your child had measles before saying 'no' to vaccination. Clinical suspicion or diagnosis of measles is often not enough as there are many illnesses that are like measles in appearance and symptoms. If there is any doubt that your child really had measles, it is better to vaccinate.

Contraindications

Many parents, especially the 'strictly' vegetarian ones, are worried when told by a doctor or a nurse that feeding an egg to check for egg allergy is a must before giving the measles or MMR vaccine. Experts clearly recommend that feeding an egg before the measles or MMR vaccine is not necessary. This wrong belief comes from the fact that the measles vaccine is prepared using hen's chick embryo cells and, therefore, can introduce antigens from the egg. But reaction to the measles vaccine is seen only in cases of severe egg allergy (shock, collapse, breathlessness). This particular type of allergy to eggs is extremely rare (less than 1 per 100,000 population).

A mild egg allergy (skin rashes or stomach upsets) is in no way considered a contraindication for the vaccine. Still, if you have observed mild egg allergy in your child, notify your doctor who can be prepared to deal with any adverse reaction.

Nowadays an 'eggless' measles vaccine (made up of the virus grown on human diploid cells) is available and can be given even to individuals with severe egg allergy.

As these vaccines are made from live but attenuated (weakened so as not to cause disease) viruses, they are not advisable in immune deficiency states, cancers and in patients on steroids or anti-cancer drugs. Any acute active illness, any severe reaction to earlier dose and pregnancy are other contraindications.

Side effects

Mild fever and rash after 5–7 days (due to the measles component), salivary gland swelling after 10 days (due to the mumps component) and joint pains and lymph node swellings (due to the rubella component) are possible side effects of vaccination.

Interactions with other vaccines

Most of the common vaccines can be safely administered along with measles and MMR vaccines. Live vaccines (such as OPV and chickenpox) should be given either on the same day or after a gap of at least 4 weeks. BCG is one live vaccine that should not be given on the same day as other live vaccines as its efficacy might be reduced. It can be given after a gap of 4–6 weeks.

MMRV vaccine

The recommended schedule of MMR and chickenpox or varicella vaccine is the same— the first dose at 12–15 months and the second at 5–6 years. To ease their administration, a combined MMR-varicella (MMRV) vaccine was introduced.

It has been observed in some studies that this combined MMRV vaccine increases the risk of febrile fits in 12–15-month-old children. These febrile fits are associated with vaccine-induced fever that is seen 7–10 days after vaccination. That is why experts now recommend that in 12–15-month-old children, MMR and varicella vaccines should be given separately and not as a combined MMRV vaccine.

There is no such problem observed in children in the 4–6 years age group, which is the recommended age for the second doses of MMR and varicella. So MMRV can be safely used in children of that and older age groups.

MMR vaccine and autism

One study reported in 1998 blamed the MMR vaccine as a risk factor for autism. This report has since been disproved by many subsequent studies. All the major international bodies now categorically state that MMR vaccination does not increase the risk for autism. Parents who needlessly keep their children away from MMR vaccination for fear of autism, risk exposing them to measles epidemics.

6

Rotavirus Vaccine

Rotavirus is a virus that causes gastroenteritis, or infection of the stomach and intestines. It is a leading cause of diarrhoea in children and causes half a million deaths in infants and young children worldwide.

Symptoms and signs

- Fever
- Vomiting
- Watery loose motions
- Abdominal pain
- Dehydration

Prevention

Hand-washing and good personal hygiene are general preventive measures. Rotavirus vaccination is the most important and most specific preventive measure.

The Rotavirus vaccine is given orally.

There are two Rotavirus vaccine types, one which requires two doses and the other which requires three doses. Confirm with your doctor which type he is administering to your baby.

The doses are given at least 4 weeks apart. The first dose should be given between 6–14 weeks of age and the last dose should be given at the latest by the end of 8 months.

Rotavirus vaccination prevents 75–87% of all types of rotavirus infections. The protection rate is even higher against severe infections (85–98% vaccinated babies).

The vaccine can be safely administered with other vaccines such as polio (OPV and IPV), DPT, Hib, hepatitis B, pneumococcal and inactivated influenza vaccine. It can be safely given to a breastfed baby.

Side effects

The side effects of this vaccine are rare and mild. These include fussiness, irritability, runny nose, cough, fever, loss of appetite and vomiting.

7

Pneumococcal Vaccines

Pneumococcal vaccines offer protection against diseases caused by pneumococci (streptococcus pneumoniae). Pneumococci are bacteria that are commonly found in many normal people's noses and throats. They are transmitted when the carrier or infected person coughs or sneezes and releases droplets in the air. They can also be transmitted through direct contact with respiratory secretions.

Pneumococci can cause infections of the lungs (pneumonia), brain (meningitis), ears (otitis media) and even blood stream (generalised sepsis). These illnesses are serious and at times even fatal. They can lead to long-term complications such as brain damage, hearing loss or gangrene (limb loss).

Currently, there are two main types of pneumococcal vaccines: pneumococcal conjugate vaccine (PCV 13) and pneumococcal polysaccharide vaccine (PPSV23). Both vaccines are given as IM injections. The number in the vaccine's name denotes the number of strains (types) of the bacteria it protects against.

The major difference between these two types is the age of administration. The conjugate vaccine can be given from 2 months onwards, whereas the polysaccharide vaccine can be given only after 2 years of age.

There are previous versions of conjugate vaccine (PCV 7 and PCV 10) which are still in use in many places and their schedule, use and other recommendations are similar to PCV 13.

Schedules

For children up to 2 years of age, **PCV 13** is recommended to be given in a series of 4 doses at 2, 4, 6 and 12–15 months of age.

For healthy children of 2–4 years who have not completed PCV vaccination, a single dose of PCV 13 is recommended.

For children in the 2–5-year age group who are suffering from certain medical conditions, 1 or 2 doses of PCV 13 are recommended, depending on the number of previous PCV doses. The medical conditions include damaged or absent spleen, sickle cell disease, chronic heart or lung disease, diabetes, cochlear (inner ear) implants and any disease or medicines reducing overall immunity.

For the 6–18-year age group patients suffering from any of these conditions, only one dose of PCV 13 is recommended, with or without previous pneumococcal vaccination.

PPSV 23 is usually not necessary for healthy children. A single dose of PPSV 23 is usually advised for children over the age of 2 years suffering from conditions such as damaged or absent spleen, chronic lung, heart, or kidney disease, diabetes, sickle cell disease, cochlear implant or any major disease or medicine lowering the body's immunity.

Final word of advice

Pneumococcal vaccines protect against bacteria causing serious and potentially deadly infections of the lungs, brain, ears and blood stream.

There are two types of pneumococcal vaccines, one that can be given to children from 2 months of age and the other that can only be given to after 2 years of age.

PCV 13 is used right from infancy and requires 4 doses before 2 years to complete the protective schedule. It is now recommended for all healthy children below 2 years.

PPSV 23 can only be used in children older than 2 years but needs to be given only to those suffering specific major medical conditions or using certain types of medicines.

Discuss with your doctor which type of pneumococcal vaccine is suitable for your child.

8

Chickenpox Vaccine

Scenario

Prita is explaining her dilemma to the doctor, "I really tried convincing Vishwesh's granny that the chickenpox vaccine is now considered very important. But she just refuses to accept that. She says it won't do him any good and that it is good if he gets chickenpox! That's why now I have got her here. Please try to convince her to allow chickenpox vaccination for Vishwesh."

The doctor has faced this situation a number of times. So he starts his well-rehearsed explanation!

Discussion

Don't ever lock horns with granny's wisdom.—Old jungle saying! Yes, I read comics and enjoy 'old jungle sayings' at times. But I am going to disagree with this particular saying and lock my horns with granny's wisdom! I am sick and tired of hearing again and again from parents that grandma told them, "Let the kids have chickenpox. It's good for them to have it in childhood."

I have to say it loud and clear, "Dear granny, I know you are the loveliest person on earth. You have nothing but the wellbeing of your children and grandchildren at your heart. But by saying this about a disease like chickenpox, you are doing a great disservice to them." Let me say that granny's view is not entirely wrong; it has some logic. It is a fact that chickenpox is a milder disease in childhood as compared to adulthood when it could be much more severe and serious. It is also true that chickenpox usually offers lifelong immunity once it occurs in an individual.

So there is a reason granny says that it is 'good' to have chickenpox in childhood. But one cannot assume that one will get chickenpox in childhood. It is possible that the disease would spare a person in childhood and strike later in life when it is much more dangerous. But my objection is on different grounds. How can one ever say that it is good to have a disease, any disease?

Disease, illness, sickness—call it what you will—means pain and misery. It means loss of productive hours and quality time for the patient and the family. It could also mean disability or death. In an illness like chickenpox, all these negative consequences are possible.

Chickenpox

Chickenpox is an illness caused by the virus varicella zoster. It is transmitted through droplets of respiratory secretions and through direct contact with the infected person. It is a highly contagious disease.

Of the people who never had the infection, those who come into contact with a patient at home have 80–90% probability of catching the illness and those who come into contact at school have 30% probability. Winter and spring seasons are known for chickenpox epidemics.

There is an incubation period, or a latent gap, of about 2 weeks after the exposure. Then start non-specific symptoms like fever, reduced appetite, lethargy, weakness, headache and abdominal pain.

The rash starts on the face, scalp, chest or back. It is initially in the form of flat, reddish spots. Soon, the characteristic pearl-like teardrop vesicles (blisters) start appearing in crops. This process goes on for the next 1 week. Then the vesicles are crusted and slowly disappear, leaving temporary scars, which finally clear up totally.

Complications

It is not just the itchy, scratchy blisters and the confinement to home that makes chickenpox such a worrisome illness. It is associated with many complications, especially in infants, adolescents, adults, pregnant women and patients with weak immunity. These complications can affect almost every system of the body and can even cause death.

Secondary bacterial infections of the skin, lung infection, liver inflammation, brain inflammation, disturbances of blood-clotting, kidney problems, generalised sepsis—the list of probable complications of chickenpox is enough to frighten any sane person. And if that is not enough, the chickenpox virus remains hidden in the sensory nerve roots and can get activated later in life giving rise to an extremely painful condition called herpes zoster.

Treatment

In most cases, chickenpox is a mild illness and requires only symptomatic treatment such as medicines to control fever and a soothing lotion like calamine for itching. Popular measures like avoiding certain foods and using neem leaves—either orally or in the bath—are of no particular use.

In severe or complicated cases, some specific anti-viral medicines are used. If used early in the disease, these anti-viral medicines limit the spread and severity of the infection. But they cannot be used for prevention against chickenpox.

Prevention

Prevention of the disease cannot be achieved only by isolating the patient as the infection can be transmitted for almost 48 hours before the rash appears and up to the stage of crusting after 3–7 days.

As far as the general population is concerned, the focus of prevention is vaccination. The latest chickenpox vaccine is safe and effective and gives almost 95% protection. It is a live attenuated vaccine, meaning that it is made from live but weakened chickenpox virus. It is given subcutaneously (below the skin) either on the arm or the thigh. The vaccine is usually well-tolerated and serious side-effects are very rare.

Even people who get chickenpox after vaccination get partial benefit. Their illness is much milder compared to the natural infection. Their rash consists of fewer spots and heals within a short period, usually a week.

Any person above the age of one year who has not had chickenpox earlier should be vaccinated. Children as well as adults need two doses, given at least one month apart. The recommended schedule for children is to give the first dose at 1 year and the second at 5–6 years at the time of school-entry.

With intensive vaccination programmes, it is quite possible that we may get rid of chickenpox forever. The only thing left now is to convince granny that it is never good to have chickenpox!

Myth	Reality
Chickenpox is a harmless disease.	Chickenpox is a prolonged (10–14 days) illness with many serious, even life-threatening, complications.
Chickenpox vaccine is useless.	Chickenpox vaccine protects in 90–95% cases. Even the ones who get the illness despite vaccination benefit by getting a much milder disease.
We have to use neem leaves and make many dietary changes for the chickenpox patient.	Using neem leaves and making diet changes are needless and useless customs.
Chickenpox leaves permanent scars.	Chickenpox scars are temporary.

9

Preventing 'Infectious' Jaundice

A-B-C-D-E and still counting. No, it's not about the English alphabet. I am counting the types of hepatitis viruses that cause jaundice.

To refresh your memory, jaundice (also called icterus in medical terms) by itself is not a disease. It is a yellow discolouration of the eyes, skin and mucus membranes caused by increased blood level of a yellow pigment called bilirubin. Bilirubin is a routine waste product in the body, produced mainly by the destruction of old red blood cells. It is metabolised by the liver and excreted through urine and stools.

Jaundice in children and adults is mostly caused by liver inflammation, which in turn is caused by a viral infection. Hepatitis viruses are the main culprits in this respect. This 'infectious' jaundice is different from the 'physiologic' jaundice in newborn babies that we discussed earlier.

Types of hepatitis viruses

Hepatitis A causes the most common and well-known form of infectious jaundice. Water and food contaminated with human waste are the primary sources of this infection. After exposure, there is an incubation period of 2–6 weeks and then jaundice develops. It is more common under the age of 15 years.

Hepatitis B is sometimes called 'serum hepatitis' because it is transmitted through transfusion of contaminated blood or blood products or through the use of inadequately sterilised needles and medical instruments. It can also be transmitted sexually and across the placenta (from the mother to the foetus). The incubation period of this type is longer at 2–6 months.

This type is more common in patients undergoing dialysis, critical care or chemotherapy; in patients suffering from certain blood-clotting diseases and in intravenous drug users. Chronic carriers of hepatitis B virus have HbsAg (hepatitis B surface antigen) in their blood and are the biggest stores of this infection.

For many years, viruses causing hepatitis except A and B types were called NANB (Non-A, non-B hepatitis) viruses. Technological advances now make it possible to identify these NANB viruses and so we have **hepatitis C**, a virus with similar tendencies as hepatitis B, **hepatitis D**, an incomplete virus which can only infect in the presence of hepatitis B and **hepatitis E**, a virus with some similarities to hepatitis A but more common in adults.

This series is being further extended to include more and more viruses as newer techniques for identification develop.

Symptoms

In children, acute liver infections are usually milder and shorter. In infants and toddlers (and sometimes in older patients), the typical yellowness may not appear at all. This condition is called 'anicteric hepatitis' meaning 'colourless hepatitis'.

Many times, there is a pre-jaundice phase of 1–5 days with fever, lethargy, reduced appetite, headache, abdominal pain, nausea and vomiting. The liver may become enlarged and painful. Enlargement of the spleen and lymph nodes is also possible. In hepatitis B, skin rashes and joint pains or swelling can occur.

The jaundice phase begins as the fever subsides. Eyes appear yellow. Urine becomes dark, and stools are often clay-coloured. In younger children, the general symptoms usually subside with the appearance of jaundice. But in older children and adults, these symptoms usually worsen. The average duration of this phase is around 10 days in children and around a month in adults.

Acute complications such as fulminant (severe) hepatitis and liver failure are possible with any kind of hepatitis.

Long-term complications like virus carrier state, chronic hepatitis, cirrhosis and liver cancer can occur only in B, C and D varieties. A and E varieties are usually without such long-term complications.

Treatment

There is no specific treatment for jaundice due to hepatitis. Bed rest is usually not necessary except perhaps in the pre-jaundice stage with severe symptoms. No particular dietary restriction (e. g., avoiding fatty foods and meat) is found to have any great benefit. Juices and soups are usually well tolerated and useful to counter dehydration because of lack of desire for food. The normal diet should be resumed once the appetite returns to normal.

Prevention

In case of hepatitis A and E, general preventive measures are good personal hygiene, especially hand-washing before eating and after using the toilet, avoiding food from food handlers and using clean boiled water.

In case of hepatitis B, C and D, stringent check of blood and blood products, using disposable needles and good sterilisation of medical instruments will reduce incidence.

Vaccines

As always, vaccination is the key to prevent hepatitis infections.

Vaccination against **hepatitis A** (two injections taken six months apart) is the safest and most effective way of preventing this infection. The vaccine can be given to anyone over the age of 1 year. No further booster is required after completing these 2 doses.

Vaccination against **hepatitis B** is included in the universal program of immunisation and has been found to be extremely effective. The primary course of the hepatitis B vaccine is of a minimum of three injections. Nowadays all newborn babies receive these doses: just after birth and then at 2, 4 and 6 months. Children and adults who missed out on hepatitis B vaccine earlier are given a three-dose primary schedule at 0, 1 and 6 months. Hepatitis B booster injection is only needed for patients undergoing dialysis and those with weakened immunity.

Vaccination is not available at present against other types of hepatitis viruses.

Final word of advice

Different types of hepatitis viruses infect and inflame liver to cause jaundice.

Hepatitis A and E viruses are transmitted through contaminated food and water. They usually do not have serious or long-term complications.

Hepatitis B, C and D are transmitted through infected blood, blood products, sexual contact and contaminated injection needles or medical instruments. They can also transmit across the placenta. They are often associated with long-term carrier state or complications.

Good personal and medical hygiene practices are important preventive measures. Vaccines against hepatitis A and B are very effective protective measures. Currently there are no vaccines available against hepatitis C, D and E.

V

General Parenting Tips

1

Child Safety

Scenario

Scene 1

The mother is busy tidying away clothes. The child is playing with her toys. Suddenly, the mother notices that the girl has put a part of a toy part in her mouth.

Scene 2

A father is reading a newspaper with a cup of hot tea in hand. The child jumps on him, spilling the hot liquid.

Scene 3

A 4-year-old child is walking with parents on the footpath. Suddenly, he decides to run into the busy road.

Discussion

In daily life, one comes across many situations in which children have accidents. Their incompletely developed physical and mental skills, natural curiosity about the environment, urge to do new things and total ignorance of and disregard for the dangers of their actions make children of all ages susceptible to accidents, whether at home or outside. Add to that parents' or caretakers' neglect of the child, carelessness and ignorance of safety measures, and the risk of childhood accidents increases exponentially.

The best way to avoid mishaps is to be aware of the possibilities of accidents in otherwise perfectly normal scenes. Bear in mind Murphy's law: If something can go wrong, it will. Be aware and remain alert to that possibility, particularly when you are looking after children.

Let us understand the possible areas prone to accidents involving children so that we can avoid them.

Accidents at home

Falls, bumps and jumps

Rolling off the bed or tumbling off it while trying to stand with support are common accidents in small babies. As they grow up, running, jumping and bumping into things become common routines.

Wet floor is a danger area with the potential to slip and fall, so keep the floor dry.

Falls from steep stairs or out of balconies or windows are often dangerous possibilities for children. Take care to restrict their access to such areas with protective doors and grills.

Walkers are a major source of accidents and should be avoided. Don't believe the false notion that, by using a walker, the baby will walk sooner. Walkers do not make babies learn walking early.

Falls and bumps are usually minor, but occasionally they can be nasty!

Household objects

Clothes, ornaments, lucky charms, toys, plastic or cloth bags, curtain cords and beddings can cause accidents. Surprised? Yes, these common things can often lead to accidents if you are not careful. Tight knots (around the neck or waist), pins, pointed or sharp buttons and zips can make some clothes dangerous to small babies and toddlers. Ornaments and lucky charms (black threads, talismans, etc.) can physically injure a child if they are sharp-edged or are tightly wound around a body part. Similarly, sharp parts of a toy can cause injury. There is also a risk of choking if the child accidentally puts a small button, balloon, ornamental bead or toy-part in the mouth or nose.

Pulling a tight plastic or cloth bag over the head or playing with curtain cords (and winding them around the neck) can cause suffocation.

Use of soft or loose beddings (blankets or pillows) has been pointed out as a risk for a condition called SIDS (sudden infant death syndrome).

Heat and fire

Always be careful when you are handling hot things near children. Hot irons, hot food vessels and hot beverages are common causes of domestic accidents. Smoking a cigarette near a child not only causes the child harm from passive smoking but also creates the risk of burns.

Kitchen burners and lighters should be kept away from kids. Fire crackers are an important hazard.

The bathroom heater and hot water taps are particularly dangerous to children. Always supervise their bathroom visits in early years.

Electrical appliances

Wires, plugs, electrical points and switches of electronic equipment always fascinate children, and you have to be constantly on guard to make sure that they do not harm themselves in their exploration of those things.

Washing machines, particularly front loading ones, are tempting to an inquisitive child, who will get into the machine and have an accident.

Medicines and chemicals

The medicine capsules, tablets, syrups, sprays, drops and inhalers always seem to attract the young ones, who end up ingesting or inhaling them, sometimes attracted by their colour or taste, sometimes to imitate the adults and sometimes just for experimentation. If a child does ingest or inhale a medicine, it could necessitate emergency medical intervention.

Insecticides, cleaning chemicals and even strong aerosol sprays are potential poisoning hazards.

As preventive measures, make sure that you keep medicines and chemicals in a place where children cannot access them, do not use these substances in front of young children (so as not to spark off imitation) and keep them in child-proof containers.

Sharp things

Every normal house has sharp things like scissors, razor blades, kitchen knives and sharp pointed pencils. Cuts and scratches with them are common accidents. Holding the sharp end of the instrument pointed upwards or outwards is dangerous if the child bumps into you! So always be careful while handling such things.

Try to shave behind closed doors. Imitation often acts as a strong stimulus, and a small child impressed by the sight of dad shaving might just start 'shaving' with dad's razor!

Bed and furniture corners should be rounded. If they are sharp, get rounded edge-protectors to cover them.

Broken glass is a major risk. Make sure that the glass in windows, doors and furniture is safety standards approved toughened (shatter-proof) glass.

If any glass does break, immediately and carefully remove any broken glass pieces and wrap them in paper.

Water

Bathtub, swimming pool, and any large container of water represents a potential drowning risk. Parents have to be careful that children, especially infants and toddlers, do not reach such places unattended by an adult.

Water from taps and showerheads should be checked for temperature as extremes of temperature can lead to burns or hypothermia.

Child-proofing your house

Child-proofing is a modern and slightly misleading term that means making the home environment safe for children. Here is a simple plan to child-proof your home.

1. Keep the floors dry.
2. Keep sharp objects, small objects, breakable objects, medicines and chemicals out of children's reach.
3. Restrict children's access to dangerous areas like kitchen, bathroom, balcony, windows, staircases and swimming pool with appropriate partitions, doors and grills.
4. Keep all electric points properly covered.
5. Use firm, properly fitted beddings and a safety-certified baby-cot for infants.
6. Do not use a walker for infants.
7. Make sure that safety-certified toughened glass is used in windows, doors and furniture.

Accidents outside the home

Outside the home, the most important type of accidents are traffic accidents. Road traffic accidents are the most dreadful accidents and are continuously on the rise thanks to the increase in the number of vehicles and the resultant increase in traffic congestion.

Disregard for traffic rules is an important factor in these accidents. Start teaching traffic rules to children from a very young age.

I have seen drivers holding their child in their lap. How someone can be so stupid and negligent and expose a child to the risk of accident is beyond me! Forget the driver's lap, never let a child sit in the front seat of the car. Properly fitted and appropriate sized baby or child car seat is the safest option. Even if you are not using a special baby or child car seat, the back seat is the only safe option in the early years. It is a safer option even for school-age children.

Keep in mind these important tips to avoid accidents:

- Follow traffic rules carefully.
- Firmly hold a small child's hand while crossing the road.
- Keep the child on the side away from oncoming traffic (child on your left if the vehicles are coming from your right and vice versa).
- Take care that the child does not cross the road in front of the school-bus after getting off it.
- Check to make sure that there is no child behind your car before reversing it.

While walking on the road, point out to your child the importance of staying away from the manholes, potholes, electric poles and electric wires along the road. Do this several times to make sure the child learns it well.

Drowning is another major type of outdoor accident. Children should always swim under supervision in a swimming pool where a lifeguard is present. Swimming in unknown waters like sea, river or lake is not a good idea.

Final word of advice

Whenever you are minding children, be aware of and remain alert to the possibility of accidents in various everyday situations whether you are at home or outside.

Falls, heat, fire, water, electricity, sharp objects, medicines and chemicals are common dangers at home.

Even seemingly harmless things like clothes, ornaments, lucky charms, talismans, toys, bags and beddings can sometimes cause serious accidents through suffocation or choking.

Follow traffic safety rules while driving or walking with kids on road.

2

Understanding Sleep in Children

Go to sleep my baby! Laurel and Hardy fans love the funny and ultimately futile attempts of the comic duo to put their children to sleep in their short film *Brats*. If you have not seen it, please do. It will put your troubled mind at rest by making you realise that you are not the only parents facing difficulty in making their children fall asleep! Coaxing, cajoling, cooing, cavorting—parents will try anything to make their children sleep, but usually in vain.

Parents with bloodshot, sleep-deprived eyes describing their baby's or child's awful sleep patterns is a common sight, but there is no simple solution. But let me give you a few bright ideas to tackle this difficult problem.

Counting the hours of sleep

The average sleep time differs according to the individual's age. Rough estimates of sleep hours according to age are shown in the table. The figures show that in the first 3 months, even though the total time of sleep is greater, most of it occurs during the day. The duration of sleep at night starts increasing only after 3 months. As always, these numbers serve as guidelines rather than absolute truths. To put it simply, sleep is a very individual trait and the average sleep required to refresh the body and mind differs greatly from person to person.

Age	Average Total Sleep (hours per day)	Average Night Sleep (hours)
1st month	17–18	3–4
1–3 months	16–17	4–5
3–6 months	15–16	8–10
6–12 months	14–15	10–11
1–3 years	12–13	11–12
3–6 years	10–12	10–11
6–12 years	10	10
13–19 years	8–9	8–9

Reasons for child 'not sleeping'

Different day-night sleep rhythm: The main reason why the mother (and even the father) starts to feel the sleep deficit in the first few months of the baby's life is that the baby's sleep cycle is so different from the adult sleep cycle. Continuing their sleep schedule inside the womb, babies, in the first few months of life, sleep a lot but do so in the day rather than at night when mere mortals like Ma and Pa sleep.

Just when you start feeling that your night vigils would never end, at about 3 months of age, the baby usually decides that enough is enough. It is ready to follow the adult pattern of sleeping at night and provide some respite to parents!

Light sleep: The human sleep cycle consists of stages like drowsiness, light sleep (also called REM or rapid eye movement sleep) and deep sleep (non-REM sleep). In the first 3 months, almost half the baby's sleep hours consist of light sleep. This is why the baby might wake up at the slightest stimulus and demand your attention!

Frequent need of feeds: In the first 6 months, babies sleep in short naps, each lasting 3–4 hours since they need frequent feeds. Later, as the diet pattern changes towards more solid foods, the need for frequent feeds decreases and the sleep period increases.

Loneliness: After 6 months, babies start to feel 'separation anxiety', and that emotion can interfere with sleep until almost the pre-school stage. Many toddlers and preschoolers go on fighting off sleep just to make sure that they don't miss out on family fun!

Other factors: Colic, cold (blocked nose), wet nappy, too cold or too hot surroundings and uncomfortable clothing or bedding are often among the factors causing sleeping troubles in infancy. Physical exertion, a heavy night meal, a scary movie or pressure at school can cause sleeping difficulties at older ages.

Effects of inadequate sleep

At younger ages, lack of sleep may manifest as hyperactivity, irritability or fretfulness. Later in life, it can cause decreased attentiveness, decreased short-term memory, delayed response and inconsistent performance at school, college or work.

Strategies to tackle sleep problems

Mental preparation: From the beginning, be mentally prepared to face some (or many!) sleepless nights. Take it as an inevitable price of becoming parents. At the same time, rest assured that these problems are temporary.

Establish a sleep routine: Maintain a consistent sleeping time schedule for the family and stick to it. When the baby is young, it would be better if the mother adapts and grabs sleep according to the baby's 'sleep packets' rather than hoping to change her baby's pattern to fit her own normal pattern.

Winding down period: Before the actual sleep time, start to prepare the baby or child for sleep. The younger the age, the longer is this preparatory stage. Giving a warm bath, tucking the child into comfortable clothes, bed and blanket, lying down beside the child (telling a bedtime story or cooing a lullaby), putting on dim lights and soothing music—these are some good preparatory rituals. Be sure that you do not excite the child or encourage any play or activity.

Do not use a feeding bottle or a sweetened pacifier as a sleeping device. It can lead to serious tooth decay. Delaying the time of the solid meal at night often prevents the need for late night feeds in infants and at later ages. Late night feeds are plain unnecessary.

Place for sleep

Where a child should sleep is a contentious issue, and the decision should be made by parents after discussing their own attitudes towards it. Western parents mostly prefer separate beds and bedrooms for their children whereas Indian and other Asian parents often prefer to sleep with their children.

In his book *Guide to Child Care,* veteran Indian paediatrician Dr. R. K. Anand says: "After going home, many mothers find following arrangements quite practical: The baby sleeps in your bed till he is 1-year-old. In the 2nd year, he sleeps on a mattress spread on the floor by the side of your bed. After he is three, he sleeps in a separate room on his own or along with his older brother or sister in separate beds. Teen-aged siblings of opposite sex should sleep in separate rooms."

Position for sleep

The scientifically recommended sleeping position for infant is supine or lying on the back. The prone position, or lying on the stomach, or the lateral position, or lying on the side, has been associated with sudden infant death syndrome (SIDS), mostly because of the possible interference with breathing in those sleeping positions.

Other sleep-related problems

Apart from the inability to fall asleep or frequently waking up from sleep, there are certain specific sleep-related problems like nightmares, night terrors and night walking (somnambulism).

Nightmares are frightening dreams which happen in the REM (light) sleep stage. The child (usually a preschooler) wakes up frightened after the bad dream and can remember the details of the dream. After a parent reassuring, the child can go back to sleep in most cases.

Night terrors happen in the non-REM deep sleep stage. The child (usually a preschooler) suddenly sits up in bed and appears terrified. The child might scream or make thrashing movements. There is sweating, and the heart beats fast. The child cannot be reassured but usually settles down by himself or herself after about half an hour and goes back to deep sleep. Later, the child does not remember a thing about the episode.

Night walking takes place in the non-REM deep sleep stage and usually happens in school-age children. The child gets out of bed and starts walking in deep sleep, with glazed eyes and incomprehensible speech.

Thankfully, most of these sleep problems are temporary and self-limited. If they seem to be persistent or prolonged, specialist opinion might be needed.

3

Choosing Toys and Games

Considering much-publicised incidents like major toy manufacturers Mattel and Toys-R-Us calling back millions of toys for possible excessive lead content, it is clear that parents need to be more watchful and more knowledgeable in choosing toys for their children. An intricately draped, emaciated looking Barbie doll, a realistic toy gun with a bang, a remote-controlled toy racing car or a miniature train winding its way on a miniature railway track—attractive and expensive toys have always been objects of desire for children.

Parents try to give these fancy toys to make their children happy, sometimes unwisely stretching the family budgets. But does an expensive toy make a child happier than a relatively inexpensive toy? I would categorically say: No!

This discussion is limited to introducing young children to simple toys and games and does not cover the newer electronic gadgets or formal sports training. Here are some simple practical guidelines for buying toys and games.

Choose a toy according to the child's age and interest. Younger children love colourful and musical toys whereas older ones are more interested in something that tests their physical or mental ability.

Gender often plays a role in toy selection. Boys often prefer objects like guns and cars, and girls prefer dolls and household objects like kitchen sets and jewellery boxes.

Choose a toy that is sturdy and likely to last. Children are not careful handlers of things and do throw and drop things. Avoid too delicate and breakable toys. Make sure that the toy has no sharp edges, pointed corners or loose small parts. Small breakable toy parts often cause childhood accidents when children put them in their mouth, nose or ears.

Avoid toys making a loud noise because that can lead to damaged hearing in the long run.

Under the age of 3 years, choking is an important danger. That is why you should avoid marbles, coins, balls and games that use balls of 1.75 inches (4.4 centimetres) in diameter or less because they present choking hazards.

Stuffed toys tend to gather dust and can often lead to dust allergy. That is why you should choose stuffed toys that are washable.

Make sure that the paint on the toy is not coming off and that the paint is stated to be lead-free on the manufacturer's label.

While choosing a bicycle or a skateboard for older children, make sure your child has adequate skill to use these or make sure the child learns under supervision. A helmet and wrist and shin guards are recommended safety gear.

Don't opt for the most expensive, most exclusive kind of toys. A child's joy and happiness in getting something new is the same whether you give something expensive or something relatively inexpensive. Novelty wears off too quickly in young minds, and your precious birthday gift may soon end up at the bottom of the toy pile.

Choose toys that stimulate the imagination rather than those which have repetitive mechanical actions. Animal or action figurines and building blocks or bricks are good choices for fostering imaginative play.

Always keep an eye on your child's toys to check for wear and tear and breakage. Repair or discard the broken toy at the earliest as the broken parts could cause injuries.

As the children grow older, they will enjoy card games, jigsaw puzzles and board games like chess, scrabble, snakes and ladders and carom. These are always good options to have at home.

A ball of the right size for football, basketball or throw-ball is the simplest and usually the most popular indoor and outdoor toy for which you don't have to spend a fortune.

When it comes to toys, more important than spending a lot of money is parents spending more time in enjoying play time with their children.

4

Travelling with Children

The moment for which you were waiting so eagerly has finally arrived. It is vacation time, and, yes, that means travel time. Travelling to another city or another country, especially with children, involves care and planning not only as regards to finance and logistics but, more importantly, health.

The new and unfamiliar environment is likely to pose challenges and problems for health. But if one anticipates and prepares for them, most problems can be easily prevented so that you enjoy your vacation rather than running from clinic to clinic.

Here are some tips to help you prepare for travelling with children.

Water

Clean and pure drinking water that is free of germs is still a pipe dream in many countries (no pun intended). You cannot possibly carry a month's supply of bottled mineral water. So when the drinking water at your vacation spot is of questionable quality, boil the water before using it for drinking, cooking or washing the mouth. You can carry an immersion coil which electrically boils water. Avoid using ice prepared from non-boiled water.

If you must use bottled mineral water, try to buy it from a major shop rather than a small roadside shop where there is a risk of getting fake or adulterated products.

For swimming, select chlorinated pools or unpolluted beaches which are declared safe for swimming. Avoid swimming in strong currents or unknown waters.

Food

Try to eat home-cooked meals or eat at clean, well-known restaurants. Don't eat at road-side food vendors.

Food should be well cooked, hot and freshly prepared. Don't eat undercooked or cold meat, poultry or fish. Avoid eating raw fruits and vegetables as they may carry germs even after you have washed them thoroughly in running water. Preferably, eat fruits, nuts and vegetables with thick skins or shells that you have peeled yourself.

Weather

Pack clothes according to the anticipated weather conditions at the place you are visiting.

For hot, sunny climates, choose light-weight, light coloured and preferably cotton clothes.

At places with very cold weather, dress in layers, with cotton on the inside and woollens on the outside, as layers make an insulation pad for the body. Take woollen clothes like sweaters, overcoats, gloves, socks and caps when travelling to cold places.

Insects

Insects such as mosquitoes, ticks, fleas and flies are carriers of many infections. To prevent insect bites, take precautions like wearing long-sleeved clothes and shoes with socks; sleeping in sheltered, preferably air-conditioned rooms; and using protective bed nets and insect repellents (sprays, coils, mats and creams).

Malaria, which is spread by mosquitoes, remains a major health risk in developing countries. Taking preventive medicines like chloroquine or mefloquine is one way of tackling this risk. Prophylaxis—or prevention—should start 1 week before travelling to an endemic area and should continue for four weeks after returning, with a maximum of 12 weeks in all. The medicine needs to be taken once weekly, on the same day every week. For the correct dose and precautions, consult your doctor.

Medicines

Carry a well-stocked medicine box when you travel. Make sure to carry a doctor's prescription to justify their presence in your luggage.

Here's a list of what you should carry after discussing the specific details with your doctor:

- Paracetamol (for fever, mild pain and inflammation)
- Ibuprofen (for fever, severe pains and inflammation)
- Antihistaminic medicine (for colds, motion sickness, skin allergy and insect bites)

- Antibiotic ointment or cream (for scrapes, cuts and boils)
- Analgesic cream or spray (for muscle pains and sprains)
- Disposable readymade dressings (for small cuts and wounds)
- Insect repellents (creams and sprays)
- Sun-protection creams, lotions and sprays (Sun-protection factor of at least 25)
- Skin moisturizing cream or lotion
- Any regular medicines taken for chronic problems such as thyroid problem, asthma, diabetes or high blood pressure

Vaccinations

Ensure that your child's age-specific routine vaccinations are completed as per schedule before you start your journey.

In addition to the regular vaccination, it is advisable to take vaccinations against typhoid, hepatitis A and meningococcal meningitis when travelling to most developing countries. When travelling to Africa and South America, it is better to take a vaccine against yellow fever.

Vaccinate against influenza if you travel during the flu season. Specific vaccines against diseases such as cholera and Japanese encephalitis are advised if you are travelling to high-risk areas.

Jet-lag

Travelling across time zones in a relatively short period upsets the body's rhythm and leads to jet lag. The affected person experiences severe exhaustion, irritability, sleeplessness, headache, bodyache and sometimes even stomach upsets. To avoid jet lag, start adjusting to the anticipated schedule 2 to 3 days in advance.

Take the following precautions during lengthy flights:

- Drink plenty of fluids. Plain water and fruit juices are the best choices.
- Avoid beverages and fizzy drinks containing caffeine.
- Stretch your body intermittently.
- Take short walks.
- Eat light meals.
- Take small naps.

On reaching the destination, expose yourself to sunlight if possible and preferably schedule the 1st day for resting.

Motion sickness

In motion sickness, a person in a moving vehicle starts feeling giddy and nauseated and often ends up vomiting. To avoid motion sickness, keep in mind these tips:

- Take light meals when travelling.
- Sit leaning slightly forward in the most stable part of a vehicle, which is the midsection of a bus or plane, the front of a boat or the front seat of a car and the car-seat in the back for the child.
- Fix your gaze at a stationery point on the horizon rather than looking at nearer objects that pass rapidly. Better still, keep your eyes closed or covered with dark glasses.
- Some anti-histaminic medicines are useful if taken 30–60 minutes before starting the journey. Consult your doctor about them.

Schedules

Make an itinerary that gives enough time to relax and enjoy. Too tight a schedule with too many places to visit just leaves everyone exhausted and prone to illness.

If you are travelling with small babies, make an early request for comfortable seats and special meals at your travel agency. Use identity tags for every child.

Recreation

Be sure to carry some of your children's favourite toys, board games, card games, gadgets and books and keep them handy while travelling. Hopefully, that should keep the children happy and busy in their little world and give you time to relax and enjoy the journey.

Happy holidays!

5

Dental Care in Children

The functions of our teeth are to chew food, help in speech and shape the structure and appearance of the face.

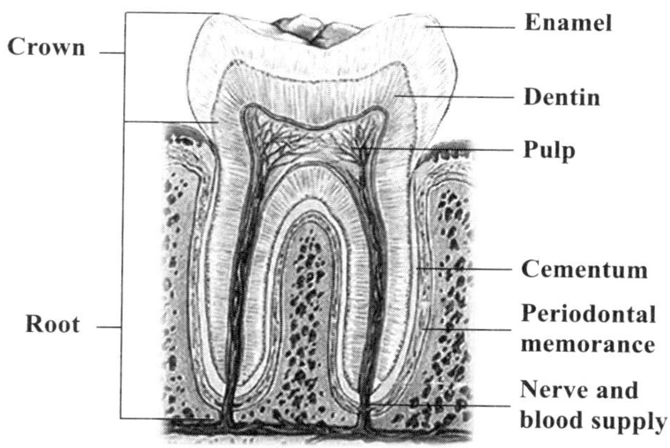

The figure shows the parts of a tooth. The visible portion of the tooth is called the **crown**. The rest of the tooth—about two-thirds the total length of the tooth—is the **root**, which is hidden by the gums. The root anchors the tooth in the jawbone.

The **enamel** is the hard outer covering of the tooth's crown. It is the hardest tissue in the body and protects the inner part of the tooth from being worn away by chewing. Directly beneath the enamel is the **dentin**, a bonelike tissue that makes up the bulk of the tooth. Within the dentin, at the centre of the crown and root is the **pulp**, which is a soft tissue that contains nerves, blood vessels, and lymph vessels.

Your teeth have different shapes because they perform different functions when you are eating. When you chew, the cusps of the teeth in one (upper or lower) jaw fit into the depressions of the teeth in the opposing (lower or upper) jaw to bite, tear, crush or grind food.

Situated symmetrically on right and left, from the front to the back of the jaw, are different types of teeth: **incisors** (to cut the food), **canines** (to tear the food), **premolars** (to crush and tear the food) and **molars** (to grind the food).

Human beings develop two sets of teeth in their life. The first set is of 20 teeth, which are called **primary teeth**. These erupt from the age of 6 months to 3 years. These teeth are shed periodically from the age of 6 to 21 years and are replaced by the second set of 32 **permanent teeth**.

Teething

Teething is the process of primary teeth erupting or breaking through the baby's gums. Typically, it starts by 6 months and completes by 2½ years. But this period can range from 3 months to 3 years.

Lower teeth appear first, followed by their upper counterparts. Central teeth (incisors) appear first and side teeth (canines) and back teeth (premolars and molars) follow them later.

The majority of babies go through the teething process without any problem. Some babies show excessive fussiness and irritability, which may begin a few days before the breaking out of teeth. It usually subsides once the eruption process is complete. Some babies start drooling, that is, bringing out more saliva, which may irritate the skin near the mouth and cause rashes.

Fever or loose motions during teething are not directly related to that process but are a result of mild infections, which commonly occur at that age.

To manage teething problems, simple painkillers like paracetamol could be occasionally used to soothe teething pain in fussy babies. Rubbing the baby's gum with a clean finger or with a small, cool spoon may provide some relief. Giving the baby something to bite on, such as a teething ring, is also soothing.

Teething gels contain local anaesthetics that numb the gums. Even though they are widely used, their efficacy is questionable.

Teething troubles have been exaggerated by the general public. There are many needless and useless teething treatments, ranging from wearing black threads or talismans to giving daily homeopathic or herbal medicines. As stated earlier, most teething babies do fine without any treatment.

Oral hygiene

Even before teeth begin to appear, you should start cleaning the baby's mouth to keep food residue and bacteria from damaging newly erupting teeth. In infants as young as 3 months, the gums, all interior surfaces of the mouth (inside of the cheeks, the roof of the mouth, the tongue) and the space between gums and mouth should be cleaned with a sweeping motion of a wet finger or a "finger brush".

After the teeth erupt, after every feeding, wipe the baby's teeth and gums with a damp soft cloth to remove harmful plaque. You can sit with the baby's head in your lap or lay the baby face up on a flat surface to make sure you can easily see into the baby's mouth.

If plaque is allowed to build on the baby's teeth, the tooth enamel could become decayed. If the decay is left untreated, the primary teeth may be prematurely lost. Children need all 20 of their primary teeth for proper eating, speaking, and appearance. These teeth also reserve space in the jaw for the permanent teeth that later erupt. A complete set of healthy primary teeth allows proper development of a child's jaw and face.

You should begin brushing and flossing your child's teeth after each meal or snack and before bedtime when all the primary teeth have erupted—usually when the child is between 2 and 3 year old.

Dental plaque

Plaque is a thin yellow or colourless film that forms over teeth. Bacteria inside the mouth secrete sticky chemicals (mucopolysaccharides) to form this film and then live inside it.

Plaque can be brushed or flossed away easily. If it is not regularly cleaned, the bacteria staying inside the film secrete acids and destroy enamel and dentin. This leads to tooth cavities.

Accumulated plaque can harden over a period and form tartar, which causes gum disease (gingivitis). Tartar cannot be brushed or flossed away. It needs to be professionally cleaned by the dentist.

Feeding bottle and tooth development

Your doctor may have told you never to put your baby to bed with a bottle. Here's why. If you put your baby to bed with a bottle, you risk development of 'rampant caries', also known as "nursing bottle mouth" or "bottle baby teeth decay", a dental condition that destroys the child's teeth through early, serious decay.

Nursing bottle mouth occurs when a bottle containing a sweetened liquid—milk, formula milk, fruit juice, sweetened water, or soft drinks—is given to the child frequently, especially before the child goes to sleep.

The sugar in the liquid mixes with bacteria in the dental plaque to form acids that attack the teeth. When children are awake, their saliva tends to carry away the liquid. But during sleep, the saliva flow decreases and these harmful liquids pool around the child's teeth for long periods, bathing the teeth in acid.

It is no solution to substitute the bottle with a pacifier dipped in honey or sugar; it can be just as damaging to the teeth. If your baby needs a bottle for comfort before falling asleep, fill the bottle with plain water.

Brushing the teeth

Cleaning the mouth requires some skill. By 2 years, your child will be learning to handle a toothbrush and may imitate you. By 4 or 5 years, children are able to brush by themselves. Flossing should be done by parents from toddler years.

However, until your child reaches about 8 years, you must supervise and help with brushing and flossing to make sure your child is doing a thorough job. With your guidance, your children should be able to do a thorough job of brushing and flossing on their own by about age 8 or 9.

It is a good idea to periodically check whether the children are brushing and flossing effectively by using disclosing agents. Disclosing agents colour dental plaque so that it can be seen. When the stained plaque is removed by brushing and flossing, you and your children will know their teeth are clean.

Toothpastes and toothbrushes for the child

Special toothpastes are now formulated with 100% ingestible ingredients, and without preservatives, for infants and toddlers.

Finger toothbrush and gum massager are gentler than the softest toothbrush. They can be worn on the mother's finger. They are made of rubber and can be used as early as the 3rd month.

Later, ask your dentist to recommend a toothbrush for your child. Generally, a brush with soft, rounded or polished bristles is recommended because it is less likely to injure the gums. Children often need smaller brushes than those designed for adults.

Toothbrushes must be replaced when the bristles because bent or frayed, usually every 3 months, because worn-out bristles do not remove plaque effectively. Preschoolers often wear out toothbrushes quicker because they brush imperfectly and chew on the brush. Inspect your child's brush often.

General tips for brushing

- Use a toothbrush with soft, rounded bristles.
- Place a pea-sized amount of baby- or child-specific toothpaste on the wet bristles.
- Use smooth, circular strokes to clean upper, lower, outer and inner surfaces of all the teeth.
- Spend a minimum of 2 minutes on brushing.
- Rinse the mouth well before and after brushing.
- Brush at least twice a day, once on getting up in the morning and once at night before bedtime. Ideally, teeth should be brushed after each meal. If you don't do that, make sure to rinse the mouth well after each meal.
- Change the toothbrush every 3 months. Do it even earlier if the bristles become bent or frayed.
- Consider electric power-brush for older children. Discuss it with your dentist first to learn the correct technique of using an electric brush.

Flossing

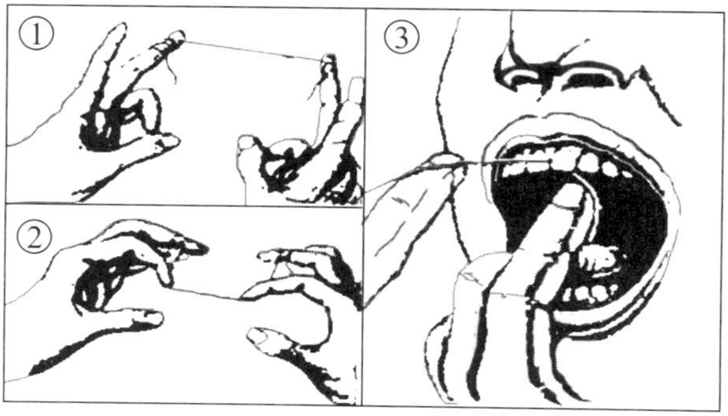

Flossing is cleaning the teeth and gums with a strand or string. The floss reaches where the toothbrush cannot and is important for healthy teeth and gums.

In developing countries like India flossing is almost unknown. Parental ignorance, lack of family tradition and avoidance of dental visits are to blame for this.

Dental flossing removes plaque from between the teeth and from the space between the teeth and the gum margins. There are different types of floss ranging from thin unwaxed strands to thicker waxed tapes. Floss holders and newer devices are also available.

Foods or dietary supplements for teeth

Dietary supplements should not be given to a child without a dentist's or physician's advice. If your child eats a balanced diet, with proper servings of milk or dairy products, he or she will receive all the calcium and phosphorous necessary for developing teeth.

Try to keep your child's sugar intake low, and that includes honey, brown sugar and sugary syrups that are just as harmful as refined sugars. Avoid sticky sugary snacks (chocolates, cakes, donuts) and make sure to rinse the mouth and brush after when the child does eat them.

Crunchy raw fruits and vegetables such as carrots, cucumbers and apples act like natural brushes. So use them regularly in the child's diet.

Fluorides

Children drinking fluoridated water have up to 65% fewer cavities than children whose drinking water is not fluoridated at optimal levels. If your area does not receive fluoridated drinking water, ask your dentist about fluoride supplements. The dentist may apply a fluoride solution or gel to your child's teeth during office visits as an additional precaution against tooth decay.

At home, the use of a fluoride toothpaste is effective in reducing dental caries.

Remember, though, that excess fluoride can sometimes cause patchy stains on teeth.

Injury to a tooth

School age children may accidentally injure their teeth. Teeth can be broken, cracked or pushed out of alignment. If this happens, consult your dentist immediately.

If a permanent tooth is knocked out, save it. A dentist may be able to replant the tooth and apply a splint that will keep it in position until it reattaches itself to the jaw and is able to function normally. What you need to do is to keep the tooth safe and go quickly to the dentist.

If the knocked out tooth is dirty, gently rinse it but do not scrub. Insert the tooth into its socket (the hollow in the gum) and hold it in place. If the tooth cannot be positioned in this way, place it in a container of milk or cool water or gently wrap it in a clean, wet cloth. Then, rush your child and the tooth to the dentist, within 30 minutes if possible. This type of accident is an emergency, so call your dentist even if it happens at night or on a weekend. If you cannot reach your dentist, go to a hospital that may have a dentist on call.

If a tooth is broken, gently clean any dirt or debris from the injured area with warm water. Apply cold compresses on the face over the injured tooth to keep the swelling down, and seek dental care immediately.

If your child accidentally bites his tongue or lip, apply direct pressure to the bleeding area with a clean cloth. If the lip is swollen, use cold compresses. If you cannot stop the bleeding, go to a hospital.

Final word of advice

Follow these guidelines for your child's dental health.

- Regular dental check-ups starting from infancy
- Balanced diet
- Early stoppage of bottle-feeding
- Avoiding sticky sugary snacks
- Using plenty of crunchy raw fruits and vegetables in diet
- Rinsing mouth well after every meal
- Minimum twice a day brushing (morning and night) and flossing
- Brushing time of minimum 2 minutes
- Toothbrush with soft rounded bristles, changed regularly, and children's toothpaste
- Good brushing technique
- Professional dental cleaning once a year
- Parental involvement and establishing a good role model

(This chapter has been adapted from the write-up by Dr. Sanjay Kalvani, a specialist dentist and a maxillofacial surgeon, currently based in Sharjah, UAE.)

6

Don't Demand Medicines

The doctor who writes a prescription of half a dozen medicines is usually far more popular than the one who tries to advise that the illness can be treated without medicines. No, this is not a research-based fact but just a general observation!

Parents, and patients in general, seem to have a belief imprinted on their minds that only medicines can cure illnesses. Whenever they see some symptoms, their first action is to seek medicines with or without a doctor's prescription.

I am not questioning the role of medicines and advanced technology in the process of cure but just pointing out a disturbing tendency of over-reliance on such treatment. What bothers me is the way we are neglecting the most important part of treatment, which is to respect the human body's own defence system.

The role of medicines is to aid the body's defence mechanisms to counter illnesses. It is unfortunate that public awareness of this fact is practically non-existent, and the medical fraternity has not been forthcoming in explaining it.

In many instances, medicines are unnecessary and could even worsen the situation. Still, all over the world, scores of patients and parents keep demanding medicines like antibiotics, cough or cold syrups, stool binders, anti-vomiting agents and appetite stimulants. More often than not, they find a person in a white coat with an impressive medical degree who nonchalantly hands over such prescriptions.

Let us examine some common childhood problems where rushing for medicines is mostly counter-productive.

Fever

The most commonly encountered fevers are caused by viral infections and last 3–5 days. The treatment required is just to provide a simple fever medicine such as paracetamol (acetaminophen), plenty of warm fluids and rest. Antibiotics are unnecessary in most cases unless there is definite evidence of bacterial infection.

Perhaps the most common cause of fever not coming down after giving a fever medicine is inadequate dosage and infrequent administration. So, first check those details with your doctor.

Do not rely on the doses advised on the label of the bottle. They are often misleading as no consideration is given to the weight of the child, which decides the dose in children.

Cold and cough

Once again, the explanation is almost the same as for fever. Most upper respiratory tract infections are viral and do not need any antibiotic. They are self-limiting, lasting 5–7 days. Just use the tried and trusted triad of rest, warm fluids and simple fever medicine such as paracetamol. Other simple but effective measures are cold mist inhalation, saline nasal drops and warm water gargles.

Cough and cold medicines available in the market are more or less similar. Most of them are mixtures with ingredients to lessen nasal congestion, to thin the secretions and to help those secretions come out. Changing from one to another of these medicines usually does not make much sense.

The advice from the experts is very clear. Over-the-counter cough and cold medicines should be avoided below 6 years of age. This is to avoid needless use of potentially harmful chemicals.

Simple herbal and honey preparations, which act as soothers, are much safer and effective in any type of cough.

Diarrhoea

Common causes of diarrhoea in childhood are gastrointestinal infections (mostly viral in origin), food poisoning and antibiotic induced diarrhoea.

Antibiotics and anti-parasitic medicines are routinely given in such cases, which could in fact prolong the course of illness. Medicines slowing down intestinal movement and medicines that thicken or bind the stools (bismuth preparations, kaolin-pectin combination) are also often used, but they can prove dangerous in cases of infective diarrhoea by allowing the germs to stay longer in the body.

In most cases, replacing the fluid loss, adjusting the diet and giving the child time to recover are the only measures needed.

Vomiting and abdominal pain

The cause of vomiting can be as simple as a mild episode of an upper respiratory or gastrointestinal infection but also as serious as an appendix problem or a brain infection. So the priority is to find out and treat the cause rather than giving medicines to suppress the symptom.

Almost the same logic applies to abdominal pain where the causes vary from simple to serious and taking painkillers becomes dangerous as it masks the cause.

Appetite

I have seen very few parents who are satisfied with their child's appetite. "Doesn't eat anything" is one of the commonest complaints and comes from parents of toddlers and preschoolers. Actually, children in these age groups naturally have slower growth rates (as compared to infancy), reduced appetites and negative behaviour (opposing parental commands).

So, in most cases, there is nothing wrong with the so-called 'not eating' child if the child's growth, activity and development are within expected norms.

Appetite stimulants are not recommended in children as they can cause serious side effects. A daily multivitamin and mineral supplement may be given to avoid nutritional deficiencies in fussy eaters. But do not expect such 'tonics' to improve your child's appetite!

In fact, experts recommend that balanced diet alone should provide the daily requirement of vitamins and minerals.

Final word of advice

There are many common situations for which medicines are routinely 'expected', and the expectations are often fulfilled with a prescription full of useless medicines. It is necessary to keep this 'medicine mentality' in check and to understand that best treatment is the one that relies on the least medicines.

7

Medicines for Children

There are certain general precautions for giving any medicine to a child. A few things parents should know are explained here.

As far as possible, do not give any medicines on your own or even give medicines on your pharmacist's (chemist shop) advice. Always consult your doctor and get a proper prescription for medicines.

Make sure that the pharmacy is dispensing the correct medicine that was prescribed to you. If the name seems to be different, always confirm with your doctor that the suggested replacement is correct.

Properly check the medicine bottle or pack for label information and expiry. Check that there are no tears or breaks in the medicine package. Read the medicine information on the leaflet inside the pack.

Take liquid medicine in the cap or spoon measure supplied with it and fill the measure up to the prescribed dose level. Do not use your own spoons because their sizes vary. The standard is that 1 teaspoonful is 5 ml and 1 tablespoonful is 15 ml. But because of differing sizes of spoons, giving medicines in kitchen spoons can lead to under-dosing or over-dosing.

After giving a medicine, close the medicine bottle tightly with a child-proof cap and keep it securely in a cool, dry, closed cabinet out of reach of children.

Give medicine doses according to medical advice and do not change it according to your whim. Maintain regular timings for giving medicines.

Each medicine is metabolised in our body, and its active component works inside the body for a certain number of hours. After that, the medicine either becomes inactive or is excreted. Taking the duration of these processes into account, the doses and intervals of major medicines are decided in pharmacological studies.

The doses and intervals are such that the active component of the medicine retains its activity throughout the day.

Giving the correct amount of dose at the correct time is important for the medicine to remain active inside the body throughout its complete course.

Commonly used medicines

Fever and pain medicines

Paracetamol (acetaminophen) is the commonest fever and pain medicine. It is available in different preparations such as infant drops, syrup, suspension, suppository and tablet. These preparations are of different strengths. Check the type of preparation and its correct dose with your doctor. Paracetamol overdose can cause serious liver damage and needs specialised treatment.

Ibuprofen is another popular fever and pain medicine, which can sometimes cause stomach upsets (including ulcers and bleeding) and trigger asthma attacks.

Aspirin is not used in children as it can cause a serious liver problem called Reye's syndrome.

OTC (over-the-counter) cough and cold medicines are useless, needless and potentially harmful in children below the age of 2 years. Even in older patients, they do not shorten colds. They just mask the symptoms without curing the actual illness.

An accidental overdose of these medicines creates a confusing mixed picture of symptoms because there are multiple components in them, each with its peculiar effects and side effects.

Increasing fluid intake, clearing the nose with saline nasal drops and simple paracetamol are often enough to treat routine colds. Simple herbal concoctions have been found to be as effective as any OTC cough syrups and they are much safer.

Allergy medications are mainly of two types—sedative and non-sedative. The first type may cause some sleepiness and needs multiple doses per day to remain effective. The second type usually needs a single dose, which remains effective for a whole day and usually does not make the patient sleepy.

Medicines for diarrhoea are needless in most cases. A popular diarrhoea medicine combines two chemicals—kaolin (to adsorb the toxins) and pectin (to thicken the stool). Similar actions can be easily achieved through food items such as slightly burnt toast (charcoal) and semi-ripe fruits (pectin).

Powder sachets of helpful bacteria (lactobacilli) are often prescribed in diarrhoea, but giving yoghurt (curds) in food serves the same purpose because yoghurt contains the same bacteria.

Most diarrhoea cases are caused by viral infections and need only dietary adjustment, fluid replacement and a little bit of patience.

Medicines for constipation come as syrups, suppositories or enemas. These laxatives are only to be used for short-term relief of severe constipation and should be avoided for long-term use as they can cause electrolyte and mineral imbalance in the body.

Most cases of constipation are because of faulty bowel habits and need to be treated through a fibre-rich and balanced diet, increased fluid intake, exercise and learning good toilet habits.

Medicines for asthma are given as syrups, chewable tablets, inhalers and nebulisers. People are often needlessly worried about using inhalers and nebulisers. They are more effective and much safer than oral bronchodilator medicines. Overdose of oral bronchodilators can cause tremors and fast or irregular heartbeats.

While using inhalers in children, a special apparatus called a spacer is used along with a mask. This ensures that the child inhales the proper dose of the medicine.

Multivitamin and mineral supplements are often used in the hope that they would increase appetite or make the individual more energetic. Well, they don't!

If we give more than the recommended daily allowances of water-soluble vitamins such as Vitamin C and Vitamin B-complex, they will simply be flushed out through the urine. Overdose of fat-soluble Vitamins A and D can cause serious side effects as these vitamins can accumulate in the body. One serious side effect is increased pressure inside the skull, which affects the brain (benign intracranial hypertension). Iron overdose can cause multi-organ failure. Calcium overdose can cause kidney stones or kidney damage in the long term.

Homeopathic medicines are by themselves safe to use. The only danger is when patients switching to homeopathy suddenly stop allopathic medicines in conditions such as asthma or diabetes. This practice often leads to unnecessary serious complications, which are invariably treated by allopathic doctors. If your child is already taking allopathic medicines for a condition and you are considering homeopathic medicine for another reason, then discuss the implications with your doctor.

Herbal medicines are popular because they claim to have no side effects. It is a myth! When herbs are made into marketable medicines, they have active chemical ingredients, which can have side effects similar to any other medicine. After all, if they claim 'action', there has to be a 'reaction'. It is the rule of nature.

Antibiotics are almost entirely wrapped in myths and misconceptions. Use them only under the doctor's advice and always complete the full course. 'Understanding Antibiotics: Popular Myths' has more information on this topic.

Medicine overdose

Medicine overdose can happen if the parent inadvertently administers a wrong medicine or a higher dose; if the child consumes or inhales the medicine for fun or when a high dose is taken for experimentation or in an attempt at suicide.

If there is an overdose, take the child away from the medicines and take the child for a check-up to the hospital. Do not induce vomiting. If the child has vomited, collect a sample to show the doctor.

Take the medicines and their container along with you for inspection at the hospital. Try to get an exact estimate of how much medicine the child has ingested or inhaled.

At the hospitals, in cases where the medicine is harmless or the quantity is small, only observation for few hours is needed.

When the medicine or the dose is potentially dangerous, the patient is kept in a special care unit and needs many investigations and treatments such as washing the stomach (gastric lavage) or administration of activated charcoal.

Prevention is always better than cure. To prevent accidental medicine overdose, always follow the doctor's prescription. Always use the measure supplied with the medicine to correctly administer doses. Always maintain the suggested dose timings. Never change doses by yourself.

Keep the medicine containers tightly closed with child-proof caps. Keep medicines secure and out of children's reach.

8

Antibiotics: Popular Myths

Despite their widespread use all over the world, antibiotics remain the most misunderstood medicines. I have seen two typical parental reactions when it comes to antibiotics usage in children. Some parents look worriedly at all antibiotics as if they are dreaded monsters! The other type see antibiotics as miracle drugs and expect them to be prescribed for every possible illness. Both these extremes are wrong, and what is needed is a sensible 'middle path' where antibiotics are used when necessary and avoided when unnecessary.

Let's consider some widespread myths about antibiotics.

Myth 1: "Who needs Antibiotics? They are useless."

Let's start with the extreme negative reaction. Many people sincerely believe that antibiotics have no place in the prescription. That is not at all true.

Since 1940 when Alexander Fleming discovered penicillin–the first ever antibiotic—antibiotics have occupied a pride of place in modern medicine. Thanks to them, millions of lives have been saved from deadly infections. Like any other important medicines, antibiotics are indispensable when they are actually needed!

Myth 2: "Antibiotics can cure any infection."

Antibiotics are useful only in bacterial infections. Urinary infections, chest infections, middle ear infections and CNS infections often need antibiotics.

Common infections of various body organ systems are caused by viruses or by bacteria. In children, as well as in adults, almost 90–95% infections are viral in origin. Antibiotics are unnecessary in viral infections as they do not have any effect on viruses. Sometimes in a viral infection, antibiotics may be given to prevent secondary bacterial infection.

Myth 3: "All antibiotics are much the same!"

There are many different groups of antibiotics like penicillins, cephalosporins, macrolides, aminoglycosides, tetracyclines and fluoroquinolones. Each group is effective against particular types of bacteria and is used according to the suspected type of infection.

In cases of severe or multiple infections, more than one antibiotic is used to launch a multipronged attack on bacteria. By aiding each other's action, by working on the bacteria through different routes and by broadening the treatment spectrum, these combinations eradicate infections.

Myth 4: "The latest antibiotics are always superior."

The main aim in the development of any new antibiotic is to improve its activity, broaden its spectrum and lessen its side effects. But not all new antibiotics are better than their older predecessors, and they are usually costlier.

Myth 5: "Antibiotics are needed for every severe medical symptom."

Every case of severe fever, cough, loose motions or vomiting does not need antibiotics. As explained earlier, if these symptoms are caused by a viral infection, antibiotics have no role to play. The symptoms may be caused by medical conditions other than an infection and may need totally different treatment.

Myth 6: "If I don't start antibiotic early, then I risk worsening the illness."

Most of the unwanted and unwarranted use of antibiotics happens because parents or patients assume that by starting the antibiotic immediately, they are avoiding further complications. Of course, this assumption is most of the times wrong!

Myth 7: "Antibiotics can easily be taken on our own. We just ask the pharmacist!"

This is the worst mistake of all! Antibiotic should never be taken without a doctor's advice. Through a clinical examination and sometimes through laboratory tests, doctors first ascertain the medical condition causing the symptoms. They differentiate viral from bacterial infections. They deduce the type of bacteria most likely to have caused the symptoms. And then they decide the best possible antibiotic and its correct dosage and duration according the patient's need.

Myth 8: "I have a previous antibiotic prescription. I just use it whenever similar symptoms recur."

Many people keep repeating the same prescription over and over again if they experience similar symptoms for which their doctor had earlier prescribed an antibiotic. This is a dangerous practice as the similar symptoms may have been caused by different medical conditions. Another reason is that, by using the same antibiotic again and again, we reduce its efficacy in the long run because the bacteria become resistant to the effect of that antibiotic.

Myth 9: "Antibiotics can be stopped once the patient starts feeling better."

This is another common mistake patients make. Every antibiotic has a prescribed course, which must be completed, of a certain number of days (3, 5, 7, 10, 14 etc.) according to the type of medicine and the type of infection. Unless that course is completed, the infection is not completely eradicated and can recur. Incomplete course also leads to development of antibiotic resistance in bacteria.

Myth 10: "We can modify antibiotic dosage on our own."

Antibiotic doses are decided in clinical studies. In children, these doses are calculated according to body weight. The doses of various antibiotics are different and so are their strengths. There is little sense in comparing 10 mg of one antibiotic with 100 mg of another antibiotic. Modifying the dose on your own for any reason is wrong. If you are worried or unsure about the dosage, always consult your doctor.

Myth 11: "Antibiotics have a lot of side effects."

Like any other important medicine, an antibiotic is given because its benefits are far greater than its side effects and risks. Yes, there are side effects of antibiotics, but the doctor chooses the correct antibiotic, dosage and duration to avoid or minimise most of them.

Gastrointestinal disturbances (nausea, vomiting and diarrhoea) and skin rashes are the commonest side effects of antibiotics and can be seen in some degree with almost any antibiotic.

Penicillin injection and occasionally oral penicillin can cause severe anaphylactic allergic reactions. Aminoglycosides can cause adverse effects on the kidney and hearing. Tetracyclines cause a permanent yellow staining of teeth. Chloramphenicol can cause bone marrow depression and a drop in blood counts. Sulfa drugs can lead to a severe reaction called Steven-Johnson syndrome. The quinolone group of antibiotics can cause joint damage. Many of these 'risky' antibiotics are usually avoided in children.

Long-term antibiotic therapy can cause pseudomembranous colitis, or an inflammation of the colon.

Most of the commonly used contemporary antibiotics are quite safe and are well tolerated by the patients if they are prescribed and taken in the correct manner.

Final word of advice

The most important problem associated with repeated use of antibiotics is the development of bacterial resistance. Because of rampant antibiotic use, bacteria are fast getting 'used to' and developing resistance to most commonly used antibiotics.

The major cause of bacterial resistance is people's tendency to use incomplete or inadequate antibiotic courses. If this continues, the day will come when we will not have any effective antibiotics to tackle serious bacterial infections.

For responsible use of antibiotics, follow these simple rules.

- Never take an antibiotic on your own.
- Never demand an antibiotic prescription from your doctor.
- Ask the doctor 'why' and 'which' questions about the antibiotic prescription.
- Discuss side effects and ask any relevant questions.
- Costlier, newer antibiotics are not always the best choices. Ask the doctor if there is an alternative.
- Follow the dosage and duration of antibiotic schedule as advised.
- Do not repeat the same antibiotic over and over again.

Remember, antibiotics are not monsters. They really are miracle medicines but only to be used when they are absolutely necessary.

9

Getting the Best out of the Paediatrician

Meeting the doctor for medical reasons is not an experience anyone looks forward to. This is especially true for the parents who visit a paediatrician for their child's problems. Many parents do not get the best out of their doctor because they do not know how to do it. Well, here are a paediatrician's tips for getting the best out of a paediatrician.

Check out the doctor.

By this, I don't mean that you ask your doctor to lie on his back and stick his tongue out! I mean that you should check out his credentials. Make sure to look at his degree and if possible get feedback from his other patients.

Don't be unduly impressed by a posh setup or a sky-high fee. It does not guarantee anything. The qualities you should be looking for are confidence, sincerity, caring attitude and compassion.

A doctor criticising other doctor's treatment and decisions is usually not a good sign. Be careful about such 'judgmental' doctors.

The doctor I would recommend is one who gives time to listen to you and then offers you guidance rather than just a quickly scribbled prescription.

Wear sensible clothes.

This instruction is not for the parents but for the child, though many parents could do with this tip.

Bear in mind that you are not entering your baby in a fancy dress competition. Layered clothing that is difficult to take off is an absolute no-no. Before the doctor can examine the baby, the mother struggles and stretches to get the baby out of the tight clothes. It wastes time and ends up in making the baby cry.

The baby's clothes should be loose and easy to open so that they provide easy access for the doctor to check various body parts for thorough inspection, palpation and auscultation.

Sit properly in front of your doctor.

Don't think that I am playing a schoolmaster. But many parents do make a hash of this simple thing.

Holding the child in the mother's lap with the face towards the doctor is the ideal position for a check-up. But many parents keep the child's face turned towards themselves, perhaps admiring it, and let the doc have a rear view.

To restrain the child for a throat inspection, the parent should contain the child's arms with one hand and restrain the forehead with the other hand. Never press the child's mouth to force him to open it. That only makes it more difficult.

When the doctor is examining the child's throat or ear, please do not peer to look inside. You would be obstructing the doctor's view.

There is no need for you to tell your kid to breathe in and out. The doctor would like to check the spontaneous breathing pattern, rather than a forced one.

Mind your language!

Try to be pleasant and do not let your anxiety dominate your conversation with the doctor. Anxiety often communicates itself to other people and worsens the matters rather than improving them.

Answer the doctor's questions completely and honestly without holding back any information. Be precise and to the point. Avoid repeating the same things over and over. Keep a paper with your queries ready, so you do not forget to ask something.

Don't show off *your* medical knowledge. That is a sure turn off for the doctor. Instead, give the doctor a chance to show off *his or her* knowledge by asking your questions in an 'innocent' but 'leading' manner to clear any doubts in your mind.

Don't ever demand medicines like antibiotics, appetite stimulants or vitamins if the doctor has not prescribed them. A good paediatrician might explain and convince you about their uselessness, but another might just quickly follow *your* advice and you would pump unnecessary medicines into your child, besides losing precious money to the pharmacist!

Keep good records.

Maintain a good file of previous and present medical records containing information about the child's birth, development, vaccination, illnesses, allergies, medicines and investigations. Bring this file whenever you visit a clinic or a hospital.

Follow the instructions.

The doctor's instructions about rest, diet and medicines must be followed sincerely. Complete the course of medicines as advised. Do not modify the dosage or duration of medicines on your own.

Don't make telephone calls for every small doubt.

You should contact a doctor on the telephone and seek advice only for real medical emergencies. And don't forget social courtesies like saying 'please' and 'thank you'.

Don't shop for doctors.

Trust your doctor. If you don't, there is no sense in going to that doctor. Medicines do not work like miracles, and an illness subsides only after a particular duration. So be patient until the medicines work on the illness. If you don't see immediate improvement, don't rush to the next available doctor.

Be friends!

Develop a friendly rapport with the doctor and also include your child in that friendship. One way to ensure that is to do away with using the word 'injection' to frighten the child.

Show your appreciation.

Like any other person, your doctor, too, would be very happy if you showed your appreciation for his work. Let it be genuine appreciation and not the forced fake kind!

10

Telephonic Consultation

Scenario

"Doc, it's my baby, you know, she is having fever and she vomited just now."

The doctor, who has been rudely awakened, sleepily looks at the time. It's 3 am! Gathering his wits, he asks, "When did I last see her?"

The harried voice at the other end replies, "Oh, it was about 6 months ago."

By now the doctor is wide awake. The exchange proceeds.

Doctor: "What's her age now?"

Father: "I think two—no—three."

Doctor: "What's her temperature?"

Father: "Umm … I haven't checked it."

Doctor: "Have you given her any medicines?"

Father: "No, I mean yes, doc. Those prescribed by the last doctor don't seem to be working."

Doctor: "What are those medicines? What food did she have at night?"

Father: "Just wait, huh, I am not sure. I will ask my wife."

So on and so forth!

Discussion

If you think I am writing a comic piece, you are justified in thinking so. But mind you, this kind of situation is very real and very common. Telephonic medical consultation has been going on since Graham Bell invented the telephone and presented a convenient chatterbox to the human race. Everybody has used this kind of medical advice sometime. As parents and as patients, you have to be aware of the do's and don'ts of telephonic medical consultation to get the best out of it. Here are some tips.

Over the telephone, consult the doctor whom you visit regularly. There is no point in asking for advice if you have not seen the doctor for a long time. It is unlikely that the doctor would have an idea of your recent health or even remember you at all.

Make sure that your doctor is willing to offer advice over the telephone. In your first meeting with the doctor at a clinic, ask about the doctor's views on subject. Ask about the doctor's willingness to take calls from patients, timings for calls and the nature of illness necessitating a call.

Use this facility sparingly and only in an emergency. Telephonic consultation is not for superficial or cosmetic problems like a child not eating well or a long-standing mole on the skin. "Could the symptom be this condition or that illness?" is a guessing game question and is absurd to ask over the telephone.

Be polite when you call. Always initiate the conversation by first apologising for the intrusion and end the call by expressing gratitude. You may be wondering why I harp on such basic manners and courtesy. But I have seen, or rather heard, too many patients asking for telephonic advice with an attitude that says: 'I own you; you are at my beck and call.' Many of my professional colleagues, too, have seen this attitude.

Once the consultation begins, give a brief and accurate description of symptoms, signs and treatment tried at home. Keep all relevant information handy for quick reference. Write down the advice given by the doctor. Take care with the spellings and doses of medicines and read them back to confirm them. Don't forget to ask about any danger signs to watch for. Ask the doctor's opinion about the possible need for hospitalisation or emergency treatment and where it would be available.

Keep the conversation to the absolute necessary minimum. If you call during clinic timings, be aware that another patient may be present with the doctor and waiting for the doctor's attention. Keep out idle chatter and unnecessary repetition of the same points.

Talk to the doctor in the language that you are most comfortable with. If the doctor knows your mother tongue, use it. English is not the best language to express your medical problems if you don't know it well.

Always make it a point to inform the doctor of the patient's progress. Most often, after using telephonic medical advice, patients forget to call back the doctor to say that the patient has recovered. Even if there is deterioration in the patient's condition necessitating hospitalisation, make it a point to convey that information at some point.

Never use this facility for a countercheck. Many patients want to crosscheck one doctor's diagnosis and treatment with another. This is unethical to say the least.

"Doctor, the last time my son suffered from a chest infection, you gave him such-and-such medicine. Can I use it again? I think he is having similar problems." This is one of the commonest calls a doctor gets (just substitute 'chest infection' with other illnesses). If the doctor responds by giving you the general guidelines of management over the telephone, which are based on a presumptive diagnosis made on the information provided by a medically untrained person (that's you), the doctor's advice is not likely to be accurate and may even prove dangerous. In most cases, it is better to get a hands-on, 'eyes-on' consultation to get an accurate diagnosis of the problem.

Many patients routinely use telephonic consultation, thinking it is a way to get free medical advice. What can I say about this? I would just say that medical professionals are using their expertise to make their living like any other professionals. It is morally wrong to 'use' that expertise without paying for it. Anyway, if there are patients trying to find a way out of paying fees, doctors are not so dumb that they do not notice the ruse. Life is all about 'give and take'!

And last but not the least, never give your doctor a missed call and expect it to be returned!

VI

Child Habits, Behaviour and Psychology

1

Disciplining Children: Start Early

Scenario

Case 1: Gurmeet is a toddler. He throws a flower vase on the floor and breaks it into pieces. Not satisfied with the spectacular results, he goes for another one.

Case 2: Parineeti is a pre-schooler. She is visiting her aunt's home, where she is scribbling furiously with crayons on the drawing room wall. Her aunt tries to stop her, but she doesn't pay attention!

Case 3: Srinivas has just entered his KG class. The teacher complains that he bites other children when he is angry.

In all three cases, the parents make hardly any effort to control their erring wards and just watch them with bemused expressions.

Discussion

Sounds familiar? Yes, these are common scenes in today's homes. Are these problem children or are the parents right to dismiss these problems with "Oh, it's just the age. They are too small to understand"?

The answer to both these questions is 'no'. The misbehaving children are certainly not problem children, at least not yet. But no, parents must not ignore these problems. In fact, the very occurrence of such behaviour reflects on the confused attitude of an increasing number of new-age parents who have not correctly understood the concept of 'discipline'.

Discipline is essential

The word 'discipline' has traditionally been associated with a bitter aftertaste of verbal and even physical punishments and a power struggle over what should be done or shouldn't be done. Today's parents were once children themselves, and they had once faced this power struggle with their own parents. Carrying the memories of their 'harsher', 'stricter' upbringing, many of them now decide on a 'softer', 'friendlier' approach as parents. In principle, it certainly is a laudable concept; but in reality, it often ends up horribly wrong because the soft, friendly approach is put into practice as a 'no discipline at all' approach.

Whether one likes it or not, discipline is an essential part of life and needs to be taught and instilled in the psyche early in life. Parents are not going to need this concept in the first 6 months of infancy when the baby indulges in just two main activities—feeding and sleeping. Once past this age, the parents see noticeable changes in their baby's behaviour. With every passing week, the baby acquires an increasing ability to master his environment. Increasing mobility, exploring nearby things and refusing to obey parental commands (especially at feeding times) becomes the new routine for the growing baby. This is the correct time for introducing the concept of discipline.

Simple approach

The baby cannot understand complex commands or the logic behind any decision. But one thing the baby understands very soon is which of his or her acts make the parents smile and give praise. Parental appreciation is the cornerstone of child psychology, and that appreciation should be used as a tool for instilling discipline.

Throwing away a bottle or a spoon, playing with food or pulling at electric plugs or wires are often the first acts of a rebellious baby. This is a normal part of development when the baby explores everything in his environment. But in this phase, he needs to learn the limits of this exploration.

A simple, firm 'no' with a clear facial expression of disapproval when the baby is doing something wrong, and a 'yes' with a pleased expression when he stops doing it is the way to begin to teach what is allowed and not allowed.

The baby will not immediately respond to these expressions and learn to obey your commands. Consistency is the key here. Every time the baby does something wrong and sees a negative response from her beloved mother or father, he begins to grasp the cause and effect relationship between his action and the parents' reaction. This is soon followed by an understanding of the concept of right and wrong behaviour through the positive or negative response of the parents to each type of behaviour.

It is parents' duty to say 'no' and show displeasure at certain actions like breaking or spilling things, approaching a danger area, touching dangerous objects, putting dangerous objects in the mouth or throwing temper tantrums. In the course of that duty, it is but natural that the baby will cry and be unhappy for a moment. Parents who are over-protective and avoid this momentary unhappiness are wasting a great opportunity to teach their little one to differentiate good from bad behaviour.

Crying is okay

'Keep the baby smiling' is fine as a parental motto, but many parents mistake its meaning for 'Never let the baby cry'. This attitude often results in letting the baby do whatever he wishes to do. Inadvertently, these parents foster in the baby the sense that 'whatever I do is right; it can never be wrong or unacceptable to others'.

If your child cries because you have not accepted his negative behaviour, you should not feel guilty because what you are doing is good for the child in the long run. Every such episode of crying or disappointment after a negative behaviour is teaching the baby an important lesson in life: 'Not everything in life is going to go your way, and you have to be ready for rejection and dejection, too.' So, every such crying episode is in fact making your child emotionally stronger and teaching the wisdom of following rules.

Don't misuse authority

As parents, you certainly have the power to say 'yes' or 'no', but as the superheroes keep saying, "with power comes responsibility." How to exercise your power is the key to successful parenting.

- When the baby is small, try to keep the environment free of 'no' objects such as electric plugs and wires and other dangerous objects.
- As your child grows older, he begins to understand the logic behind your positive and negative command, so make sure that your commands are consistent in their logic and execution. Permitting certain things at one time and objecting to them at other times is going to confuse your child as to what he should do in those situations.

- Clearly define your set of rules regarding issues like food and eating habits; school work; language usage; playing activity; television, computer and gadget use; pocket money and bedtime.
- Be considerate of your child's changing emotional needs and growing independence and modify the rules as necessary.
- Don't contradict your spouse or undermine your spouse's authority by questioning his or her decision in front of the child. Discuss any contentious issues in private.
- Discipline is not only about criticism of wrong behaviour; it is also about appreciation of good behaviour. Be sure to show appreciation when your child does something right.
- Parents are the role models for children; so practice what you preach.

Punishment

Physical punishment has been proved to have no use in correcting wrong behaviour. In fact, it sends the wrong signal that it is okay to hit another person. Sometimes it leads to repetition of negative acts as a means of seeking attention. More than the physical harm such punishment causes, it is the emotional harm that is deeper.

Verbal punishments in the form of shouting or taunting can also lead to emotional scarring and usually serve no purpose.

Time-outs (at 1 minute per year of age) and taking away privileges (like pocket money or television, computer or gadget time or night out) are good strategies to curb negative behaviour in children above 2 years of age.

Time-out puts the errant child in a solitary place without distractions and give him a chance to cool down and think about his negative behaviour. Taking away privileges teaches him that there is a price to pay for wrong behaviour.

When it comes to children's discipline, always start early. Starting late might be too late!

2

Temper Tantrums

Scenario

The entire supermarket is watching Mrs. Naidu and she wishes she could just hide. Gopi, her toddler son, the love of her life, the apple of her eye, is squatting on the floor and letting out a full-blown emotional hailstorm. He is screaming, crying and kicking—right there in the middle of the main aisle—chanting "I want that toy."

Discussion

Substitute Mr. Singh for Mrs. Naidu, a theatre for the supermarket, a daughter for the son and a chocolate for the toy and the scene would still look pretty similar. This is the typical temper tantrum seen in children.

Temper tantrums are prolonged emotional outbursts with relatively minor causes (stimuli) that are seen primarily in the age group of 1–3 years but can occur earlier or later. Boys and girls are equally 'good' at throwing tantrums. Up to a limit, temper tantrums are to be considered a normal stage in the child development.

Reasons

Before thinking of strategies to tackle temper tantrums, parents should understand why children are prone to these unpleasant outbursts.

From the child's point of view, most of these tantrums are power struggles for control. As infancy (the 1st year) comes to an end and the toddler phase (the 2nd and 3rd year) begins, the child's mental make-up changes. Many new skills are constantly being acquired, such as walking, running, speaking, feeding and other daily activities. The child feels ready to take on the world with this repertoire.

'I can do everything' and 'I can have everything' is the child's attitude, but this newfound confidence and independence is challenged by parental authority. Parents exercise their authority because they are unsure of their child's ability or feel the activity might be dangerous or destructive. A child with an aggressive, active personality is more liable to feel frustration at such parental interference and might resort to tantrums.

Sometimes, these tantrums are as a result of the child's **craving parental attention.**

Indulgent, ignorant, impatient, insensitive and inconsistent parenting is often at the root of the problem of temper tantrums. Parents who lavish toys, sweets and gifts without a reason; who allow certain liberties at times and then change the rules; who are too strict or too lenient; who are unhappy, fatigued or impatient; who fail to understand the individuality of their children and who are prone to public displays of anger are the ones most likely to see tantrums in their children.

Frequent temper tantrums could sometimes be **manifestations of a disorder or illness** in the child, such as a hearing, speech or vision problem; a learning disorder; a psychiatric illness or any other chronic illness.

Parental response

The first rule for managing a child's temper tantrum is for the parent to keep cool. Your anger and frustration will make the situation worse.

Perhaps the best way to deal with it is to ignore the tantrum completely. Make no fuss and avoid any positive or negative reaction, while remaining close by to make sure the child does not hurt herself.

If there is a possibility of injury to the child or to others, remove the child from the place and bring her to a quiet, safe place. Try to distract her by changing the environment and offering a new interesting activity.

In either case, analyse the cause of the tantrum. If it is about some forbidden activity (e.g., 'Don't touch that thing!'), judge how significant that decision is for you and your child (a knife versus a spoon). If that activity is likely to be dangerous or destructive, stick to your decision but remove the desired object out of sight. If you feel you have been too harsh in your original decision, revise it. Make sure to explain that you made the change based on your own re-thinking and not because of the pressure of the tantrum.

Reasoning or intelligent negotiations are not strong points of small children. So don't waste your time doing that.

If you want to shout, keep it short and snappy. Express your anger and then leave the scene for a while to cool off.

Physical punishments are useless and might reinforce the negative behaviour.

In many children (older than 2 years), an option of a time-out alone to cool down is often possible. Praise them after they gain control.

Further investigations

Further psychiatric or medical investigations are indicated in the following conditions:

- Too frequent, too severe and too prolonged temper tantrums
- Destructive tendencies
- Frequent mood changes
- Anxious or withdrawn child
- Associated physical symptoms like headache, vomiting or speech, vision, or walking gait disturbances

Prevention

While temper tantrums are a normal stage in development, you could do certain things to prevent as many of the episodes as possible.

Define your disciplinary limits clearly and consistently. Keep in mind that 'She is still a kid' and try to modulate her behaviour. Every child is an individual, and you have to be flexible in your approach to control each one. Children should clearly understand that you love them. Express your love through words and deeds. Showering them with gifts and goodies is not necessary and is in fact detrimental.

Make sure that your child's sleeping hours are adequate for the age. Inadequate sleep leads to tiredness and crankiness.

3

Sibling Rivalry

Scenario

Mrs. Mamta Desai is worried. Her 7-year-old son Prashant has changed a lot since the birth of her daughter Rashmi. All of a sudden, he has started to stammer. He has also started wetting the bed at night. He often tries to pinch his infant sister or pulls her hair when no one is watching. Mrs. Desai knows that this is sibling rivalry but doesn't know how to deal with it!

Discussion

Frayed tempers, frowning faces, stuck-out tongues, name-calling, hair-pulling. All of us have seen how sibling rivalry unfolds. This natural part of development in children with siblings can be disastrous for the family if it reaches an extreme.

Reasons

Rivalry is inherent to human nature. To prove one's superiority and to feel jealous of others' achievements are two traits from which no human mind is exempt; only the intensity of these feelings differs from individual to individual.

In a way, sibling rivalry starts from the moment of news that a new family member is on the way. The elder child, who has been the centre of attention in the family until then, suddenly finds himself relegated to the second spot. He sees a tiny tot, who doesn't even know what it is doing, hog all attention.

As the new baby grows, she sees the elder sibling as somebody 'powerful' and 'skilful' at things which she cannot do. These two conflicting perspectives of elder and younger siblings and the social compulsion of having to stay together and share everything—including parental love and attention—forms the basis of sibling rivalry.

Personalities of siblings play an important role. Children who are fussy, get easily frustrated or are aggressive are more likely to engage in such conflicts.

Family environment is another important determinant. Parents who show overt favouritism amongst their children on the basis of gender, appearance or achievement; who frequently have arguments or fights and who fail to devote enough time and attention to children are more likely to face this problem.

Manifestations

In the early years, siblings fight over things like toys or sometimes for a father's lap or a mother's breast. As they grow older, the rivalry takes a different course. There might be conflicts over using shared things like a room, books, television or computer. There are negative remarks passed on each other's appearances, achievements or friends. There is bullying to get the daily chores done.

Parental response

Preparing the elder children for the arrival of the new baby is the first step in managing the problem of sibling rivalry. Let the child know well in advance (by the second trimester) about the delivery. Encourage him to voice his views and concerns. If you are comfortable with the idea, let him 'see' the baby during ultrasound tests or let them 'feel' the baby's kicking.

Emphasise the first child's 'big brother' or 'big sister' role and role in caring for and protecting the young baby. Reassure him that your love for him is not going to be any less. At the same time, also tell him that mother would be busy looking after the small baby for some time and would find it difficult to give him the same time and attention.

Be prepared to face the child's negative remarks about siblings ('He is not nice!' 'She is ugly!') and about your parenting ('You are unfair!'). Remember that these remarks are coming from children who are not yet emotionally mature.

Make your child understand the concept of 'family' and also that physically injuring (pinching or hitting) or yelling at the other child is not going to be permitted. Make both children appreciate each other's good points. Never indulge in comparisons between the children and ensure that your attention, affection and appreciation are evenly distributed.

Don't take sides in a sibling fight. Firmly make both children understand that what they are doing is wrong and would not be tolerated. Give them time to cool off and then make them shake hands or give them a shared activity.

If sharing common things is the problem area, set a timetable to share things like toys, games, television time or computer time.

At younger ages, serious sibling rivalry may manifest itself as temper tantrums, play acting as a baby (baby talk, crawling, crying for bottle or breast feeding, etc.), bed wetting, stammering or withdrawn and depressed mental states. Older children and adolescents could show difficulties at school, anxiety, depression or rage attacks.

Most of these manifestations are manageable by parents showing more understanding, patience and affection. If they persist, the family needs expert guidance from a child psychologist or psychiatrist.

Final word of advice

The key to solve this problem is for you to understand—and then make your children understand—that everyone has one's individual strengths and weaknesses and must use the strengths and overcome the weaknesses to succeed in life, instead of comparing oneself to someone else. Feelings of jealousy and rivalry are not unnatural, but we have to use them as spurs to try harder and reach higher, instead of being sucked into the whirlpool of despair and dejection!

4

Breath Holding Spells

Scenario

Diksha is 8 months old. She is happily playing with her rattle. Her mother takes the rattle away because it is feeding time. But something goes horribly wrong. Diksha starts wailing loudly and, while crying, suddenly stops breathing and goes blue and limp.

Tearful and panicky, the mother immediately rushes her to the doctor. The doctor asks her a few questions while examining the baby, who is already coming back to normal.

"Oh, don't worry. This is your first brush with a breath-holding spell—a scary sight but a harmless condition of early childhood," the doctor announces.

Discussion

Let's see what these breath-holding spells actually are and what can be done to treat and avoid them.

A breath-holding spell is a sudden involuntary temporary stoppage of breathing in an otherwise normal child. These spells typically follow violent crying as a result of anger, frustration or pain. These spells usually start by 6 months, peak by around 2 years and disappear by around 5–6 years. They are more common in girls.

There are two distinct types of breath-holding spells.

Cyanotic or blue breath-holding spell is the commonest variety. In this, the baby or child cries excessively and passionately. The crying is followed by brief breath-holding for a few seconds, and the face turns blue and the body goes limp. Usually, after some time, normal breathing resumes and the body colour and activity return to normal. Occasionally the blueness is followed by the body becoming taut and going into a minor jerky fit which, too, is self-limited.

This type of breath-holding is seen in more assertive, aggressive and stubborn babies and children. It usually happens when such children become angry or frustrated on being disciplined or on being denied something.

Pallid or white breath-holding spell is the less common variety. In this, the child suddenly stops breathing and turns limp and white. This usually happens following sudden fright, startle response or pain and with practically no initial crying. This type of breath-holding is not really associated with any particular behaviour pattern and is thought to be a result of physiological aberrations.

Management of breath-holding spells

During the spell, do these things:

- Don't panic.
- Roll the child over to her side and keep her in a safe, clear space.
- Check her mouth to make sure that there is no object inside that would cause choking.
- These spells are not life-threatening, and most of them stop within few seconds without any treatment.
- Prolonged spells may need resuscitation measures.
- Blowing air on the face or sprinkling water on the face or turning the child upside down are some measures often tried by parents, but you are better off without them.

To avoid spells, keep these things in mind.

Get the child evaluated by a doctor to avoid any confusion about similar conditions like a cyanotic heart disease or a seizure disorder. Once the harmless nature of breath-holding is confirmed, just take it in your stride and don't make unnecessary fuss over their occurrence.

Many parents try a non-confrontational approach by taking care to not offend such a child and let her do whatever she wants to do in order to avoid the crying and resultant breath-holding spells. But this is not needed and will worsen the child's behaviour. Just be consistent and set the proper disciplining limits.

No medicines have proved effective for breath-holding and none is needed. By 6 years, almost all sufferers of this condition come out of this frightening habit.

5

Thumb-Sucking, Nail Biting and Pacifiers

Scenario

Mrs. Sahai is agitated. "My daughter Shilpa is driving me crazy. Either she sucks her thumb or she keeps biting her nails. It is so embarrassing. I want to get rid of that habit at the earliest! I really wish I had given her a pacifier when she was a baby."

Her doctor friend Meenu asks her, "How old is Shilpa?"

"She just completed 3 years!" the mother replies.

Meenu immediately says, "But, then, I don't think there is any problem with her. And I also don't think a pacifier would have helped her in any way."

The surprised mother mumbles, "Oh, really?"

Discussion

Thumb-sucking

A baby inside the mother's womb starts sucking its thumb after 29 weeks. So, there is nothing unnatural about this habit. This so-called non-nutritive sucking is perfectly normal and natural. It happens because the baby associates the pleasurable stimulation of lips and mouth with pleasant feelings like satiety (being full after feeds) or being held. However, the persistence of this habit often indicates underlying anxiety, emotional stress or frustration in the child.

As a majority of children up to the age of 4 years suck thumbs at least occasionally, clinically, the habit is considered significant only after that age.

In most thumb-sucking children above the age of 4 years, this habit is annoying but not worrisome. But in some children the duration, frequency and intensity of thumb-sucking are greater, and in them, adverse long-term effects are possible.

Long-term effects

A severe habit of thumb-sucking could lead to problems in teeth, facial structure and obviously in the thumb.

Dental malalignment, disturbances in jaw bones and joints, disturbed placement and function of lips or tongue and injuries to soft tissue in the mouth are possible effects in the mouth and face.

The thumb that is sucked vigorously could become bent or deformed. Thumb soreness, callosities (thickened skin), irritant eczema and acute or chronic nail infections (e. g., herpetic whitlow) are also possible.

Psychosocial effects of thumb-sucking are much more damaging. In one study of school children, thumb-suckers were found to be unpopular and were considered less intelligent and attractive by peers. Add to this the stress of having to endure the taunts and reprimands by parents, teachers and schoolmates.

Management

In a majority of cases, just assuring the child of parental love and support is enough to rid the child of the habit. Parents should try and ignore the habit without making it a major issue as it usually subsides on its own. They should encourage the child's own efforts in tackling this habit.

Parents should make an effort to identify and remove any underlying cause of anxiety or stress.

Parental scolding and negative attitude make the problem worse. That is why the famous paediatrician Dr. Spock once said, "The danger of thumb sucking is not in the habit itself but in what parents do about it."

Professional treatment of thumb-sucking is needed only in children over 4 years of age, who show adverse effects of the habit. Physical barriers like mittens, socks or bandages; orthodontic appliances; aversive taste formula applications and in some cases psychotherapy are the treatment modalities available.

Aversive taste formula is bitter or sour and is applied on the thumb so that the child's aversion for the taste discourages sucking the thumb. Application of the formula, coupled with a reward system for not sucking the thumb, should be used after taking the child into confidence about what is being done and why. This method has a very good success rate.

Nail-biting

Nail-biting and thumb-sucking are quite similar as regards to the causes, effects and treatment. Here, too, one has to understand the self-limited and essentially benign (harmless) nature of the condition and identify and remove the underlying emotional stress.

Pacifier to avoid thumb-sucking

The so-called pacifier (also called soother or dummy) is usually a ringed nipple offered to a crying baby, who seems to be crying simply to be carried or held. Many parents introduce it in the early weeks of the baby's life to reduce having to hold and soothe the baby. Some start it a little later in infancy to provide an alternative to thumb-sucking. But a baby sucking on its own thumb is better off compared to a baby sucking a pacifier!

The pacifier is not a habit to recommend for it offers no real emotional benefit to the baby. It might provide some minor comfort but is never a substitute for the parent holding and soothing the baby. Pacifiers carry an increased risk of infection (particularly fungal infection of the mouth) and oral injuries. Besides, they often become an annoying and prolonged habit, which proves more difficult to stop than thumb-sucking.

If pacifiers are dipped in sweet, syrupy substances like honey or glucose syrup, there is a risk of tooth decay in the long run. Constant prolonged use of a pacifier extending into toddler years might even cause faulty alignment of teeth.

Final word of advice

Thumb-sucking is considered normal up to the age of 4 years.

Identify and correct any underlying stress or anxiety in the child. Assure the child of parental love and support. Avoid scolding and negative attitude.

Avoid using pacifiers to prevent thumb-sucking. They often become an annoying, prolonged habit and may cause infection, injury or dental problems.

5

Pica (Dirt Eating)

Scenario

Dipti is 4 years old. Her mother is noticing that Dipti often scratches the wall and eats paint. At times, she has also been eating stranger things such as crayons, tissue paper and even sand.

When Dipti's mother voices her concern, her doctor tells her that it is a case of pica and needs to be properly investigated.

Discussion

Pica is an annoying and potentially dangerous habit in which a person regularly eats unusual non-food items from the environment. To be medically significant, the habit has to last more than a month.

Usually, pica is seen in children. Almost 10–30% children between 1–6 years of age suffer from this condition at some point. Even adult pregnant mothers may sometimes get into this habit.

The substances most commonly eaten by pica patients are mud, clay or wall paint. Other things eaten habitually are plaster, pebbles, ash, wallpaper, strings, rags, stationery (paper, pencils, crayons), shoe soles, hair and stools.

Causes and complications

Parental neglect is often an underlying cause of pica, but there may be no particular cause in many cases. Developmental, behavioural or psychological problems such as mental retardation or autism are often associated with pica.

The potential complications of pica are the harm that the ingested objects can do. Common dangers are poisoning, particularly lead poisoning from wall paint and pencils, and worm infestation. Surgery is needed when hard or sharp objects cause internal injuries or hair or other objects accumulate to form bezoars, which are ball-like tumours in the stomach.

Diagnostic tests

A complete blood count with blood picture is ordered to check for iron deficiency anaemia. Stool tests are done to check for worm infestation.

If lead poisoning is suspected, the blood is tested for lead levels.

If surgical complication is suspected, x-rays and ultrasound scans may be required.

Treatment

Eating right is the primary cure for eating the wrong things. Patient and family education about good nutritional habits is central to the treatment of pica. Parents must establish a balanced diet for the child.

The non-food items the child craves should be removed from the child's environment. The child may also need behaviour modification treatments.

Treatment is needed for associated problems such as nutritional deficiency (iron supplements) or worm infestation (wormicidal medicines).

Prognosis

In most normal individuals, pica is a temporary problem that lasts for months but responds well to proper management. Pica in pregnancy usually stops after delivery.

Pica can persist for years in individuals suffering from developmental and psychological problems.

7

Toilet Training

Scenario

To go from soiling anytime, anywhere to passing urine and stools in the toilet or a potty is a big milestone in your baby's development. Parents tired of changing dirty nappies and cleaning soiled floors are always eagerly waiting for this landmark. But as always, there is a right way and a wrong way of doing things, and potty training is no exception! So, let's learn the right way of teaching this important step to your toddler.

Remember the three Rs—not the three Rs of education but of toilet training.

- The first R is 'recognising the child's readiness'.
- The second R is a 'relaxed approach'.
- The third R is 'routine establishment'.

If you follow these three Rs, then the fourth R—'reward'—is not too far.

Age to start toilet training

By 1½ years, most toddlers start indicating the urge to pass urine or stools either through words or through action. That is the ideal time to start potty training or toilet training. Here, recognising your child's readiness is important.

The overall understanding, attitude and developmental level of the child are important factors in deciding the timing. Some babies will always be more mature, expressive and co-operative than others, and they will be the ideal candidates for learning this new skill. If these qualities are slow to develop in your baby, there is no harm in waiting up to 2½ years or later to start potty training.

Duration

The time required for toilet training varies from individual to individual. Usually, the basic process takes a few weeks to a few months.

Remember the relaxed approach. Don't be a pushy control freak. To master a new skill, each child takes its own time. You should be prepared to be patient and tolerant of your child's failed attempts. Sometimes, it could take months before the child masters the process, and there could be occasional mishaps even after the child has apparently mastered it.

Equipment

A receptacle potty is the commonest device used for toilet training. The other way is to use the normal toilet with a toilet seat adapter suitable for the child's size.

Switching from the diaper to trainer pants or normal underpants is also a good idea in this phase. At first, do this switch from the nappy to the trainer pant or underpants only during the day. Start doing it at night only after a reasonable control is achieved during the day.

Actual training

There are five simple steps to toilet training a baby. Go through them one by one according to your child's readiness and response. Give a minimum of 5–10 days for each step. This is the third R, which is to establish the routine of toilet habits in a gradual and phased manner.

Step 1: Place the potty or the toilet seat in the toilet. Take your toddler to the toilet and make him sit on the potty for a while. The pants or nappies should not be removed during this step. Repeat this step a few times every day for at least a week. Make it like a game. Do not associate it with passing stools or urine.

Step 2: Once the child is used to the idea of sitting on the potty, start removing the pants when putting the child on the potty. Repeat it a few times every day. Do not associate it with passing stools or urine.

Step 3: When the child soils the pants or diaper, put the child on the potty and remove the soiled nappy into the potty. Let the child see the flushing away of the faeces. If the child is afraid of the flushing noise despite your reassurance, give him a few more days to get used to it. This step is to make the child realise that the potty or the toilet is for disposing of wastes.

Step 4: It is time for the child to practice what you preached. The shadowboxing is over, and the actual battle begins. In this step, remove the child's pants and tell the child to try to pass stools while sitting on the potty. Do this at a time when the child usually passes stools. Do it twice or thrice in a day according to the child's habit.

Slowly but surely, the child will master the skill. Show your appreciation for the child's new-found mastery of this bodily function.

Step 5: In the final step, the child is trained to go alone to the potty, independently remove the pants and pass bodily wastes in the potty.

Achieving full bowel and bladder control is a long process and happens in stages. The usual order is night-time bowel control first, followed by daytime bowel control, followed by daytime bladder control and finally night-time bladder control.

Understand well that, along the way, there will be some incidents or 'accidents' when the child soils the pants or the bed. 'No harsh negative comments or measures' is the way to deal with such episodes.

Cleaning the baby

Cleaning the child with water is perhaps a more hygienic option than using toilet paper. The direction of wiping should be from front to back to avoid passing germs to the urinary tract. Fixing a water-jet pipe in the toilet will help you teach the child to easily clean himself or herself after passing stools.

Teach the child to wash his hands with soap and water after using the toilet. That completes toilet training and you can put your feet up and relax.

8

Bedwetting

Scenario

Kshama is 7 years old. But her mother never allows her to go on any school trips. She also never lets her go for sleepovers at her friend's place. Kshama is secretly happy about this restrictive rule.

Do you want to know why? It's because Kshama still regularly wets her bed at night.

Discussion

Bed-wetting is one symptom that both the parents and the young sufferer are too embarrassed to discuss. At the same time, the problem is too sticky and troublesome to just brush under the carpet.

The medical term for bed-wetting is enuresis. It means involuntary voiding of urine after the common age of achieving adequate bladder control. When bedwetting mainly occurs at night, it is called nocturnal enuresis, and when it occurs mainly during the day, it is called diurnal enuresis.

Up to the age of 4 years, as many as one in four children wet the bed occasionally. Only after that age is reasonable bladder control achieved. Boys take even longer to achieve this control. So most experts consider bed-wetting significant only if continues after the age of 6 years.

Bed-wetting is said to be 'primary' when the child has never achieved adequate bladder control and 'secondary' when the child achieved good bladder control for 6 months or more and then lost it.

More than 85% cases of bed-wetting are nocturnal and primary, and almost 99% of such patients have no underlying disease. I will limit the discussion to this particular type of enuresis.

Primary, night-time bed-wetting

Causes

This type of bed-wetting is a developmental problem in which the brain takes more time to mature in this particular respect. The immature brain fails to recognise the full bladder's voiding signals during sleep, which is why these children fail to wake up to urinate.

Smaller bladder capacity and deeper sleep patterns have been observed in children who suffer the problem. Genetic factors are also involved, considering that many cases show a familial tendency.

Psychologically stressful events like a death in the family, birth of a sibling or a move to another place were once considered very important in the causation of enuresis. But it is now thought that such stress is mainly responsible only in the secondary type of bed-wetting.

Other conditions

Involuntary urination may be caused by other conditions such as urinary infections, congenital abnormalities of the urinary tract and the spine, diabetes, excessive water intake and constipation.

A visit to a paediatrician and a urine test are usually enough to diagnose and distinguish these conditions. Only occasionally are x-rays, ultrasonography and blood tests necessary.

Management

Managing a child with primary, nocturnal enuresis is a difficult and long process. As in any such complex disorder, it calls for patience, persistence and perseverance.

Ensure that the affected **child participates actively** in the management program. Make the child feel responsible by encouraging her to keep a record of dry and wet nights. Involve the child in the cleaning and changing of the soiled bedsheets but do that gently and tactfully.

Parents should make every effort to **preserve the child's self-esteem**, which is the first casualty of this symptom. Shouting and punishments achieve nothing. Parents must understand that the child is not doing it deliberately and that it is just a matter of time before she gets it right. A reward system for dry nights (as simple as stars on a star chart) often works wonders for the child's motivation.

Some routine measures that help are:

- Compulsory urination before going to bed
- Decreasing water or fluid intake close to bedtime
- Avoiding things like tea, coffee, chocolate or fizzy drinks close to bedtime
- Improving access to the toilet, sometimes keeping a potty near the bed
- Avoiding diapers as an easy way out because it hampers learning

Behaviour modification should aim to make the child realise that she should not be trying to hold off the urine throughout the night but rather should get up, go to the toilet and urinate there when she feels the impulse.

This patient self-awakening program uses techniques like progressive behaviour modification and self-hypnosis; in the latter, the patient imagines having a night free of bed-wetting. This method, when successful, has the lowest relapse rates.

Sometimes this method is combined with a parent-awakening program in which the parent wakes up during the night, not to carry the child to toilet but just to wake her up and make her go to toilet to urinate.

Bedwetting alarms are small, wearable alarms. When the patient starts to wet the bed, the alarm starts to buzz by detecting moisture. These alarms have a success rate of 70% in curing the condition and a low relapse rate. But for this therapy to be successful, it requires motivation on the part of the patient and parents and a trial of at least 23 months.

A particular antidepressant (which helps to relax the bladder) and a synthetic form of a hormone (which helps to concentrate and reduce the volume of urine) are the two most popular **medication options** for bed-wetting.

Neither medicine gives a complete cure and both have a high (>90%) relapse rate. They are useful in combination with other techniques and as a short-term benefit in certain situations like school trips and scout camps.

Final word of advice

Self-motivation, supportive parental attitude, self-awakening program—with the aid of bedwetting alarms and short-term judicious use of medicines—is the answer to this tricky problem.

Many less motivated parents and patients lose heart midway in this long-drawn battle, being riddled with shame, guilt and frustration. For them I have one reassuring statistic. With every passing year after the age of 6 years, 15% of these patients are cured spontaneously. At that rate, practically every patient is cured by the age of 15 years!

So just hang in there; time will cure it.

9

Understanding Teenagers

Scenario

Family 1

Mr. and Mrs. Walia are exasperated. They feel driven to the wall by the way their teenage daughter Suparna is behaving lately. Actually, Suparna has the same feelings about her mom and dad!

Family 2

Sunil Vohra is angry. He feels that his parents just don't understand him. His parents say that they, too, have been experiencing the same feelings since he became a teenager!

Discussion

These scenes are representative of the common parent versus teenager conflicts happening all over the world. Like any other conflict, this too could be resolved if each side made a sincere attempt to understand the other side's viewpoints. Since I currently count myself amongst parents (and not anymore amongst teenagers!), I will try and demystify some of the things that usually baffle the parent community.

Different, detached, defiant, deviant—these 4 Ds need to be understood to understand teenagers.

Teenagers are 'different'.

Teenage or adolescence is a stage midway between childhood and adulthood. In a teenager, we see someone who is not yet an adult, yet no longer a child. This stage is perhaps the most complex stage in life.

Let's start with the basics. In teenage years, there are hormonal changes, and the body is changing because of that. Teenagers are growing taller, heavier and developing secondary sexual characteristics (pubic and armpit hair, breast enlargement in girls, facial hair and hoarseness of voice in boys).

These physical changes are accompanied by changes in thinking and behaviour patterns. They are becoming more aware of their external appearance. They are becoming more interested in the opposite sex. Insecurities about own body image or social worth are quite common. Food fads (diets) and exercise could suddenly become parts of their routines.

The prevailing pop teen culture often attracts them to adopt drastically different clothes, make-up, music, movies, technology and even language. All this is nothing but their way of emphasising the fact that they are now 'different' and that their world is different from the others'.

Teenagers are 'detached'.

Teenagers' detachment is directly a result of their feeling 'different' and shows at many levels.

Detachment from family: The teenagers' fashions, their 'cool' or 'hot' pop icons, their language and their likes and dislikes are so different from the rest of the family that they feel 'disconnected'. They start feeling uncomfortable with their 'Mama's boy' or 'Dad's girl' image and are embarrassed by public display of affection by parents. They often start avoiding their parents' or siblings' company and feel at home with their own friends and peers.

Detachment from real world: Teenagers are not much interested in the daily nitty-gritty of the real world and are quite comfortable in their own world of friends and fantasies. The virtual world offered by the Internet and related technology often becomes their preferred abode.

Detachment from responsibility: Critical self-appraisal and learning from mistakes are not the teenager's strong points. Teenagers often refuse to take responsibility for their actions and think little about possible negative consequences.

Teenagers are 'defiant'.

Teenagers are much more likely to engage in confrontation with their parents by refusing to follow their rules and directions. Fighting over dress codes, curfew timings, studies and television or Internet use is often observed. Many times, they reject everything associated with their parents' 'old world'.

Once again, this trait follows from their 'different' and 'detached' thinking patterns and their need to assert their independent individual image.

Teenagers are at risk to be 'deviant'.

Teenagers are reaching adult physical sizes, proportions and capabilities, but their minds still have quite a distance to cover to reach adult maturity. Peer pressure is the strongest force driving them. A wrong friend circle may cause a teenager to engage in risky experiments or practices with sex, tobacco, alcohol, drugs, crime, rash driving, or neglect of studies and so on, without realising their long-term consequences. Unfortunately, at that age, they are not yet ready to critically look at their own actions. The defiant 'So what ?' attitude and detachment from responsibility puts them in danger of losing their way in life.

Tips for parents

Understand and respect teenager's individuality. Give them the necessary time and space to discover their own identity.

Clearly define family rules and limits and be consistent in their interpretation and implementation. Remain aware of the social, cultural and technological changes happening around you. Only then will your rules, regulations and interactions be relevant.

Discuss prickly topics in a friendly but firm manner. It is okay to feel frustrated, even sad, at the changes you observe in your teenager. It is a major transition period and is bound to be turbulent at times. Everyone involved is going to experience insecurities.

But remember that, at core, they still are your babies and expect your love and acceptance! Only, you need to modify how you express your feelings.

Be observant without being nosey. Make a point to know their friends and their backgrounds.

You may have to seek professional help if you see danger signals like neglecting studies, dropping school performance, social withdrawal, anti-social behaviour, frequent family fights, too much indulgence in virtual world activities (SMSing, chatting, surfing etc.), or excessive weight gain or weight loss. A doctor may use the HEADDSS assessment which assesses the teenager's mental well-being by asking questions about home, education, activities, drugs, drinking, sex and suicidal tendency.

Final word of advice

Do you remember the turbulent times when you were teenagers and how you felt back then? Life does move in a circle, doesn't it? The turbulence has come again, though you are on the other side now. Don't worry because you did fine with your life and so will your children. Do not keep trying to control every aspect of their life. Let them explore the world; let them make their own decisions and let them even make their own mistakes. All these things are going to make them learn more about their strengths and weaknesses and finally make them better individuals in the end.

There is nothing wrong if you discreetly watch them from a distance. Just make sure that they know that you will always be there to offer a helping hand and compassionate guidance whenever they need it.

10

Television and Children

Since the time it entered human lives, television has been an extremely influential device. 'Idiot box', 'surrogate nanny' and 'electronic baby-sitter' are some unflattering names given to it. But its value as an entertainer, informer and informal educator has remained undiminished.

In recent years, computers, multimedia games, the Internet and mobile gadgets have been snapping at its heels in terms of popularity, but television retains its place as the prime infotainment home appliance. In fact, the increasing availability of gadgets and internet connectivity has resulted in more television (video) viewing on these 'second screens'.

In the US, a child usually spends one full day out of a week sitting in front of the screen beaming moving pictures and that statistic does not include time spent on computers, multimedia gaming devices and other mobile gadgets. With such a powerful hold over children, television is bound to have a considerable influence on their mental and physical wellbeing.

Effects

School performance: Most experts do not think that the so-called educational television programs significantly improve children's school performance. Studies have proved that too much television-viewing definitely impairs children's school performance.

Couch potatoes: The first thing television does to children is to stop activity and hold them in their seats as wide-eyed spectators. The increasing incidence of childhood obesity is undoubtedly related to these 'idle' television times. More often than not, these television times also become 'junk food times', with crunching chips and cookies and munching on chocolates and donuts.

Children sitting glued to televisions are more likely to be deprived of playful physical activities necessary to keep them fit. Such children also spend much less time on activities such as imaginative play and socialising with friends and family. Reading books, a habit so important for improving the imagination and knowledge, is declining thanks to television.

Emotion and behaviour effects: Films and television serials, especially cartoon shows, often portray characters as 'good' and 'bad'. Such simplistic black and white demarcation of the world is often perceived as the 'reality' by children in their formative years.

More importantly, the 'good guys' often use violence as a means to overcome the 'baddies', and the guns and gore become 'normal' and 'routine' in the growing minds. Horror shows with their scary images can scar the young mind and induce irrational fears. Psychologists and sociologists have expressed worry and published research linking television violence to aggressive behaviour.

Increasingly overt portrayals of sex and promiscuity in television programs is harmful to the developing minds that have not yet reached the level of maturity needed to deal with such complex issues. Older children and adolescents are liable to 'act' out such fantasies in real life without realising the implications and complications.

The continuous barrage of advertisements, often specifically targeting children, promotes a senseless consumer culture resulting in demands for unnecessary things that are projected with a 'must have' tone.

Other probable effects: Television viewing time often cuts into a child's sleep time and causes sleep deficit and tiredness. The flickering television screen is known to precipitate attacks of migraine and even fits of epilepsy.

Effects on toddlers: Excessive television exposure deprives babies of the human interaction that is so important for their neurological development, especially language and speech acquisition, and can cause delay in those areas. The American Academy of Pediatrics, a reputed medical association, strongly recommends that toddlers, or babies up to 2 years of age, should not be allowed to view television at all.

Role of parents

In view of all these dangers and harmful effects of television, parental role in guiding and supervising children's television viewing assumes great importance. Here's what parents can do:

- Limit children's television viewing time to a maximum of 2 hours per day of quality content.
- Plan a programme schedule for viewing to make sure that the content is suitable for children. For that, you will also have to keep track of current television programmes and timings.
- Preferably, sit with children when they watch television. This will give you a chance to monitor the programmes as well as a chance to enjoy them with the children.
- Discuss the viewed programmes. Talk about the real and imaginary world and how one should not mistake television images for reality.
- Keep the television out of the bedroom and children's room if possible.
- Switch off television at meal times.
- Promote other recreational activities like reading and indoor and outdoor games.

Final word of advice

Minimising the negative influence of television isn't only about switching channels and setting time limits. The most important thing is to be 'with' your children whenever you are free, both physically and emotionally. Rather than entertainment, children need interaction.

Too often, television is used as an instrument to keep inquisitive children occupied when parents 'want to be left alone and not be bothered for some time'. Beware that this could prove to be the disastrous first step to being left alone forever by your children.

11

Children in the Cyberworld

Scenario

Scene 1

Animesh is 2 years old. He regularly plays on his swanky white tablet computer and when bored, switches to his latest game console. His parents are very proud of his techno-savvy.

Scene 2

Archana is 9 years old. She has an account on a popular social networking site. She created it by giving a false birthdate that makes her 14 years old. She has also assumed a false name on that network. She says that all her classmates have done it and they all share each other's passwords. She spends a lot of time following her friends' statuses and is disappointed when her posts or photos don't get enough likes.

Scene 3

Salman is 15 years old. When he is done with his studies, and even when he is studying, he keeps checking his mobile phone. Every few minutes, it flashes his friends' SMSs or chat updates. He doesn't feel that he is wasting time because he thumb-types his responses quite fast. He especially enjoys sending and receiving multimedia messages. And yes, he also loves downloading music and movies in his free time.

Discussion

The Internet really has entangled the world in its web, especially the young. First, the Internet could only be accessed through big, box-like computers sitting on the desks. Later, it appeared on portable laptops and then on gaming consoles, mobile phones and tablet computers. Now, around the clock, we are surrounded by this web! But this uncontrolled progression, expansion, and invasion of technology have also raised many questions about its role in children's development. Many researchers strongly recommend that children under 3 years should not use computers. According to them, children of that age learn through their bodily organs, namely, eyes, ears, mouths, hands and legs. Children at this stage are still learning to master walking, running, talking, and making friends. Computers and gadgets are not a good choice for the development of their basic life skills.

Even when children are older and developmentally ready to use computers and the Internet, there are certain good and bad points about technology that parents should bear in mind.

Effects of technology

The Good

If used properly, computers and the Internet are priceless sources of quality education and entertainment content.

The Internet has become a platform without boundaries where one can display one's creative talents without needing any backer or where one can communicate with people across the globe.

Early exposure to technology allows children to master many adult technical skills at much earlier ages.

The Bad

Physical effects: The increasing amounts of time that children spend in front of a computer screen give them less time to play, study and sleep. This puts them at risk of obesity, impaired school performance, eye strain and sleep problems.

Faulty postures while sitting for long hours in front of the computer screen and the continuous typing or thumb-typing can cause serious muscle, bone and joint problems in heavy gadget users.

Psychological and behavioural effects: Use of computers may blur a child's ability to distinguish real world from the virtual world.

Excessive use of computers and gadgets often has a negative impact on children's friendships and family relationships. They may become prone to emotional and psychological problems.

Playing violent computer games may increase aggressiveness and desensitise a child to human suffering.

The Internet could expose children to text, image, audio or video content that is inappropriate. Sexually explicit content or intolerance-filled propaganda could lead to deviant and dangerous behaviours.

The large number of 'likes' and positive comments for doing something as insignificant as posting a photograph or stating a current activity may give a false sense of accomplishment and a bloated self-esteem. Agreed, all humans are narcissistic to some degree and need that occasional boost of appreciation. But the Internet and social networking sites are making that self-love far too bad for our own good!

Computers and the Internet have taken away many children from the extremely enjoyable and enlightening habit of reading books or newspapers. Many children today instead prefer 'viewing' stories as videos on gadgets.

The wealth of information stored on the Internet and the ease of its retrieval have led people (especially the young students) to look at it as the ultimate source of knowledge. That is why plagiarism and an unwillingness to explore traditional sources of information have been increasingly observed in students' work. Students often overlook the possibility that a lot of the information found on the Internet may be coming from unauthenticated and dubious sources. Everything learnt by using a search engine and confirmed by an online encyclopaedia may not be true.

The invasion of technology can be easily felt in fields like music, movies, art and design where individual hands-on creativity is giving way to mass-produced software-based output.

Habits such as constant multitasking and the expectation of instant gratification are making many youngsters unfocused and impatient with short attention spans. ("Why is this webpage taking so long to load?")

The technology-induced shortening and distortion of language through tweets, SMSs and net chats is a serious challenge to traditional languages.

Social and legal problems: Through Internet chat-rooms, emails and social networks, children and teenagers may encounter dangerous anti-social elements. Identity theft, cyber-bullying, cyber-stalking, financial scams and theft, sexual abuse and computer virus attacks are some major dangers.

Virtual identity sometimes gives users a false sense of invisibility and unaccountability. That is why some Internet users lose simple civic sense. But provocative, criminal or illegal Internet-based actions can be easily tracked by authorities and can lead to unpleasant social or legal consequences. Even a seemingly harmless activity like music or movie download may leave a younger in violation of intellectual property laws and liable for legal action.

The 'posts' on virtual networks remain archived for years, and the wrong ones could affect social or career prospects even years later!

Tips for parents

Set clear guidelines about gadget and Internet use.

Age limits: Avoid introducing gadgets (computers, tablets, game consoles, mobile phones) before the age of 3 years, even as a toy. Let children first get acquainted with the real world, real people, real games and real activities. Allow 3–10-year-old children to use gadgets only in your presence. Do not allow any social network use before 13 years of age.

Time limit: Total screen time should be up to 20–30 minutes per day in the 3–6 year age-group, gradually increased to a maximum of 1–2 hours per day, with priority for educational use.

Tip: Include television viewing time in the calculation of total screen time.

Content limit: Introduce age-appropriate games, software programs and websites. Activate your browser's pop-up blocker. Child-safety filtering software programs allow you to monitor your children's online activity, set healthy time limits and ensure safe content access. But your personal presence is the best filter and monitor.

Location limit: Strictly forbid any closed-door Internet or gadget use. Children as well as teenagers should be allowed to access the Internet only in the common area of the house.

Activity limits: Ensure that children take regular relaxation breaks while using the computer. Family lunch, dinner and outings should be gadget-free periods.

Educate, encourage, engage and enrich

Be involved in your children's cyber-world experience. Educate yourself about gadgets and online activities. When you introduce children to gadgets, teach the basic do's and don'ts from an early age. Encourage them to freely share their positive and negative online experiences.

Encourage children to use the Internet as a library of enriching educational and multimedia content and as a platform to display their talents rather than just a place for chats and games.

Encourage children in creative and productive activities such as making a website, creating a blog, joining an online hobby or learning group or making imaginative videos. But teach them not to share too many personal and family details in such activities.

Online safety tips

Teach your children basic online usage rules.

- To protect identity use a screen name, share the email account with a parent in pre-teen years and use proper privacy settings on social networks in latter ages.
- Do not accept any chat or friendship requests from strangers.
- Never meet an unknown 'virtual friend' alone anywhere.
- Never share passwords, personal information or images or credit card details with anyone.
- Never make unauthorised online downloads or online purchases.
- Be responsible 'netizens' and understand that one's online activities should always be within social, cultural and legal limits and that one is accountable for any transgression.
- Freely discuss any unpleasant online incidence with parents.

Make sure that you are part of your children's social network but just as an observer. Do not try to enter their Internet interactions by posting comments or opinions.

Warning signs

Act immediately, compassionately and decisively if you observe any of the following warning signs.

- Increasing time spent on online activities
- Excessive secrecy about online activities (e.g., password protected screen or shutting off the screen at your approach)
- Unexplained phone calls or gifts received from strangers or unknown 'friends'

- Unexplained increases in your credit card charges or telephone bills
- Missing school and deteriorating academic performance
- Noticeable negative changes in behaviour and personality
- Noticeable changes in sleep or appetite

Final word of advice

Consciously remain involved in your children's online experiences but without being intrusive. Encourage them to enjoy the Internet's full potential as an educator and entertainer but also clearly explain the lurking online dangers. Most importantly, make children aware that, when it comes to a choice between the virtual cyber-world and the real people's world, their priority should always be the real thing!

12

Advertisements and Children

Television advertisements: Today's scenario

Two mothers and their sons are arguing about which health drink (milk supplement) is better. Claims and counterclaims are made about the amount of high quality nutrients in the drinks, which apparently make children healthier, taller and more intelligent.

The same two health drinks play on exam phobia and claim that their drink improves memory.

A famous sportsman and a movie star come together and extoll the virtue of heavily salted, artificially flavoured potato crisps.

An action movie star shows that people who drink a popular fizzy drink are macho and have all the fun in life.

Mothers happily agree to their children's demands for more of an artificially flavoured sugary soft drink (available in powder form) because it now has real fruit as an ingredient.

A cereal brand is shown as a wonder recipe to reduce weight in a few weeks.

An antibacterial hygiene product is shown as sure shot protection against multiple infections.

A young woman advises her friend to use the 'day after' contraceptive pill. An ad shows the 'pleasures' of using a condom.

A popular movie-star endorses a fairness face cream.

A liquor brand, through a fizzy drink advertisement, claims that it is preferred by people who have made it big! Another liquor brand uses famous sportsmen to sing its jingle.

Discussion

From diapers to fashion accessories, from toys to toiletries, from baby-foods to alcoholic beverages and from fever medicines to contraceptives, advertisements for all kinds of things come at us around the clock and through all media.

Targeting children and teenagers has become a major advertisement strategy for most brands and products. A US-based study says that an individual is exposed to approximately 40,000 ads in a year on television alone. Add to that the advertisements on billboards; in newspapers, magazines and movies and on the Internet and we have a mind-boggling total exposure to ads.

One well-researched article on the Global Issues website (www.globalissues.org) says that in the US, 15–17 billion dollars are spent on advertisements targeting children and teens. The returns on these advertisements are handsome as they influence parental purchases of 130–670 billion dollars! The current figures are probably even higher as this article was written in 2010!

Media strategy

Teens and tweens (8–12 years) are the age groups most heavily targeted by advertisers because they strongly influence choices and decisions about family spending.

Television and the Internet are by far the commonest platforms for advertisements, far ahead of print media and billboards. Television keeps bombarding ads not only during commercial breaks but also during programs in the form of on-screen tickers.

Big sports events and entertainment events provide advertisers a huge captive audience for a significant length of time.

A good advertisement is all about making the audience recall its product (product recall). That is why advertisements use catchy jingles and memorable punch lines, often using humour, peer pressure psychology or fear-mongering as underlying themes.

High achievers such as sportspersons, movie actors and musicians are often used as brand ambassadors.

There is a strong trend of using characters resembling common people for better brand identification. Children are very often used as characters in such ads.

Cartoon characters and superhero characters are placed in ads to specifically target children.

Internet ads use social networking sites, video sharing sites, web and mobile apps and online games to target the audience.

Tie-ups between movie houses and toy, fast food, soft drink and fashion brands are quite common. Advertisements for these products appear as subtle brand placements in movies and open promotions in restaurants and shops. Fast food brands highlight attractive toys that are giveaways with their kid-meals.

Even school premises are being used for promoting fast food and other consumer items.

Advertisers often hide behind the saying: 'Consumer is king and knows what is best for him.' This is not at all true of immature children as consumers.

Products

Common products groups that directly target babies or children through advertisements are:

- Baby products: diapers, milk formulae, baby foods, wipes
- Toiletries: soaps, shampoos, oils, creams, lotions, hand washes
- Toys and games: traditional toys and games, game consoles, tablet computers and mobile phones
- Foods: cereals, biscuits, cakes, cookies, chocolates, candies, donuts, ice-creams, noodles, pizzas, burgers, crisps (practically every packaged and processed food item, that is heavily loaded with sugar, salt and unhealthy fats)
- Beverages: health drinks (milk supplements), fruit-flavoured drinks, fizzy drinks
- Medicines (for): colic, teething, appetite, growth, common symptoms, weight loss
- Fashion: clothes, shoes, bags, sunglasses
- Educational, hobby development and fitness programs

Effects on children

Up to the age of 8 years, children do not have the maturity to understand that advertisements are imaginary and made with the intention of selling products. They take ads at face value, believing their selling messages as truths! They can feel they must have an until-then perfectly unknown object after watching just a 15- or 30-second advertisement spot.

The peer pressure felt by tweens and teens is exploited to the maximum in advertisements where a popular product is shown to be consumed or owned by a group of friends or students and the person without it is presented as a loser. Further, buying that product buys the person immediate acceptance among the peers.

Imitating their sports, movie or music idols comes easy to children and so does identifying with cartoon characters and superheroes. Brands endorsed by such role models become immediate objects of desire.

Brand consciousness at an early age often makes children desire things beyond their family's means, which leads to avoidable frustration and disappointment. Such children are often not happy even when they are given cheaper and equally good unbranded substitutes. This fosters consumerism and materialism and distorts sociocultural values from a young age.

Love of fast food coupled with idle screen-time is turning millions of children into overweight and obese individuals.

A specific idea of beauty is overemphasised in advertisements through the use of slim, fair and beautiful female models and muscular male models. This often makes individuals strive for the so-called perfect body and try to achieve that goal through questionable products and therapies.

Advertisements for products such as condoms, contraceptives and deodorants often show explicit sexual content, which is inappropriate for young children and may encourage 'acting out' behaviours.

Advertisements for alcoholic beverages or cigarettes promote drinking and smoking by emphasising the so-called 'cool' factor of these habits.

Ad-based promotions of medicines and treatments distort facts, quote fake researches and foster wrong health concepts by promising quick fixes. Many such ads use blatant fear-mongering, such as the idea that germs waiting at every corner to strike.

Not all so-called educational, hobby-training and fitness programs are suitable for young children. Many are run by untrained people, offered for inappropriate age groups and may even be hazardous.

Children and adolescents are treated as 'internal pressure groups' in the family by advertisers. By targeting them and getting them hooked on to the ad-message, advertisers try to get the youngsters to pressurise the family decision-makers (read, parents) to loosen the purse strings and purchase the advertised commodity. This is not only done for products directly targeting children but for any expensive product. That is why advertisements of most major family purchases such as vacations, homes, cars, smart televisions, home appliances and electronics often show images of happy children.

Parental strategies

To counter the dangers of advertising, parents should be informed about common advertising ploys. Exaggerations, half-truths or totally baseless proclamations are common in most advertisements. Make sure that you are aware of these.

Be aware of the newer Internet-based advertisement strategies that often work in the guise of media downloads, online games or apps.

Be involved in your children's television-viewing, Internet use and reading. Know what they are watching, reading or following.

Make sure that your children are not exceeding the 2-hour limit on non-educational screen time.

Be interactive. When you see children falling for advertising messages, try to teach them how the system works and what its potential pitfalls are. Hear their views patiently and then explain in a friendly manner.

Teach children that brand visibility, brand pricing, brand quality and brand utility are different things. The most expensive, most sought-after product is not always the best possible product for their need.

Be frank about the family's financial condition and the effect of such ad-driven consumerism on the family budget.

Do not rush to satisfy your child's every 'branded' demand even if you can afford it. Instant gratification makes children impatient, and they do not learn to value things. Delayed gratification teaches them to be patient and allows them to analyse their priorities.

Raise your children to think independently, teach them strong values, make them aware of their family and social responsibilities, teach them to differentiate wants and needs and help them to resist peer pressure.

For this to happen, it is necessary for you to become good role models, who are well-informed consumers and value good quality products at reasonable prices rather than just splurging to show off meaningless brands.

If possible, create like-minded parent groups that can exchange ideas and information. Try to do your bit to exert pressure on media, corporates and governments to strictly monitor and regulate advertisements that target children or teenager. In countries like Sweden and Norway, advertisements directed at children under 12 years are forbidden.

Myth	Reality
Eating packaged, processed fast foods and drinking flavoured or fizzy drinks is no big deal. So, bring on the burgers, pizzas, chocolates, chips, ice-creams and sodas!	These foods and drinks are loaded with unessential ingredients such as sugar, salt and unhealthy fats. Their excessive consumption can lead to major health problems such as obesity, hypertension and diabetes.
Antibacterial soaps and hand washes are better than ordinary soaps to prevent infections.	Using regular mild soaps for baths and hand washing is equally effective and much safer. Antibacterial hygiene products may kill normal bacteria on the skin and promote the growth of antibiotic-resistant bacteria.
Everyone should have a perfectly chiselled beautiful body (with spotless white teeth and silky, dandruff-free hair) and it can be easily had by using the beauty products.	Beauty and good physique depend on natural attributes (genes) and lifestyle (diet, exercise, stress). No one product can transform a person, and there is no need to be obsessed by this idea of 'perfection'. The only way to achieve a beautiful body is to work for it by making positive changes in lifestyle.
Alcohol consumption, cigarette smoking and reckless sexual acts are cool.	All of these are serious health hazards.
My neighbour has it. My friend has it. My relative has it. So I have to have that branded item now!	First examine its need and utility for you. Then see if you can afford it. Don't be driven by peer-pressure.
My sports, movie, music idol uses that product. So I have to get that!	The celebrities are performing when they endorse a product in an ad. They are being paid to do that. In real life, they may not even touch that product for personal use.

In the advertisement, the cream made the person fairer. So it can do the same for me.	The model used for the ad was already fair and was made up to look dark. There was no 'fair play' there.
Those supplements, medicines and therapies are heavily advertised in the media. They must be effective.	A simple rule is to stay away from any medicines and therapies that indulge in excessive advertising. If you are still tempted, first ask your doctor. Most of these products are plain hype.
All advertisements are bad for children.	Positive advertisements focusing on social, environmental or health issues (anti-corruption, save the tiger or polio vaccination ads) are great tools for public education and awareness. Children, too, can benefit from them.

13

ADHD: Can't Sit Still

Scenario

Sujay Sharma is 7 years old, but he already has quite a 'reputation'. His teachers complain, "He is so naughty. Never attentive in class; always talking." His parents complain, "He never sits still in one place. Always on the move." His peers complain, "He is very aggressive. Just doesn't fit into the team."

When you start hearing these complaints from all quarters, it is very likely that the child is an unfortunate victim of a condition called 'attention deficit hyperactivity disorder' or ADHD.

Discussion

Before focusing our attention on ADHD, let's first understand that not all hyperactive children suffer from ADHD. Anxiety, depression, anticonvulsant and psychiatric medicines and some medical conditions like Tourette syndrome can also cause hyperactivity. Similarly, inattentiveness can be a manifestation of hearing or vision deficit, seizures (fits), conduct disorder or learning disability.

ADHD

Three I's define ADHD when they are found together and are inappropriate for the developmental level:

- Increased physical activity (hyperactivity)
- Inattention (attention deficit)
- Impulsiveness

Not all ADHD patients have all three characteristics. Some show mainly hyperactivity and impulsiveness, others mainly inattentiveness and yet others a mix of all three. The last group, showing all symptoms, is the commonest presentation.

The condition is sometimes called ADDH (attention deficit disorder with hyperactivity).

ADHD is one of the most common behavioural problems of childhood and adolescence. Some 8–10% school-age children suffer from this disorder. Boys are three times more likely to be victims, and half of them start showing symptoms before the age of four.

Causes

No one knows the exact cause of this illness. Obviously, it has got something to do with the imbalance of various chemicals in the brain. The frontal region of the brain that controls motor activity and the pre-frontal region that affects mood and attention are the likely problem areas. In ADHD patients, these brain parts develop slowly in early childhood and only catch up with normal brains by the end of adolescence.

Poor parenting skills, excessive sugar intake or vaccines are **not responsible** for ADHD.

Genes play a major role as many ADHD patients have either parents or close relatives suffering from similar conditions. Alcohol consumption or smoking during pregnancy, prematurity, low birth weight, brain injury, parental violence, excessive television exposure and certain food additives have been blamed as potential causes of ADHD in some studies.

Diagnosis

No single test or sign or symptom can establish the diagnosis of ADHD. It is a multistep approach. Here are symptoms that suggest each component of the condition. Notice the word 'often', telling us that the behaviour is normal up to a certain degree and a symptom only in excess.

Inattention

- Often does not give close attention to details or makes careless mistakes in schoolwork, work or other activities
- Often has trouble keeping attention on tasks or play activities
- Often does not seem to listen when spoken to directly
- Often does not follow through on instructions and fails to finish schoolwork and household chores or duties at work (not due to oppositional behaviour or failure to understand instructions)
- Often has trouble in organising activities

- Often avoids, dislikes or doesn't want to do things that take a lot of mental effort over a long period (such as schoolwork or homework)
- Often loses things needed for tasks and activities (e. g., toys, school assignments, pencils, books, or stationery items)
- Is often easily distracted
- Is often forgetful in daily activities

Hyperactivity

- Often fidgets with hands or feet or squirms in seat when sitting still is expected
- Often gets up from seat when remaining in seat is expected
- Often excessively runs about or climbs when and where it is not appropriate (adolescents may not do this but feel very restless)
- Often has trouble playing or doing leisure activities quietly
- Is often "on the go" or often acts as if "driven by a motor"
- Often talks excessively

Impulsiveness

- Often blurts out answers before questions are finished
- Often has trouble waiting one's turn
- Often interrupts or intrudes on others (e.g., butts into conversations or games)

To diagnose ADHD, 6 or more of the inattention group symptoms or 6 or more of hyperactivity-impulsivity group symptoms have to be present for more than 6 months to an extent that is disruptive and inappropriate for the age.

These symptoms cause significant problems at home and at school and at least some of them are detected before the age of 7 years.

Other possible conditions causing similar symptoms should be ruled out before arriving at the diagnosis of ADHD.

Difficulties in diagnosis

As you may have noticed, all these symptoms are too common in young children to be called abnormal. Furthermore, the ADHD diagnosis can seldom be made in the clinic setting and in one session. Almost 80% of such patients can behave completely normally while in the clinic for evaluation.

Repeated observations at home and at school, in structured and non-structured settings, in small and large groups and in situations of differing complexity are necessary to reach the diagnosis.

Management

Managing such child with ADHD is a complex issue. It needs a team approach involving parents, teachers and medical personnel like a paediatrician, a child psychologist and a psychiatrist. The affected child should be involved in and made to feel responsible for the management of the condition from the outset.

Behaviour modification, medicines and parental education and support are the three main aspects of ADHD management.

Behaviour modification

Behavioural changes need to be brought about both at home as well as at school. The first and most important step is to foster positive feelings between the child and the parents and teachers by setting aside special time which could be as little as half an hour. When the child knows that he is loved, he will make efforts to change his behaviour to please the people who love him. Short attention and retention in these children make it mandatory that they receive frequent feedback from caregivers.

Things to try in ADHD individuals:

- A well-set routine for the day's activities
- Setting a few simple, short-term goals (e. g., playing quietly for half an hour) and promptly rewarding with praise and affection
- Better organisation of everyday objects such as clothes, schoolbag, books and toys
- Keeping away valuable, breakable and dangerous items
- Avoiding distractions such as radio, television or computer at study time
- Limiting choices of food, clothes or toys to avoid overwhelming the mind
- Simple, straightforward communication and effective discipline
- Avoidance of overstimulation and excessive fatigue (specifically, avoiding long automobile journeys and shopping sprees)
- Occasional interaction with younger children to improve social behaviour

- Cognitive therapy (positive self-talk) and encouragement to discover a personal talent (sport or art) or to participate in social activities like scouting to improve self-esteem
- Individualised activities and games, in which ADHD children do well, rather than team activities in which they have difficulty in adjusting

Medicines

Stimulant medicines surprisingly make ADHD patients calmer, and they are being successfully used in the treatment of this condition for many years. Non-stimulant medicines and anti-depressants are also sometimes used.

One medicine that works in a particular ADHD patient may not work in another, and that is why there has to be an individual plan to choose the correct medicine. All patients require a period of at least 2–3 weeks for evaluation and dose adjustment.

Due to the side-effects of medicines, such as decreased appetite, abdominal pain, increased nervousness, jitteriness and growth suppression, medicine-free holidays for at least 2–3 weeks in a year are recommended.

Parental education and support

Dealing with ADHD children is a challenging task for any parent, which is why parental education about the condition and parental support groups are essential parts of the treatment plan.

Final word of advice

In ADHD children, there are often increased chances of poor peer relationships, personal injuries and accidents, defiant behaviour and conduct disorders. Though hyperactivity is likely to subside considerably with age and treatment, other symptoms (poor attention or organisation) are likely to persist even in adulthood, often leading to complications like adult alcoholism and anti-social behaviour.

Considerate and compassionate multilevel treatment is the only way to manage this common disorder with such far reaching, socially devastating complications and to positively transform a potentially unpleasant, unproductive and unpopular life.

14

Autism: In a World of Their Own

Scenario

Rakesh is almost 3 years old. He hardly speaks a few words. He does not smile or respond to his parents' expressions of affection. He does not mix with other children of his age. He avoids eye contact with others and prefers to play on his own. He keeps doing the same thing again and again. He throws tantrums whenever he hears loud noises. Rakesh has autism.

Discussion

Man is a social animal. Getting together to talk, play, study or work comes naturally to human beings. But autistic individuals have difficulties in relating to and communicating with the external world. It is as if they are living in their own world oblivious to what is going on outside.

According to the US Center of Disease Control and Prevention (CDC) statistics, almost 1 in 88 children suffer from autism or autism spectrum disorders (ASD). The reason for calling it a spectrum is that not all cases are similar—some are mild, others severe and many fall between these extremes. The symptoms seem to occur in different combinations in different individuals.

ASD becomes apparent during the first 3 years of life. Half of such children have slow development from the beginning, but the rest develop normally up to 18–24 months of age before parents start realising that something is amiss.

Boys are five times more likely to have this condition compared to girls. No social, racial, ethnic or economic patterns are found in the occurrence of the condition, and it can affect almost anyone.

Causes

No one knows the exact cause of ASD. What we know is that the brain of affected individuals functions differently. Both genetic and environmental factors seem to play a role in causing the 'difference'.

Vaccines, viral infections, allergies and food or environmental toxins have all been blamed for causing autism, but none of these 'causes' has been scientifically proved.

Let me make some things clear:

Autism is not a psychological problem or a mental illness but rather a case of a different kind of a mind.

- Parenting errors do not cause autism.
- Autism is not pretence or bad behaviour by the child but a real impairment.

Signs and symptoms

There is impaired social interaction. The child spends more time alone and shows minimal interest in people. He cannot develop peer relationships and does not reciprocate socially or emotionally. He withdraws on cuddling. There is poor eye contact, lack of facial expressions (including smiling) and other communicative gestures.

Speech is delayed or even totally lacking. When present, it is limited to repeating, or echoing, words spoken by others without understanding their meanings (echolalia). Even in autistic individuals with adequate language ability, there is an inability to start or sustain conversation with others.

The ability for imitative or imaginative play is severely impaired.

Stereotypic repetitive motor activities like hand flapping, rocking, head banging, teeth grinding, twisting or complex whole body movements are common.

Overactive or over-passive behaviour, temper tantrums, self-inflicted injuries and abnormal fixation for predictable and often insignificant rituals are some other notable features.

ASD children have unusual sensory responses, especially to sudden, loud, high pitched sounds and an aversion to human touch.

One interesting feature is that some people with ASD have remarkable isolated abilities in which they might outperform their normal peers. In conditions such as Asperger's syndrome, or high-functioning autism, the typical autism symptoms are milder. Here, individuals have average or above average intelligence. Their speech development is normal, and their social interactive skills are better.

Diagnosis

There are no blood tests, x-rays or scans to diagnose autism. It cannot be detected before birth by any type of screening.

The only way to diagnose autism is by observing the individual's behaviour, speech and development over a period of time. Detailed questionnaires to be filled by parents are used. Ideally, such a child should be evaluated by a multidisciplinary team made up of a developmental paediatrician, paediatric neurologist, psychologist, speech and language therapist and, if possible, an expert with specific experience in dealing with autism.

The experts may sometimes conduct certain tests to rule out other genetic, developmental or psychological conditions with similar symptoms.

Treatment

Unfortunately, autism cannot be cured. There are no specific medicines for autism, though medicines are sometimes needed to treat associated medical or psychological problems. However, with better understanding of the illness, effective strategies can be planned to cope with it and improve the functioning of affected individuals.

Early intervention is associated with the best results.

An individualised multidimensional treatment plan consisting of physical therapy, occupational therapy, speech and language therapy, early childhood education techniques and sensory stimulation is the preferred plan of action. These programs are highly structured and aim to promote social interaction, language skills and positive behaviour.

Life skills like crossing the street, shopping, cooking and asking for assistance are incorporated in the treatment plan and emphasised in such program to promote the child's independence in daily activities.

Parents need special counselling to deal with children with ASD. For them, it is almost like 'losing' a child because the child is unable to comprehend or reciprocate their love. To further complicate matters, there is no remedy. Parent support groups play an important role in offering guidance and emotional support to affected families.

The long-term outlook for this condition remains unpredictable. Some children grow up to lead relatively normal, productive adult lives while others need varying degrees of help throughout their personal and working lives.

Continuous and compassionate community care for autistic children and their parents still remains a distant goal, and only increasing awareness can change this picture.

VII

Problems in Schooling

1

Is it Dyslexia?

Scenario

Rehan seems to be an intelligent 7-year-old boy, but his parents are worried about him. His teacher says that he is lagging behind his class. He still cannot write all the alphabets properly, often writing some letters backwards, as their mirror images. He cannot fluently read simple paragraphs from his school books. He makes mistakes in simple spellings and mathematical calculations.

One day, the father's friend suggests, "Why don't you get him tested for dyslexia? Haven't you seen that movie *Taare Zameen Par?* The kid there had similar problems!"

Discussion

A child not studying or not performing well in school is a problem that could arise from various causes. Dyslexia is one important and intriguing condition affecting school performance negatively.

Probable causes of school failure

When a child of average intelligence performs below par at school, there are many possibilities to consider. The problem may be in the child or in his family environment or his school.

Among possible problems in the child are chronic illness; medication effects; vision, speech or hearing impairment; behavioural problems like ADHD (attention deficit hyperactivity disorder) or unnoticed seizures.

The family environment may be responsible for a child's failure at school through child abuse and parental neglect or conflicts that make the child anxious, depressed and unfocused.

Among common problems in school conditions are language barrier, incompetent teaching and classwork that is either too difficult or too simple.

Learning disability

Learning disability refers to a group of problems related to one or more of the basic processes involved in learning. A student with learning disability is of at least average intelligence but has problems in listening, thinking, speaking, reading, writing or doing mathematics.

The term excludes children with physical, sensory or mental impairment; emotional disturbances and cultural, socioeconomic or environmental disadvantage.

Dyslexia

Dyslexia is a learning disorder in which the child finds it difficult to read, write and spell despite normal intelligence. The condition also can make doing arithmetic difficult.

The commonest learning disorder, dyslexia accounts for 80% of all learning disorders. In the UK, 4–8% of school children are estimated to have dyslexia of varying degrees.

Dyslexia is a lifelong condition and is not 'cured'. Children suffering from it do not outgrow it, and dyslexics are seen in all age groups. But timely and appropriate intervention in childhood can help these individuals to succeed in life.

Causes

Dyslexia is caused by certain genes determining brain development. It appears to be an inherited condition and often runs in families.

The structure and functioning of the brain are different in dyslexics. The nervous connections in their brain are wired differently, and such individuals use a different part of the brain while reading than normal people.

Symptoms

Various symptoms appear during the early stages of development.

Before school

- Delayed speech
- Difficulty in learning new words
- Frequent mixing up of sounds in words
- Difficulty in rhyming

At school

- Slow reading and writing
- Difficulty in reading, spelling and memorising
- Tendency to reverse ('bog' for 'dog'), invert ('we' for 'me') or transpose ('on' for 'no') letters in a word
- Tendency to substitute similar-looking words with different meaning
- Tendency to omit, add or substitute small words and suffixes
- Tendency to misspell even when copying from the blackboard or a book
- Frequent erasures and over-writings
- Difficulty in following rapid or multiple instructions

In teens and adults

- Difficulty in reading, spelling, memorising and summarising
- Difficulty in learning new languages
- Difficulty in time management

Dysgraphia

Often, dyslexics show a tendency towards dysgraphia or poor, illegible handwriting. Unusual pencil or pen grip (too high, to low, too tight or with thumb over fingers), difficulty in cursive writing, unusual positioning of letters and a slow, laboured writing process are pointers to this condition.

There is no single definitive test to diagnose this condition. Screening tests usually combine oral and written tests.

A formal psychological and language skills test is carried out. A detailed history from parents and teachers; interview of the affected child and parents; thorough evaluation of the child's reading, writing and language processing and screening for associated disorders are a must in diagnosis.

Associated conditions

Attention deficit disorder is found in almost 40% of dyslexics. This existence of these two conditions together dramatically increases the risk that the child may engage in drug abuse and anti-social activities.

Light sensitivity (scotopic sensitivity syndrome, Irlen syndrome, perceptive dyslexia) is found in 3–8% individuals with dyslexia.

This sensitivity makes it difficult for them to see small black print on white paper. For them, the background is too bright. The printed words seem to shimmer and move and get immersed in white rivers. They show a dislike for fluorescent lights and shade a page while reading. Wearing glasses with coloured lenses or placing plastic sheets over pages or screens give relief by reducing brightness.

Dyslexic individuals are prone for frustration, anger, low self-esteem, depression and poor family and peer relationships.

Management

There is no magic cure or medicine for dyslexia. The intervention needs to be a continuous process with regular adjustments.

Phonemic awareness is an important step in teaching language. It teaches the connections between sounds and written symbols. Each word is broken into its basic sounds, the smallest sound unit being termed a 'phoneme'. Then, the relationship of each phoneme with the written symbols, or letters of the alphabet, ('grapheme') is taught. Finally, the rest of the rules of language are incorporated into the training.

For example, to teach how the word 'dog' is spoken and written, the teacher first speaks the word by breaking it into three separate sounds: 'd'-'o'-'g'. Then the child is taught how to blend these three sounds together to say the entire word 'dog' at one go. Later, the child is taught to identify and write the letters matching the individual sounds in the word.

Daily sessions of independent and supported reading and writing can greatly improve the situation. Use of audio books and special computer software is helpful.

Multisensory approach involving vision, hearing, speech, touch and motion is employed to teach writing. To learn 'A', the child sees it written on the board, hears it from the teacher, repeats it himself, draws it in the air and writes it on paper.

Dyslexics in normal schools

Milder varieties of dyslexia are common, and cases of these are likely to be present in every school. Schools can accommodate the needs of such children by introducing phonemic awareness in early classes, reducing the load of homework and writing in general and, if possible, relaxing time limits for tests. Special tutoring for scholastically weak students is desirable.

Final word of advice

Being a dyslexic does not mean the end of the world. With positive parenting and proper intervention, children with dyslexia can overcome many difficulties caused by the condition.

Besides, such individuals may have hidden strengths arising from their unusual brain. Dyslexics are found to have artistic, musical, mechanical, athletic, creative and intuitive abilities in abundance. They do well in professions like architecture, interior design, teaching, marketing, performing arts, scientific research and athletics.

If we believe historians, Mozart had dyslexia, and so did Einstein, Agatha Christie and John F. Kennedy. They didn't do too badly in life. Did they?

2

Teacher, Teacher

Scenario

Three young women are sitting in the park, chatting and watching over their children playing. The maternal discussion turns to the burning topic of their children's schools and the teachers there.

The first mother says, "The teacher in Bharat's class is really strict. She made him stand one whole class."

The second shares her story, "My daughter doesn't understand her teacher's accent at all."

The third has made up her mind, "I am planning to change my son's school next year. I am not at all happy with the teachers in his current school."

Discussion

Don't tell me you haven't heard such comments or haven't made such comments yourself at some time or the other. Teaching in the nurseries and schools is a specialised job, but it is true that specialists are not always handling it.

Knowledge of the subject and a knack for simplifying it as well as kindness, understanding and discipline are the essential qualities in this profession. Many a times, students and their parents face the problem of having to deal with teachers who lack these qualities.

Changing a class or changing a school is not a solution in most such instances. It is like changing a house every time the tap starts leaking. Instead, you should try to tackle this issue in a cool and reasoned manner, weighing the pros and cons of every action. Let's consider some aspects of handling your and your child's relationship with the teachers.

Teach your child the value of politeness, discipline and respect. These values are necessary in life and often succeed better than intelligence or wit. Being regular, obedient, punctual and thorough in classwork is to be encouraged. This is a sure-fire policy to be popular with teachers.

Race, region, religion and relations have always played a part in examinations and interviews, but the cream has always risen to the top. You have to make your child realise that one has to face unfair practices at times in life, but the best can survive. Complaining about every 'injustice' is not something you should encourage. Instead, you should teach the child to overcome such obstacles with grit and determination.

Many problems in the school stem from parent's unrealistic expectations. Parents often misjudge the innate ability and intelligence of their child. For you, your child is the best in the world, but your love and affection cannot propel your child to the top. To reach there, both inspiration and perspiration are necessary.

One thing all parents must remember is never to consider their child as themselves by proxy. Don't push your child hard to achieve the scholastic ambitions and aspirations that remained unfulfilled in your career.

It is fairly simple to judge a teacher's performance by seeing him or her through the child's eyes. Comments like "I like my teacher" or "I want to be like my teacher" are pointers that the child has accepted the teacher wholeheartedly. School phobia, imaginary complaints like headache or abdominal pain to avoid school or consistent negative remarks about teaching are signs of problems.

When a child has problems with a teacher, you should initially try to curb this tendency by making the child see the good side of teaching. If these negative signs continue, it is time to evaluate the problem in detail.

To find the root of the problem, you should try to understand why the child is not happy with the teacher. The most common reason is the teacher's attitude, which the child has perceived as unfair or unfriendly. Even a simple negative remark or gesture can sometimes lead to a student's dislike for that teacher.

You can often solve this problem just by teaching your child to ignore these minor 'offences'. A simple way to make the child realise that certain remarks or gestures don't mean that the teacher is unfriendly or unfair is to point out the child's own occasional bad behaviour at home with you or the child's siblings.

Encourage your child to develop a one-to-one rapport with the teacher. Asking for help with difficulties or questions about the subject after class is sometimes preferable but shouldn't become a routine or an attention-seeking device.

Extra-curricular activities like sports, reading, writing, drawing or singing provide opportunities to develop such student-teacher rapport as teachers are more likely to be friendly during these activities, especially if they share the same passions.

A student's quality of classwork, understanding of concepts and evaluation reports from school can tell as much about the teacher as the student and whether they are functioning well as a 'team'. If you see problems in these areas, it is time to discuss the matter with the teacher. Parent-teacher meetings with their cramped, crowded and time-bound settings are not ideal for this purpose, but you can make a start during these meetings and get an appointment for further discussion. Preferably, meet the teacher in the school and do not make a routine of asking for this kind of special favour.

While discussing the problem areas in your child's scholastic record, never start with aggressive or accusatory talk. It would just make the teacher defensive. Instead ask the teacher what the weak areas are in your child's school performance and how they can be improved. After listening, you can put forward your views. Any unfair practices (including physical or emotional punishments) should be discussed openly and forthrightly.

If and only if the unfair, unfriendly or incompetent teaching practices continue despite repeated discussions, you should take the matter to higher authorities and consider changing the class or changing the school.

Problems in teaching have many causes. A teacher may know a subject well but may not know how to present it to students in the classroom. Individualised attention is almost never possible in a class of 30–40 students. Teachers' increasing workload, personal problems and personality traits are all going to play a major role in the teaching process. Parents have to be aware of these burdens on teachers.

Teachers are the shapers of the future world, the role models for growing minds. It is not just a job to add something to the family income. Unfortunately, some teachers don't realise this great social responsibility and devalue this noble profession. But then, which profession has remained immune to these problems?

3

Bullying

Scenario

Scene 1

Ajit is in the seventh standard. He has recently started at a new school. His mother has been observing a strange thing lately. Ajit looks sad and is reluctant to go to school. In the mornings, he sometimes comes up with excuses like a headache or stomach ache and tries to avoid going to school. He has always been a good student, albeit a bit shy. These signs of avoidance of school are quite new. The mother tries to find out more from him, but he does not tell her anything specific. She thinks that he must be missing his old school friends.

After a few weeks of this, Ajit is admitted to hospital with five stitches on his head. No, he did not have an accident. He was mercilessly beaten up just outside the school compound by a gang. No, it was not a criminal gang; it was a gang of bullies made up of four of his new classmates. The same bullies had been making his life hell since he came to the new school.

Scene 2

The mother walks in to Sunita's room to find the 14-year-old ninth standard student opening a bottle of sleeping pills. Shocked, she confronts her daughter. Sunita breaks down and, sobbing hysterically, tells how she is being constantly bullied over the Internet on a popular social networking forum. Someone morphed her photograph to make it obscene and then circulated it via MMS. She has become the target of vicious jokes and crude comments not only in her school, but in the whole town. She says that she wants to end her life.

Discussion

If you think the scenarios are exaggerated, let me assure you they are not. These kinds of violent, virulent bullying assaults are becoming quite common nowadays, and they are happening all over the world.

Bullying in schools is such a common menace that estimates are that 1 in 3 students have experienced it in some form or the other. With the availability of technology, the problem has only become more complicated. Ragging in colleges is just an extension of the same problem.

Bullying

Bullying is intentional abuse or aggression against an individual by one or more peers. This abuse or aggression can be physical or emotional. It can happen in person or in the anonymity of cyberspace. It can be by a single individual or by a group of individuals.

This damaging aggressive behaviour is repetitive, unprovoked and involves a power imbalance (stronger aggressor, weaker victim).

Physical bullying can take the form of pushing, punching, pinching, kicking, hitting with objects, spitting or tripping.

Emotional bullying occurs as insults, verbal abuses, teasing, name-calling, rumour-mongering and isolating the individual.

Sometimes the bullying can take the form of damaging or stealing the victim's belongings (schoolbag, books, money, etc.).

The usual times for bullying are before school activities begin, during the recesses, after the school disperses and on the school bus. The common places for bullying are areas just outside the school's compound, the school bus, corridors, playgrounds or toilets.

Cyberbullying

With the advent of gadgets and the Internet, bullying has found new locations and methods in cyberspace. Text messages, multimedia messages, chats or social network posts on mobile phones, computers or other gadgets have become popular ways to abuse others. Many times, cyber-bullies hide their identity by using pseudonyms.

Signs in a victim

Victims of bullying may not talk to their parents about it. You should watch for these common signs of bullying in victims.

- Repeated unexplained or poorly explained injuries or bruises
- Social withdrawal
- Falling attendance or school performance
- Unexplained headaches or stomach aches
- Inability to sleep, disturbed sleep or frequent nightmares

Damage

Physical injury is an important and immediate danger of bullying, but emotional scarring is perhaps an even greater and longer-term problem.

Bullied individuals are prone to anger, frustration, loneliness, depression, 'acting out' aggression and poor peer and family relationships.

Typical bully and victim

Keep in mind these typical characteristics of a bullying aggressor.

- Physically taller and stronger than children of the same age
- Tendency to aggressive behaviour
- Preference for violence on playground, television or computer games
- Poor academic record, failures and expulsions
- Skirmishes with teachers
- Abusive or permissive home environment
- Part of a group with similar individuals

The typical bullying victim, too, has certain common characteristics.

- Shorter and weaker than children of the same age
- Physical or mental impairment
- Shy personality
- Belonging to a minority group by race, religion, language or sexual orientation
- Single parent or unconcerned parents
- Uncomfortable, unsure or unconvinced about sharing experience or seeking help from authorities

Management of the problem

To manage bullying, we must first become aware that bullying is a serious problem and that it is very common.

We must remain alert to spot bullying activity at the earliest. When bullying is seen, we must act immediately to stop the offenders and protect the victims.

Schools and colleges should establish an official anti-bullying programme involving teachers, parents and student representatives. Early education about bullying, compassionate communication, strict guidelines, zero tolerance and quick enforcement are key requirements for such a programme to succeed.

The government could help by putting in place legal measures to enable action against offenders.

VIII

Common Child-Health Problems

1

Fever: A Multifaceted Entity

Scenario

Scene 1

Mr. and Mrs. Ghosh are a young couple who were blessed with a baby boy 1 month ago. Ajay (that's the baby's name) is active and feeding well, but today his body is warmer than usual. The mother checks the temperature and the thermometer shows more than 38°C. She calls up the father, who feels that she is over-reacting and tells her to wait and watch. The mother is not convinced and insists that they visit their paediatrician. The father reluctantly agrees.

The doctor checks the baby and confirms that there is fever. He advises them to do some tests and tells them that the baby needs immediate treatment while they wait for the test results.

A urinary infection is detected through the tests and appropriate antibiotic treatment initiated.

Scene 2

Mrs. Qadir brings her 6-year-old son to the clinic and says, "Doctor, Abdulla has been having a fever for the last 3 days. It fluctuates throughout the day, sometimes going as high as 40°C. It comes down for a while after we give him the fever medication but never really goes away for good. He is eating less than usual but otherwise seems okay in his routine. I am really worried. Should we do some tests? Doesn't he need antibiotics?"

After checking Abdulla, the doctor reassures the mother that it looks like a viral infection and that there is no need for any tests or antibiotics. He asks her which fever medicine she used. The mother fumbles and says, "Oh, just the usual one." Then he asks her if she had checked the dosage, and there is an awkward silence! He tells her to adjust the fever medicine dosage and wait and watch for a day or two.

Two days later Abdulla goes back to the school hale and hearty.

Scene 3

Mr. and Mrs. Jones bring their 3-year-old daughter Sara to the clinic. According to them, Sara has been having intermittent fever for the last 3 weeks. The fever ranges between 38°C and 38.5°C and comes down after the fever medicine is given. There are no other specific symptoms, but Sara has been looking pale and feeling extremely tired and lethargic.

The doctor examines Sara and tells the Joneses that their daughter needs to undergo certain investigations for him to make a diagnosis and only after could he reassure them.

The tests reveal that Sara is suffering from a blood cancer (leukaemia) that fortunately is in the early stage and fully curable. She is referred to a specialised hospital for further treatment.

Discussion

The three representative cases should tell you that the condition 'fever' could be a symptom of so many different health problems and therefore elicits different approaches from the doctor and has different outcomes. There is no 'one size fits all' strategy to manage a fever, which is a multifaceted entity.

Fever is the most common symptom that promptly sends the patients and parents running to a doctor. It is the most overrated, overtreated and mistreated symptom. So here is an effort to clear the myths and misconceptions regarding fever.

Fever

The human body temperature is usually around 37°C (98.6°F), with a normal variation of 1°C above or below. Even in a healthy person, the normal body temperature is low early in the mornings and goes up slightly late in afternoons. A core (inner body) temperature of 38°C (100.4°F) or more usually is considered to be 'fever'. ***Fever by itself is not a disease. It is just a reaction to an underlying illness.***

The hypothalamus—a small part of the brain—acts like a thermostat to maintain body temperature within the normal range. Chemicals called pyrogens raise the set point in the hypothalamus so that the nervous system activates the mechanisms to make body temperature higher. Illnesses causing fever prompt the release of pyrogens from various cells in the body, which reach the hypothalamus through the blood stream and raise its set-point leading to fever.

The patient feels cold shivers just before the appearance of fever. This is because the hypothalamus thermostat set-point is already set higher, but the rest of the body, which is still at a lower temperature, feels cold compared to the higher set-point. In other words, the brain senses the normal body temperature as too low once the thermostat settings are changed.

Causes

Though theoretically there are several causes of fever, the most important cause in any age group is infections. So the most common cases of fever encountered in daily life are due to infections caused by viruses or bacteria.

Inflammatory disorders, immunity problems, malignancies, drugs and malingering (factitious fever) are some other important causes to be considered in specific situations.

Remember, if your child has a fever, always think about the common things first. Don't panic by assuming the worst possible cause.

Checking the temperature

The simplest way of roughly estimating fever is by touching the forehead of the patient with the back of your hand. Depending on the relative warmth of the patient's skin, you can judge whether it is a mild, moderate or high fever. This is the subjective assessment of fever which is not accurate but gives an initial idea about the presence and severity of fever.

To have an accurate and objective temperature assessment, one should always keep a thermometer handy at home. There are various types of thermometers available.

The traditionally used and fairly accurate **mercury thermometer** is nowadays not recommended for use in small children because of the risk of accidental mercury ingestion. If the thermometer breaks, the child may swallow the mercury, which is harmful when ingested.

Electronic thermometers are simple to use. When the electronic thermometer detects the correct temperature, it indicates that immediately by giving a beep or lighting up.

Aural (ear) thermometers are designed to be inserted in the ear canal. Though touted as easy and quick, they are sometimes difficult to use correctly in smaller children and could give false readings in children with small angulated ear-canals or with ear-wax.

Temperature or thermometer **strips** are easy to use, but their results are not accurate.

After buying a good thermometer, follow these tips to take the temperature.

Armpit (axilla), mouth and rectum are the usual places to check the temperature. The temperature is slightly different at each of these sites. The formula relating them is:

Core temperature = Rectal temperature = Oral temperature + 0.5°C = Axillary temperature + 1°C

This means that rectal temperature is the correct core temperature. If you check temperature in the mouth, add 0.5°C to the reading to find the core temperature. If you check at the armpit, add 1°C.

The ideal duration to keep the mercury thermometer at the site is around 1 minute for rectal, 2 minutes for oral and 4 minutes for axillary temperature. But practically, a 1-minute recording gives a fair idea of the fever. In case of an electronic thermometer, we hear a beep when it has detected the correct temperature.

Dangers

In most commonly encountered situations, fever is not risky and, indeed, might be considered beneficial to aid the body's defence mechanisms in getting rid of germs. If the child remains active, smiling and playful in spite of a fever, the outcome is most likely to be normal.

In the following situations, one needs to immediately seek medical attention:

- Age less than 6 months
- Sick look
- Lethargy
- Severe associated symptoms and signs
- Hyperpyrexia or very high fever (> 41°C)
- Fever with chills (feeling uncomfortably cold) and rigors (shivering movements)
- Continuous fever
- Rapidly swinging fever with wide temperature fluctuations

- Prolonged fever
- Presence of serious pre-existing disease (cardiac, pulmonary, neurological or metabolic)

Fits usually occur at the beginning of fever during the sudden rise of temperature, so there is no need to worry about them when the fever has already been present for some time. Moreover, these fits are practically harmless and have no long-term medical consequences despite their frightful appearance. They can occur in almost 4% of normal children between 6 months and 6 years. (The next section has more on fevers and fits.)

Treatment

Medicines

Paracetamol (acetaminophen) is the safest medicine for fever and, in proper dose, can be used every 4 to 6 hours. There are various formulations of this medicine (drops, syrup, suspension and suppositories) which have different strengths. Check the dose of the formulation you have with the doctor and do not rely on the label information. Overdose can lead to liver toxicity, and underdosing results in inadequate response.

People wrongly believe that suppositories (which are inserted in the rectum) are more effective than oral medicines in the treatment of fever. The only situation where suppositories are useful is when the child is refusing to take any medicine orally or is vomiting.

Ibuprofen should be used only sparingly and under the doctor's supervision. It has drawbacks like the possibility of damage to the stomach lining, kidney damage and triggering asthma attacks.

Aspirin is one medicine you should avoid in children as an antipyretic, especially in the presence of viral illnesses like influenza or chicken-pox, because it can cause Reye's syndrome, which is a serious liver condition.

Diclofenac, mefenamic acid and nimesulide are anti-inflammatory agents, but they are too strong and not really safe to use for the treatment of fever. Their usage is commonly a result of parental anxiety, medical overzealousness and needless fear of fever.

Tepid sponging

Bath or sponging with tepid or lukewarm water is a method of bringing down the temperature, especially when the temperature is very high or is not coming down with medicine.

Don't ever use cold water or an ice-bag for sponging. It is not the temperature of the water that brings down the body temperature. The heat of the body is used to evaporate the water on its surface and this brings down the core temperature. In this process, the temperature of the water does not matter. And believe me, a cold water bath is not a pleasant experience when you are having a fever.

Using a cloth soaked in lukewarm water, wipe the whole surface of the body. Keep the film of water on the body surface for a few seconds and then dry it. Repeat the cycle for 20–30 minutes.

If the child does not cooperate, give a quick lukewarm shower or make the child sit in a tub filled with lukewarm water and then dry the body. This will serve the same purpose as sponging.

Keeping a cologne water-soaked cloth over forehead is an age-old popular method, but it is not effective in bringing down the temperature.

Do not use alcohol or spirit to rub on the body or in the sponging water. It can cause toxicity.

Antibiotics

If the cause of the fever is not a bacterial infection, antibiotics will not help at all in treating that fever. Almost 90–95% of common infections are viral. The common wisdom of not starting any specific treatment for the first 3 days of a fever is founded on the fact that most of the simple, common viral illnesses causing fever start subsiding by that time.

Final word of advice

To understand the treatment, understand why we treat a fever. Fever is treated only to prevent or relieve associated aches, pains and misery. Some experts believe that no treatment is necessary for temperatures as high as 40°C in a well-looking child who has no risk factors.

It is very difficult to differentiate a relatively harmless illness from a severe illness just from the presence of high fever. In the earlier years of life, even a common cold can give rise to high-grade fever. So, rather than just looking at the temperature on the thermometer, we should look at the patient as a whole. If the overall appearance and activity look alright, the chances of a common, uncomplicated illness are higher.

Unfortunately this is the thing most of us forget to do and often end up making a mountain out of a molehill.

Myth	Reality
Fever is a dangerous disease.	Fever is a helpful symptom.
All fevers need treatment.	Many cases of mild fevers don't need any treatment.
Higher temperatures in fever indicate serious disorders.	The height of a fever is not always indicative of a serious underlying cause.
Antibiotics are a must for any high or prolonged fever.	Thorough medical check-up (and not uncritical faith in medicines) is a must for any high or prolonged fever.
Paracetamol is an old and mild medicine, and one should use newer and stronger medicines to immediately bring down fever.	Paracetamol is a tried and trusted medicine that, when given in the correct dosage, can safely manage most fevers. Other so-called newer and stronger fever medicines are unsafe and not officially recommended.
Suppositories are more effective than oral medicines in treating fever.	In correct dosage, oral medicines are as effective as suppositories.
Sponging should be done with cold water or at times even with ice packs.	Sponging should always be done with tepid or lukewarm water.
Bathing is to be avoided in fevers.	Bathing should be continued as usual.

2

Fever and Fit

Scenario

Mr. and Mrs. Rastogi come rushing into the doctor's room. Their faces are pale and anxious. Mr. Rastogi is carrying his 1-year-old daughter Ananya in his arms and says frantically, "Doctor, we just had her first birthday party. She was perfectly fine then. She played and danced with the other children and had a good time. Soon after the party, I noticed that she was looking different, a kind of a 'lost' expression. Then she suddenly became unresponsive. Her body became stiff, her eyes rolled up, and she started twitching. We immediately rushed here. The nurse checked her temperature and told us that she is running a high fever. But trust me—she was okay just moments ago."

The doctor checks Ananya, who is not twitching any more. She looks tired and sleepy but has recovered consciousness. As she calls out to her mother, the Rastogis heave a sigh of relief. To the teary-eyed parents, the doctor announces, "Oh, don't worry. Ananya has just suffered from a febrile fit. She should be fine."

Discussion

A febrile child throwing a fit is a common occurrence. "The fever has gone to the head (brain)" is often the colloquial description of the condition known as 'febrile convulsion'. What does really happen?

Typically, such an event begins dramatically and ends rather tamely. A child who was perfectly all right a few moments ago suddenly rolls up her eyes or stares blankly, begins jerking violently or becomes limp and is found to have high-grade fever. By the time the terrified parents rush to the nearest medical facility, the baby has almost always stopped convulsing and has either gone to sleep or regained the normal state without any treatment.

Febrile convulsion is a peculiar condition which has mystified parents and paediatricians alike from the days of Hippocrates. Medical thinking about this condition has undergone a sea change over recent years. Even some medical practitioners are not clear about the new concepts. Let's try and demystify this needlessly dreaded thing.

Febrile convulsion

Febrile convulsion (also known as febrile seizure or febrile fit) is a convulsion associated with a sudden rise of body temperature. It is typically observed in infancy and pre-school years. It is not caused by any brain-related infection such as meningitis or encephalitis and is different from epilepsy.

The condition is quite common, occurring in almost 4% of children in the age group of 6 months to 6 years. Around half of those cases occur between 1 to 2 years of age.

Causes and mechanisms

Fevers associated with colds, throat infections, ear infections or dysentery and fevers with rashes (due to viruses like roseola or measles) are some of the commonest triggers for febrile seizures.

How does fever cause the fit? The exact mechanism of action of the phenomenon is still a mystery. In the early years, the brain is relatively immature and has a low seizure threshold. The sudden rise of body temperature seems to somehow trigger simultaneous, excessive electrical discharges from the brain cells, which lead to the seizure. We can compare this event to a sudden overload on an electrical circuit, leading to a brief shutdown.

Types

Febrile seizures can be either simple or complex. A simple febrile seizure occurs within a few hours of the onset of fever, lasts less than 15 minutes, is generalised (affecting the whole body) and does not recur within 24 hours.

When the seizures are multiple, prolonged, focal (affecting only a part of the body) or are associated with focal neurologic deficit, they are called complex seizures.

Heredity

Febrile seizures tend to occur in families. But we do not know the exact genetic mode of inheritance, or how the condition is passed on through the genes. If one child in a family suffers febrile seizures, there is a 10–20% chance of its occurrence in a sibling. The chances of occurrence are even higher if the parents also suffered from febrile seizures in their childhood.

Recurrence and outcomes

Febrile seizures often do recur. One-third of patients are likely to get another febrile seizure after the first one, and almost 10% get three or more during the typical age range.

Recurrences are more likely when the first seizure happens at an early age and when there is a strong family history of febrile seizures.

Misconceptions

Parents' biggest worry is whether febrile seizures progress to epilepsy. Luckily, the outlook is positive. Epilepsy is an illness characterised by recurrent, non-febrile seizures. Most children outgrow febrile seizures and less than 5% actually progress to epilepsy in later life.

Frequent recurrences of febrile fits do not indicate increased risk of epilepsy. Cerebral palsy, delayed development, mental retardation, complex febrile seizures and a strong family history of epilepsy are the risk factors for the development of epilepsy in future.

Another parental worry is whether these seizures cause brain damage or growth problems. The answer is a big 'No'. Even in frequently recurring febrile convulsions, there is no increased risk for neurological, intellectual or growth handicaps.

Some parents ask whether **vaccinations** should be avoided in such patients. No, not at all! These children should receive all the vaccines that normal children do.

Investigations

According to the latest medical thinking, routine blood tests, lumbar punctures (to check spinal fluid), x-rays and scans are unnecessary if clinical judgment is heavily in favour of simple febrile seizures.

Complex febrile seizures, very young patients and suspicion of other possible serious causes warrant investigations.

Does an abnormal EEG mean something serious in these cases? Actually EEG (electro-encephalogram) has no value in predicting a recurrence of the febrile fit or future development of epilepsy. So an EEG abnormality has no significance. In fact, recent trends are for avoiding EEG altogether in most such cases.

Management at home

- Don't panic.
- Don't try to restrain or hold down the convulsing child.
- Place the child on a flat surface or on the floor.
- Turn the child on the side or on the stomach.
- Loosen or remove any tight clothes.
- Take care that the child does not hurt herself.
- If possible, try to gently remove any object (such as food) from the mouth.
- Don't push any object into mouth to keep it forcibly open. This is dangerous. The object can break inside the mouth and obstruct the airway.
- Sponge the body with tepid water.
- If the convulsion doesn't stop within 10 minutes, take the child to the nearest medical facility.

Medicines and prevention

In most cases of febrile seizures, no long-term preventive medicines are needed. Prolonged use of anti-epileptic drugs phenobarbitone or sodium valproate is found to have much more risk of serious side effects than advantage. These medicines are no longer used for the condition.

If febrile seizures are frequent or prolonged, doctors may prescribe medicines such as diazepam to be used orally or rectally.

One important point to note: No medicine has any role in preventing the progression of febrile seizures to epilepsy.

Precautions

To prevent febrile seizures, try to prevent or reduce the high temperatures of fever. Routine measures to bring down fever—giving the correct dose of fever medicine (like paracetamol) and tepid sponging—are more than sufficient. Vigorous fever control—stronger than the routine measures—has not been shown to have any additional benefit.

Myth	Reality
Febrile seizure is a dangerous situation.	Febrile seizure is a harmless, age-specific, self-limiting phenomenon.
It will usually progress to epilepsy.	Though it has high chances of recurrence, it does not usually progress to epilepsy.
It causes brain damage, mental retardation or growth problems.	It does not cause brain damage, mental retardation or growth problems.
It needs to be thoroughly investigated with special tests like lumbar puncture, EEG and brain scans.	In most cases, clinical diagnosis is sufficient and investigations are unnecessary.
It needs to be treated and prevented with anti-convulsion medicines.	Except for simple anti-fever measures, special medicines are hardly ever needed.

3

'Cold' War

Scenario

Sitting in front of the doctor, Mrs. Dhar looks worried. Her 2-year-old son Rajeev is blissfully unaware of his mother's anxiety. He is happily jumping around the consulting room. The mother starts sharing her concern, "This is the fourth time in the last 4 months that I am visiting a doctor. Every month, he gets a cold. It starts with sneezing, then develops into a runny nose, and sometimes even a mild fever. It goes on for a week and then subsides.

"My previous paediatrician kept telling me that I don't have to worry and these are just viral infections. He did not even prescribe any specific medicines. He'd just tell me to clear his nose with salt-water drops and advise me to give him warm fluids. No decongestants, no antibiotics, nothing! Finally, I said, I must change the doctor and find someone who could give me some real medicines to get rid of these colds!"

For a moment, the doctor looks amused, a faint smile on his face. But then he quickly wipes that off and fixes his expression in his patented serious scholarly look. After carefully examining the child, he says in a heavy voice. "Ma'am, I really hate to tell you this but I have to."

The mother's anxiety deepens. What is he about to tell her? Is it something serious?

Then the good doctor says, "I think I must agree with your previous paediatrician. This is nothing but a common cold and I, too, am going to give you the same advice that he did!"

The mother quickly calculates the consultation fees in her mind. Such a waste of time and money! She has already stopped listening to the advice the doctor is offering her. As soon as she comes out of the clinic, she calls her best friend. "Neeta, what's the name of the paediatrician you go to? The one that cured your Chintu of frequent colds?"

Discussion

"Treat it and it stays for 7 days. Leave it alone and it lasts a week." Everyone has heard this adage about the common cold, which is very irritating but so common around the planet that it carries the adjective 'common' everywhere it goes. Yes, I am talking about the 'common cold'.

Doctors sometimes like to sound knowledgeable when they call it by fancy names like coryza, acute viral nasopharyngitis and what not. But for most people, it's cool to just call it the cold.

Unfortunately, if you do not keep yourself well-informed, it is very easy to lose your cool while tackling this rather simple and harmless illness. So let's find out more about it.

Common cold

The common cold is a viral illness affecting the upper respiratory tract (the respiratory passage from the nose to the throat). It can be caused by more than 200 types of viruses, the commonest of them being the rhinovirus which is responsible for almost one-third of the cases. Because it is more common in cold climates in the winter, it has got the name 'cold'.

The common cold can occur at any age. It is common to have 5–8 such infections per year and the maximum occurrence is in the first 2 years.

Transmission

Tiny droplets are released into the air when the patient sneezes or coughs. The virus in the droplet may be directly inhaled by other people. Hands and objects contaminated by the droplets can carry the infection to other people.

Signs and symptoms

The common cold starts with sneezing, a heavy head, runny nose, watery eyes, body ache and sometimes fever. The fever is usually mild in older children and adults but can be high-grade in infants and toddlers. The nasal discharge is initially watery but later changes colour from white to yellow to green.

In small babies, the nose-block caused by the cold leads to irritability and causes difficulty in breathing, feeding and sleeping. When the baby is lying on its back, the nasal discharge drips down into the throat and causes cough. The nose blockage leads to Eustachian tube blockage and causes decreased hearing and ear pain. The noisy breathing sounds caused by the blocked nose are transmitted to the chest where they can be felt by the hand.

Danger signals

A common cold may develop complications like sinus infection, croup, chest infection, asthma flare-up or ear infection. This is why it is important for parents to recognize the danger signals to know when things are taking a turn for the worse.

In case of the following warning signs, parents should immediately seek medical opinion:

- Age less than 3 months
- High fever (more than 103°F) for more than 3 days
- Prolonged fever (101°F for more than 5 days)
- Rapid breathing
- Distressed breathing (flaring of nostrils, sucking in of the chest or abdomen)
- Increasingly noisy breathing
- Severe ear pain or ear discharge
- Persistent nasal discharge, which is foul-smelling or coloured, beyond 1 week
- Sick look
- Lethargy

Treatment

The treatment of common cold, as of any viral illness, is only supportive and symptomatic. Rest, intake of warm liquids (hot beverages, soups, etc.), increasing fluid intake and analgesics like paracetamol are usually sufficient in older children and adults.

Most of the cough-cold medicines available in the market contain anti-allergic and decongestant chemicals. They are unnecessary in most cases and have significant side effects like drowsiness and drying up of secretions and cannot be called really 'safe'. Especially under the age of 6 years, they should be avoided and if used, should be used only under doctor's supervision.

Vaporisation with cool-mist humidifier is helpful in early resolution of a cold. American Academy of Pediatrics recommends avoiding warm steam inhalation in order to avoid the risk of scalds and burns. So do not give steam inhalation to your child by holding his head under a towel and telling him to inhale the steam rising from boiling water in an open vessel.

Practically speaking, warm steam inhalation can be useful if done at a safe distance with a closed, funnelled, plastic-body steamer. The trick is to place the steamer on a table or stool near the child's bed when the child is asleep and let the steam humidify the surrounding air. The parent or care-giver should always be around while the steamer is on.

Antibiotics are not advisable and unnecessary in most cases of common cold. They are only needed when bacterial complications are suspected and should only be taken with a doctor's prescription.

Zinc and vitamin C are touted to have cold-curing properties, but their use is mostly experimental.

Treatment of nasal blockage

In children, especially in infants, the nose block remains the most irritating symptom that interferes with breathing, feeding and sleeping. But medicated nasal drops and sprays are potentially harmful in common colds and are to be avoided. Instead, the nose block is treated with normal saline nose drops or sprays.

Normal saline solution is nothing but plain salt water. It can easily be prepared at home by dissolving a quarter (¼) teaspoon of common salt in a cup of boiled water.

To administer saline solution, have the baby lie on its back. With a clean dropper or a cotton wick, put 1–2 drops of the saline solution in each nostril. The time of putting in the drops—called the instillation—should be about 15–20 minutes before feeding and before sleep. These drops can be safely used as often as 5–6 times a day.

Saline nasal sprays are available without prescription and are easier to use than drops and perhaps more efficient in relieving nasal block.

Suction bulbs can be used to suck out the secretions to relieve the nasal block. They are easier to use in young infants but toddlers may resist them.

Prevention

There is no specific vaccine to prevent colds, but we can take some simple measures to avoid its spread from person to person.

- Avoiding contact with infected persons
- Frequent hand washing with soap and water
- Teaching the child to cover the mouth with a tissue or a handkerchief when sneezing and coughing

Simple supportive measures and a patient, smiling attitude are the best methods to counter this maddening illness.

Myth	Reality
Frequent colds in the first 2 years are dangerous.	Frequent colds in first 2 years are quite normal.
Yellow or green nasal discharge in a cold is abnormal and needs immediate treatment.	The nasal discharge in common cold changes from watery to white to yellow to green over days.
Antibiotics are a must for a severe cold.	Antibiotics are not useful in most colds. They are only necessary when the doctor suspects a bacterial infection.
OTC (over-the-counter) cough-cold medicines are okay to use at any age.	Due to their potentially dangerous side effects, OTC cough-cold medicines are not advisable under 6 years of age.
Medicated nasal drops and sprays are necessary to relieve the noseblock of common colds.	Medicated nasal drops and sprays are harmful in common colds, and only normal saline drops and sprays are sufficient.

4

Fighting Flu

Scenario

Flashback to 2009.

The swine flu (H1N1) global epidemic is in full swing. The clinic's waiting-room is overflowing. Everyone is looking suspiciously at the next person who seems to be excessively sick.

In the midst of this, someone first sneezes and then coughs. He is covering his mouth with his hands. Suddenly all eyes turn to him. A non-stop stream of instructions and questions flows his way.

"Please cover your mouth with a tissue."

"Here, have this sanitizer solution. Wash your hands with that."

"Is there anybody else sick with similar symptoms in your family?"

"Have you taken the flu medicine?"

The poor fellow looks around confused by the sudden attention. Then he hesitantly says, "Actually, I am perfectly fine. I am here for my kid's vaccination. I just cannot tolerate strong perfumes!"

Now the lady sitting next to him looks embarrassed. She had thought her new perfume was mild.

From inside the consulting room, the doctor looks at the waiting room scene on his security camera monitor. He smiles to himself. He knows that the mass hysteria generated by swine flu has just claimed two more innocent victims.

Discussion

It took a global outbreak of a new influenza virus to make people aware of its deadly nature. Suddenly, people started talking about virus strains, hand washes and vaccines. Otherwise, flu was something not taken seriously. But swine flu and the worldwide deaths it caused dramatically changed public perception of this common viral illness.

Flu

What is called 'flu' in ordinary language is a very common viral infection caused by the influenza virus. This virus has got three types—A, B and C. Type A is the most important as it causes frequent and widespread outbreaks. Type B is responsible for some small-scale, localised outbreaks, and Type C occurs sporadically.

Flu is highly contagious and does not spare any age or sex. But it seems to target children much more frequently and severely.

The rainy season and winter are the most likely seasons for it.

It spreads directly from person to person through airborne droplets coughed or sneezed out or through sharing things like tissues or handkerchiefs contaminated by the respiratory secretions of the patient.

After a person has been exposed to the virus, the symptoms take around 1–4 days to manifest. Usually, the fever and pains subside in 4–5 days. The cough and weakness are usually gone by 1–2 weeks but sometimes could last longer.

Symptoms

Most of us have experienced flu symptoms at one time or another and know exactly what happens.

In older children, the manifestations are pretty much the same as in adults. Abrupt high fever (102–104°F), chills, flushed face, headache, eye pain, muscle pains, dry cough, cold, sore throat, anorexia and tiredness are the trademark pointers to flu. Diarrhoea and vomiting also might occur.

In younger children, the flu can look like the cold, croup, bronchiolitis, bronchitis, middle ear infection or pneumonia. Febrile convulsions are often associated with initial sudden surge of temperature.

In newborns, the flu takes a different form—a much more severe and disguised one. Refusal to feed, lethargy, irritability and apnoea (stoppages of breathing) make it look very similar to bacterial sepsis.

Although 'flu' and 'cold' are sometimes used as words with the same meaning, they are very different conditions. The symptoms of a cold are much milder, develop gradually and are more localised to the nose (stuffiness, runny nose). The flu, on the other hand, is much more abrupt, severe and generalised.

Complications and danger signals

Because of its commonness, the flu is often not taken seriously enough. It is, therefore, wise to emphasise a fact that a worldwide epidemic known as Spanish flu killed more than 20 million people in 1918. US outbreaks of Asian flu in 1957 and Hong Kong flu in 1968 killed thousands and so did the 2009 pandemic caused by H1N1 or swine flu virus.

Serious complications like pneumonia, middle ear infection, sinusitis and tracheitis (inflammation of the windpipe) are common in flu. Acute myositis (muscle inflammation) and acute parotitis (salivary gland inflammation) are seen in some cases.

Danger signals in flu are:

- Continuous bouts of high fever
- Prolonged fever
- Breathing difficulty
- Rapid breathing
- Increasingly noisy breathing
- Ear pain or discharge
- Lethargy, drowsiness, convulsion
- Severe body pains or headaches
- Explosive diarrhoea or vomiting
- Sick look

Management

Most cases of flu need only paracetamol (to control fever and pains), plenty of fluids and rest. Ibuprofen can be used under a doctor's guidance.

Vaporisation and saline nasal drops and sprays are helpful.

Never use aspirin in young flu patients as it could lead to a serious liver problem called Reye syndrome.

In severe or complicated cases, antiviral medicines may be prescribed by the doctor. Antibiotics are unnecessary and useless in uncomplicated flu cases.

Prevention

Hand washing to wash off any infected droplets, avoiding crowded places, avoiding kissing on the mouth or face and not sharing tissues or handkerchiefs are some simple ways to avoid contracting the flu.

It has now been proved that washing the hands with simple soap and water is more effective than sanitizer solutions.

Vaccination against the flu is the best way of preventing it. There is an injectable inactivated flu vaccine and also a live attenuated nasal vaccine. The injectable flu vaccine can be given to children over the age of 6 months. A single injection at the beginning of winter for adults and children above 8 years offers almost 60–80% protection. The nasal live vaccine can be used in healthy children older than 2 years.

When they receive the flu vaccine for the first time, children younger than 8 years need two doses taken at least 1 month apart. The next season onwards, only 1 dose is sufficient.

Unlike other vaccines that offer immunity over a much longer period, the flu vaccine offers only 1-year protection. This is because of the flu virus' ability to keep changing its antigenic structure. The vaccine is prepared every year following WHO recommendations about the strains of flu virus that are going to be more common that year.

Severe egg allergy is the only major contraindication for taking the flu vaccine. Apart from mild pain, redness at the site of the injection and occasional mild fever, there are no major side effects.

Anybody who wants to avoid the flu can opt for the vaccine to get protection against the prevalent flu strains. The American Academy of Pediatrics recommends seasonal flu vaccine for every child above the age of 6 months. Only from cost considerations, it is not recommended as a routine vaccine in other countries. The Indian Academy of Paediatrics recommends it only for high risk categories. These categories are people with the following conditions:

- Any chronic heart, lung, kidney, neurologic or blood disease
- Metabolic diseases like diabetes mellitus and cystic fibrosis
- Immune deficiency

- Undergoing chemotherapy for cancer
- Healthcare professionals
- Babies who remain in day-care centres for a significant portion of the working week
- People staying or working in closed, crowded settings
- Elderly people (over 65 years)

Myth	Reality
Flu is a harmless illness.	Flu is a potentially dangerous illness.
Antibiotics are necessary in the treatment of flu.	Antibiotics are needless and harmful in uncomplicated flu.
Antiviral medicines are necessary for all flu cases and should be started on our own.	Antiviral medicines are necessary only in certain cases and should be prescribed by a doctor.
Sanitizer hand wash is very useful in prevention of flu.	Simple soap and water hand wash is more effective in prevention of flu.
The flu vaccine is useless in the prevention of flu.	The flu vaccine is extremely useful in preventing severe and complicated cases of flu.
Giving the flu vaccine every season is needless.	The flu vaccine needs to be given every season as the virus types keep changing every season.

Final word of advice

Never take the flu lightly. Beneath its common, well-known face lurks a deadly killer. Prompt curative measures and prevention whenever appropriate are needed to counter this potentially fatal but extremely common disease.

5

Diarrhoea

Scenario

"My son has had diarrhoea for two days. Yesterday, he passed three watery loose motions, and this morning, he has already gone to the toilet thrice. He is otherwise okay but just feels some mild abdominal pain before passing the stools." Mrs. Kanojia informs the doctor.

The doctor asks: "What have you done so far?"

Mrs. Kanojia replies: "Oh, I have given him two doses of *******. Last week, too, he had the same kind of problem and the chemist suggested giving it. I just used it for a day and he got better! But it doesn't seem to be working this time."

The doctor shakes his head in despair. The mother has named a popular diarrhoea medicine, which is a combination of a strong antibiotic and anti-parasitic medicine. He thinks, 'How can people use such strong medicines and that, too, in such a wrong manner, starting and stopping them at will without bothering to complete the course?'

Checking his annoyance, the doctor says, "But, madam, do you know that medicines are not really necessary in your son's case? They are in fact harmful and may prolong his problem. What he needs is just some replenishment of fluids and electrolytes, a change in diet and waiting for a day or two."

Mrs. Kanojia looks at him in disbelief. Is the man joking?

Discussion

Do you know the origin of the word 'diarrhoea'? It comes from two Greek words—'dia' meaning 'through' and 'rhien' meaning 'flow'. Medically, it denotes an increased frequency of loose, altered, abnormal stools and is called gastroenteritis.

Acute and chronic types of diarrhoea are primarily differentiated by duration. The acute variety lasts less than 2 weeks and the chronic one persists more than 2 weeks. The causes, course and treatment of the two types differ a great deal.

Common causes

Most cases of acute diarrhoea are caused by **infections** of the gastrointestinal tract. These infections can be viral, bacterial or parasitic in nature.

Viruses (such as rotavirus), bacteria (such as E.coli, salmonella, shigella, cholera) and parasites (such as amoeba, giardia) are the main pathogens.

These infections are transmitted through the faecal-oral route, meaning through human waste contaminating water and food.

Sometimes the diarrhoea may be a result of **food intolerance** or allergy and sometimes even due to some **medicines** such as antibiotics and laxatives.

Viral and bacterial diarrhoea

The distinction between viral and bacterial diarrhoea can be confusing. By oversimplifying somewhat, it can be expressed as follows:

- Profuse, painless, watery diarrhoea with minimal systemic symptoms is more likely to have a viral origin.
- Scanty, frequent, painful diarrhoea with severe systemic symptoms like fever is more likely to be bacterial.
- Bloody diarrhoea or dysentery is more likely to be bacterial in origin.
- Viral diarrhoea is more likely in winter and the bacterial type in summer.

Food poisoning

This type of diarrhoea occurs within a short period after consuming food items contaminated with certain germs or their toxins. Food poisoning is usually suspected when a group of people who have eaten the same food suffer from similar gastrointestinal symptoms within a few hours of ingestion of that food.

Salmonella (through dairy or meat products and eggs), staphylococci (through meat, eggs, pastries or salads), clostridium perfringens (through meat and gravy) and clostridium botulinum (through canned food, honey and fish) are the major offenders.

Dehydration

The diarrhoea patient loses water in the body through loose motions, which is a problem in itself. As the patient loses more and more body water, the symptoms of dehydration worsen and may be as serious as coma in severe cases.

Type of dehydration	Body water loss	Signs and symptoms
Mild	Up to 5%	Lethargy, thirst and irritability
Moderate	5–10%	Sunken eyes, dry mouth and lips, absence of tears, decreased skin elasticity, rapid pulse, reduced urine output and sometimes drowsiness in infants, depressed fontanelles (soft spots) of the skull
Severe	More than 10%	All these signs exaggerated; shock and even coma

Oral rehydration solution (ORS) is a scientifically proven and simple way of providing fluids and correcting electrolyte imbalance in situations like diarrhoea and vomiting. It is available free in government hospitals and commercial preparations based on the same principles are available in pharmacies. Most cases of mild and moderate dehydration can be adequately handled at home by using ORS under medical guidance.

The current ORS composition recommended by WHO and UNICEF is as follows:

Sodium chloride	2.6 gm
Tri-sodium citrate	2.9 gm
Potassium chloride	1.5 gm
Glucose	13.5 gm
Water	1 litre

This formula is called hypo-osmolar ORS formula, which provides the necessary fluid and electrolytes and is found to be effective in reducing the volume and duration of diarrhoea.

Home remedy

A salt-and-sugar solution, in the following proportion, serves the purpose of ORS in most cases of uncomplicated diarrhoea. Salt contains sodium and chlorides, and sugar contains glucose.

Salt	2.5 gm (½ teaspoonful)
Sugar	30 gm (6 teaspoonful)
Water	1 litre (5 cups)

The teaspoon measurement is for a flat level in the teaspoon and not a heaped measure. You can squeeze a lemon or sweet lime in this solution to give it flavour. The standard taste of ORS is similar to the taste of tears.

Zinc supplements

Zinc supplements along with ORS have been shown to be effective in reducing the duration and severity of diarrhoea, the need for hospitalisation, the chances of later pneumonia and mortality.

Zinc supplements are typically given for 10–14 days in diarrhoea cases. The recommended doses are:

Less than 6 months: 10 mg/day
From 6 months to 5 years: 20 mg/day

Discuss with your doctor whether zinc supplements are necessary in your child's case.

Intravenous fluids

Intravenous (IV) fluids are only necessary in conditions like

- Severe dehydration
- Shock
- Persistent vomiting
- Refusal to accept oral rehydration
- Very large and frequent stools
- Extreme fatigue
- Abdominal distension (bloated abdomen)
- Altered mental state or other significant complications

Lab tests

As a routine case of acute diarrhoea is mostly self-limiting and requires only precautions regarding food and fluids, no particular lab test is necessary. Only in cases of bloody diarrhoea, severe associated symptoms, significant dehydration or persistent diarrhoea, do stool and blood need to be tested in a lab to get to the root of the problem.

Diet

The important thing to understand is that food should not be denied to a diarrhoea patient but it should be modified.

Avoid foods that are too starchy, too fatty or too sugary foods; non-vegetarian foods such as meat, poultry, fish and egg and fresh animal milk (cow or buffalo milk).

To replace fluid do not use sugared fruit juices, fizzy cola drinks or even plain water. These may worsen the situation by causing electrolyte imbalance.

In my practice, I advise the following items in the diet:

- Rice-kanjee or rice-water with salt (improves absorption of electrolytes and provides fluids and electrolytes)
- Clear vegetable or chicken-broth with salt (provides fluids and electrolytes)
- Yogurt or buttermilk with salt (provides lactobacillus, a useful type of bacteria that can displace the harmful ones)
- Dark toasted bread (activated carbon adsorbs toxins)
- Sliced or mashed semi-ripe fruits like banana, apple or pear (provide potassium; pectin helps in binding the stools)
- Non-sugared fruit juices, like 100% natural apple or orange juice, in small quantities

Milk-feeds for babies

Breast-feeding should be continued normally when a child has diarrhoea. In formula-fed babies, either a diluted milk formula or a lactose-free milk formula should be used.

Cow's milk should be avoided or offered in small quantity in diluted form.

Medicines

The unfortunate tendency is for parents to demand medicines and for unscrupulous medical practitioners to supply them. This has led to a number of unnecessary medicines being used routinely in cases of diarrhoea.

The most commonly used medicines are:

- Anti-motility agents (to slow down intestinal movement)
- Anti-spasmodics (to counter intestinal spasms or colic)
- Anti-secretory agents like bismuth preparations (to reduce intestinal secretions)
- Stool binders like kaolin-pectin (to thicken stools)
- Lactobacillus preparations (to provide useful bacteria)

You can avoid these medicines in most acute diarrhoea cases.

The important thing is that using medicines to reduce the frequency or improve the consistency of stools is not only unnecessary but could even prove dangerous due to some unwanted side effects of these medicines. The stools formed after using such medicines could still carry a high water-load but give a false sense of security, which would delay the requisite fluid replacement.

Antibiotics (like co-trimoxazole, nitrofurantoin, ciprofloxacin and norfloxacin) and anti-parasitic medicines (like metronidazole) are also often used quite recklessly. It would be prudent to ask the doctor why he considers them necessary. Even in bacterial diarrhoeas, antibiotics are seldom required and, in many instances, their use prolongs diarrhoea.

Instead of taking medicines, you can take these preventive measures against diarrhoea:

- Breast feeding (in infancy)
- Avoiding or limiting bottle feeding
- In case of bottle feeding, making sure that bottles and nipples are sterilised properly
- Washing hands with soap and water after using the toilet and before preparing or eating food
- Using clean drinking water
- Avoiding outside food
- Properly cleaning and washing foods like meat and vegetables
- Eating freshly prepared and properly cooked food

Myth	Reality
Diarrhoea needs immediate medications.	Diarrhoea mainly needs only fluid and electrolyte replacement and food modification.
Breast feeding should be discontinued in diarrhoea.	Breast feeding should be continued as it is.
Food is to be denied to the diarrhoea patient.	Food should not be denied, just modified.
Plain water, sugared juices and fizzy cola drinks are useful as replacement fluids.	Such drinks can lead to electrolyte imbalance, instead use properly made ORS or salt-sugar solution.
Over-the-counter diarrhoea medicines should be regularly used.	OTC diarrhoea medicines are mostly needless and potentially harmful.

Final word of advice

Most cases of acute diarrhoea—whether viral or bacterial—are self-limited and last 3–7 days. ORS and sensible dietary changes are the only measures required for such cases. Lab tests and medicines are mostly unnecessary.

6

Constipation

Scenario

Mrs. Hamid brings in her 5-year-old son Ismail into the consulting room. Even before she says anything, the doctor asks, "So how is his constipation now?"

Maternal concern overflows, and Mrs. Hamid starts recounting her tale of woes, "What should I do, doctor? It has been so many months since I have been coming to you, but Ismail's constipation is showing no signs of improvement. I have been regularly giving him laxatives and even using enemas at times. But he just cannot pass stools normally. He doesn't pass stools for many days and when he does, it is very little and very hard. He is constantly complaining of stomach pain and gases. Sometimes, he ends up soiling his pants. He doesn't feel like eating. I am at my wits' end."

The doctor looks at the boy. Ismail is looking chubbier than before. He is busy playing a game on a mobile phone. He howls angrily when his mother takes away the gadget from his hand but then becomes quiet when she hands him a pack of potato chips.

The doctor shakes his head and asks in a resigned tone, "Mrs. Hamid, I had told you to make certain changes in his eating habits and his daily routine. Have you done that?"

The mother indignantly says, "Oh, doctor, please. I am trying very hard, but he just doesn't listen. Why don't you change some medicines? Give me something stronger which would get rid of this problem once for all!"

Discussion

In an age where children's diet has centred on chips, chocolates, candies, cookies and colas and their daily activity has been reduced to being couch potatoes hooked to the television, the Internet and mobile devices, constipation has become an increasingly annoying problem.

Managing constipation is a task that needs clear understanding of the underlying mechanism and often, it requires changes in the child's lifestyle. Let's see what exactly goes wrong when your child is habitually constipated and how to solve that problem.

Constipation

Constipation is not just about the reduced frequency of stools. Babies who are mainly on milk feeds may pass stools every 3–5 days, but so long as the consistency of the stools is soft and normal, this doesn't constitute constipation.

When infrequent passage of stools is also associated with dry and hard stools that are difficult to pass, only then does the condition qualify as constipation.

Encopresis is involuntary passage of stools beyond the age when bowel control is usually achieved. This kind of day- or night-time soiling of formed stools beyond the anticipated age of toilet training (4–5 years) is often a complication associated with constipation.

Certain other problems are associated with constipation.

Passage of very hard stools can lead to injury and cause bleeding and fissure formation in anal region.

Abdominal distension, abdominal pain and anorexia are also commonly associated with constipation.

Overflow diarrhoea can occur when the accumulated fluid leaks around the hard masses of the stools.

In very severe cases, there may be stool impaction and intestinal obstruction.

As the stool-loaded bowels exert pressure on urethra and partially obstruct it, there is increased risk of developing urinary tract infections.

Causes

The commonest variety of constipation encountered is called functional (habitual) constipation, in which there is no organic abnormality responsible for the condition. This type accounts for 90–95% of constipation cases above the age of 1 month.

Organic causes include congenital abnormalities (of the gastrointestinal tract or of the spinal cord), metabolic abnormalities (such as dehydration, hypothyroidism and cystic fibrosis), drugs (such as iron preparations) and painful conditions of the anus (such as an abscess or a fissure).

As a rule, constipation in the newborn period and infancy needs to be evaluated more carefully to rule out these organic causes. At later ages, the functional variety is more likely.

Functional constipation

The following factors are involved in functional constipation in children:

Faulty toilet training: Development of functional constipation has a psychological basis and is mostly related to faulty toilet training. If such training is too vigorous and coercive, passing stools becomes a negative experience for the toddler. Such a toddler then starts voluntarily withholding stools as a method of expressing his rebellion or sometimes simply fearing that the soiling might be punished by parents.

Unfamiliar surroundings such as a hospital, a relative's house or a school often induce reluctance to void stools in older children.

Retention-pain vicious cycle: Hard stools are painful and difficult to pass. This painful passage of stools causes fear of voiding stools in the child's mind. This quickly develops into a vicious cycle where the child voluntarily holds and retains stools to avoid painful voiding. This excessive stool-retention distends the rectum and reduces its sensitivity, making it even more difficult to void stools.

Faulty lifestyle: The wrong diet (less fruits, vegetables and unrefined grains; more dairy, meats, poultry and unessential foods) and lack of exercise are usually found in children with constipation, and they serve only to worsen the situation.

Management

A thorough physical examination and a good history usually provide enough information to the paediatrician to rule out serious organic causes. Investigations like barium enema and other tests are needed only when such causes are suspected.

For the functional, non-organic type of constipation, management involves participation of both the parents and the child sufferer. All of them should be given the explanation of how constipation develops and should be asked to identify the problem areas in their particular case.

Rigid parental attitudes about bowel control often need correction. It cannot be emphasised too strongly that this is not a problem that will vanish if the patient pops pills; it needs a permanent change in lifestyle to correct itself.

Regular physical exercise, ensuring adequate water and fluid intake, and improving the fibre content in the diet are the cornerstones of treatment.

Cut down on fast foods. Fruits (orange, ripe banana, melon, papaya), bran, cereals and green leafy vegetables should form the main part of the diet. In infants, addition of fruit juices to milk feeds is often necessary.

Don't make the toilet seat a battleground. Pressurising the child about having 'good' bowel habits is counter-productive. Explain the things gently and be patient about the result which often takes long (a few weeks to a few months) to achieve.

The child should be made to understand that he has to follow toilet timings, which should be the same time every day. Usually a 10-minute period on the toilet seat is sufficient.

Medicines such as laxatives (lactulose, magnesium preparations, bisacodyl), lubricants (mineral oil, glycerine suppositories) and enemas have only a limited role in management. Only your doctor should decide how these medicines are to be used. Usually, these medicines are used to break the 'retention-pain' vicious cycle. But after that, it is the changes in diet, activity and psychological make-up which finally cure this problem.

Myth	Reality
The earlier we start and finish the toilet training, the better the result. It is better to take control early.	Be relaxed about the whole exercise of toilet training. Depending on the child's age and readiness, it may take a few weeks to a few months.
Passing infrequent stools (less than once a day) means constipation.	It is constipation only when infrequent stools are hard in consistency and difficult to pass.

Laxatives, suppositories and enemas are the most important treatment measures in constipation.	Medicines are never the solutions to constipation. Regular physical exercise, adequate water and fluid intake and fibre-rich foods are the cornerstones of treatment.
Special tests like barium enema x-rays are always necessary in a case of constipation.	Special x-rays and other tests are only necessary when the doctor suspects a serious organic cause and not functional or habitual constipation.

7

Vomiting

Scenario

Scene 1

Pratiksha is a 5-month-old baby on bottle-feeds. From time to time, she throws up or rather, spits out curdled milk in small amounts.

Scene 2

Devansh is 6 weeks old. He was perfectly fine until recently. But he now throws up after every milk-feed. It is quite forceful vomiting, which seems odd.

Scene 3

Daksh is 2 years old. In the last few hours, he has vomited five times and is looking tired now. Last night, he had been given a fried chicken piece at a fast food joint.

Discussion

The three scenes are associated with three different causes, three different treatment approaches and three different outcomes.

Vomiting is that kind of a symptom. A baby or a child throwing up is never a pretty sight. It has multiple causes, some common and harmless but others serious and potentially dangerous.

That is why any repeated vomiting in a baby or a child should never be taken lightly. It demands prompt medical attention and evaluation.

Vomiting in newborns and infants

For this age group, it is important for parents to understand the difference between simple regurgitation (reflux) and vomiting. Vomiting is a much more forceful and projectile ejection (or throwing out) of the entire stomach contents whereas in reflux, a small quantity of stomach contents slowly dribbles out of the mouth. Most of the reported cases of 'vomiting' in this period are actually regurgitation or reflux.

Gastroesophageal reflux (GER): Food passes in one direction from the mouth through the digestive system. There are mechanisms to stop it passing in the reverse direction. Among these is the valve (sphincter) situated at the lower end of the food pipe which guards against the upward or reverse movement of stomach contents. In the early months of life, this valve is slightly lax. Whenever there is any increase in intra-abdominal pressure while coughing, crying, laughing, moving or passing stools, it can cause this valve to relax further, resulting in upward movement of stomach contents.

Because infants are mainly on liquid milk feeds in this age, their stomach contents move upward more easily.

In usual cases of simple GER, the babies occasionally spit out small amounts of curdled milk. They do not show any outward ill effects and are happy and playful. Their weight gain pattern is normal.

Usually, these cases of mild reflux need no treatment. The condition improves with passing months and after the introduction of semisolid foods.

Gastroesophageal reflux disease (GERD) is a term used for severe cases of reflux. In such cases, the reflux frequency is higher, the regurgitated amounts are greater and the baby is often irritable and either not gaining weight or losing weight.

The treatment of GERD may need special milk formulas, specific medicines and sometimes even surgery.

Other important causes: Feeding errors (wrong feeding position, not burping well after feeds and overfeeding) are common simple causes of vomiting in this age group. Correction of these errors usually solves the problem of vomiting.

Among serious causes of vomiting in newborn and early infancy period are:

- Congenital abnormalities such as congenital hypertrophic pyloric stenosis and metabolic errors
- Surgical conditions such as intessusception
- Significant infection, which may be anywhere in the body

These cases show severe vomiting and associated symptoms and signs. They need urgent medical attention and management of the underlying cause.

Vomiting in toddlers and children

Common causes of vomiting above 1 year are common infections (viral or bacterial gastroenteritis and upper respiratory infections), motion sickness, food intolerance or allergy and medicinal side effects.

Some **unusual causes** are serious infections (meningitis, typhoid, viral hepatitis), surgical conditions (like appendicitis) and accidental poisonings.

Watch out for these danger signals in an infant or child who is vomiting:

- Sick look
- High fever
- Lethargy or drowsiness
- Greenish bile-stained vomiting
- Severe abdominal pain, distention or a lump
- Severe diarrhoea or constipation
- Bloody stools
- Headache or neck pain or rigidity
- Less urination
- Refusal to accept feeds or fluids
- Signs of dehydration

Management

Just administering anti-vomiting medicines is not the right way of treating vomiting. One must identify and treat the underlying condition causing vomiting.

Seek a medical opinion if the vomiting is frequent or severe.

Don't stop feeding the child unless your doctor has advised you to do so. In breastfed babies, breastfeeding should be continued as usual. In formula-fed babies, it is better to dilute the formula. In children, semisolid foods (rice *kanjee, khichri,* soups, mashed fruits, fruit juices and yoghurt) are good options.

Don't stop giving fluids but give them (paediatric ORS and similar fluids) in small sips.

Sometimes urgent investigations like blood and urine tests and x-rays and ultrasonography might be necessary to find the cause of vomiting.

8

Acute Abdominal Pain

Scenario

"Doctor, I want to ask you a question."

The doctor looked at his newly joined staff nurse in surprise. She was never prone to asking questions. But today, she was standing before him like a curious student, waiting eagerly for his permission to ask a question.

"Yes, sister, go ahead. What do you want to know?"

"Doctor, in the last 3 days, we got about 15 children with acute abdominal pain. To some, you just gave reassurance; for others, you prescribed medicines; for yet others, you advised admission and observation and, finally, you sent some straightaway for an emergency surgery. How do you make these judgments? In these infants and children, it must be difficult to judge what is causing the acute abdominal pain, since they are not able express their symptoms clearly."

The doctor was pleased. The new staff nurse was indeed quite observant and intelligent. Her question was very important and deserved a detailed answer.

Discussion

Sudden, severe pain in the abdomen is a common symptom in childhood. Most such episodes may be self-limited and harmless, but some may have a serious underlying condition. The cause of such pain is often difficult to diagnose at the first visit and may require repeated examinations, sometimes backed up by hospitalisation and lab tests to judge the progression of symptoms and signs.

The common causes of acute abdominal pain differ in different age group. **Infantile colic** in newborns and infants and **functional recurrent abdominal pain** in the 5–15 years age group are the essentially harmless and common causes. They do not need much medical intervention.

Acute gastroenteritis and **urinary tract infection** are other common causes, and they need immediate appropriate treatment.

Abdominal pain is sometimes caused by a condition outside the abdomen. Throat infections, ear infections, chest infections and diabetic ketoacidosis are some such causes.

What makes acute abdominal pain a worrisome problem is the possibility of conditions that may require surgery. Abdominal injury, intussusception and appendicitis are most important conditions in this respect. Kidney and gall bladder stones also come under this category, and these can occur in children.

Intussusception is a condition in which one part of the intestine telescopes into another and causes obstruction. If left untreated, it can lead to gangrene (sloughing) of the affected intestine. The usual age group when this condition is seen is 6–18 months.

Intermittent colicky (cramp-like) pain causes the infant to suddenly cry and draw up its knees. Vomiting, lethargy, mild fever, currant-jelly stools (blood and mucus in stools that are dark red or black jelly-like in appearance) and a long and narrow shaped abdominal lump complete the clinical picture.

A specialized x-ray procedure—the barium enema—is used to confirm the diagnosis. Many a times, the diagnostic procedure of barium enema itself can reverse the abnormal telescoping of the intestine. In severe cases, surgery is required.

Appendicitis

The appendix is a small finger-like appendage attached to the first part of the large intestine. It does not serve any known physiologic function. When its cavity is blocked by anything, most commonly by a small piece of stool, infection and inflammation set in and that is appendicitis.

Acute appendicitis is the most common surgical cause of abdominal pain in older children and adolescents. It affects 4 in 1,000 children below the age of 16 years. This is an important thing to note because many parents seem to think that appendicitis occurs only in adults.

In a typical case of appendicitis, dull or cramp-like pain starts around the umbilicus or navel. It is followed by nausea, anorexia, vomiting and mild fever (38°–38.5°C). Within a day or two, the pain and tenderness localise into the lower-right quadrant of the abdomen, being the highest at a medically defined McBurney's point.

This classical triad of pain, vomiting and fever may not be always present in children. With unusual appendix location in the some patients, the pain and tenderness may be felt at different places. Frequent urination or diarrhoea also can occur in such cases.

In case the appendix ruptures, there is initial relief from pain but soon the peritoneum (the membrane covering abdominal organs) gets inflamed and manifestations like high fever and generalised abdominal guarding (tightness) and rigidity become apparent.

The treatment of appendicitis is surgical removal of the inflamed appendix. In a case where perforation of the appendix is suspected or has occurred, antibiotics are also needed.

The location of the abdominal pain often gives the doctor a general idea of the organ that is likely to be affected, but it is just a rough idea.

Pain in the stomach, pancreas, and initial parts of the small intestine is felt in the central 'hollow' of the abdomen above the umbilicus (navel). Liver and gall bladder pains are felt just below the right lower edge of the ribcage. Pain from distal parts of the small intestine and the right side of the large intestine are felt around the umbilicus. Pain from urinary tract infection, genitals or the left side of the large intestine is often felt in the lower central abdomen below the umbilicus and just above the pubic bony prominence. Pain from the kidneys is felt around the loins or the flanks.

Diagnosis

Parents report a child's problem to the doctor and should carefully note the symptoms. Note down the location, duration, frequency and severity of the pain episodes. Note their relationship with food ingestion, that is, whether the pain happens before or after eating. If the child is older, ask about the character of the pain such as whether it is dull or sharp. Any associated symptoms like vomiting, diarrhoea, constipation, bloody stools, urinary frequency or burning or fever should be noted. It is also important to tell the doctor about any acute or chronic illness or recent injury.

As acute abdominal pain has so many probable causes and complications, it is often not possible to pinpoint the diagnosis immediately. Many times, the causative condition evolves over a period of 24–48 hours. In such cases, hospitalisation is a good option as it allows constant medical supervision and monitoring of the condition. When it is not clear whether the cause is surgical or non-surgical, the patient is kept on an empty stomach and on intravenous fluids so to be ready for a potential operation should surgery be necessary.

Investigations like blood, stool and urine tests; x-rays and ultrasound are often necessary to arrive at a diagnosis. Sometimes, these may be needed even after diagnosis to monitor the course of the condition.

Painkiller medicines reduce the pain but do not correct the underlying disease. They might mask the progression of symptoms and induce a false sense of security, delaying proper treatment.

Final word of advice

Acute abdominal pain can be caused by many medical or surgical conditions, some mild, some serious and some even from outside the abdomen.

Never take any acute severe abdominal pain lightly. Never try to manage it at home with home remedies and painkillers. Always seek prompt medical opinion. Never hesitate when hospitalisation or investigations are ordered in such cases.

9

Recurrent Abdominal Pain

Scenario

Mrs. Mathur is worried about her son. He is 10 years old and, for the last few months, has had repeated attacks of abdominal pain. She has already taken him to three specialists for evaluation. They have checked him and even done some tests. All that they tell her is not to worry and that it is just a case of recurrent abdominal pain without any specific cause.

They all have told her, "It's nothing serious! It is just a case of functional RAP."

But Mrs. Mathur is still worried. She wants to know more about this functional RAP thing.

Discussion

RAP (recurrent abdominal pain) is diagnosed when at least one episode of abdominal pain happens per month over a period of 3 months, each episode severe enough to disrupt the daily routine.

An underlying cause is not found in most such cases. Almost 90% of RAP cases are without cause and are termed functional RAP.

Functional RAP is quite common in the 5–15-year age group in which as many as 10–15% children may suffer from it. Girls tend to suffer more.

Causes

The very fact that these recurrent pains are called 'functional' means that there is no known underlying physical cause. This is where it starts getting mysterious. On the one hand, there is a child who is having abdominal pains severe enough to disrupt daily activities. On the other hand, there is a diagnosis proclaiming 'There is no disease.' So what exactly is going wrong?

No one knows the exact cause of this pain. One thing is sure that this abdominal pain is real and not faked to imitate adults or to gain advantages like parental sympathy or a day off from school.

The following factors may be responsible for such pain.

- Physical and psychological stress
- Disturbed intestinal movement because of dysfunction in hormones or autonomic nerves
- Genes (Many family members have similar problems.)
- Personality
- Emotional status

Symptoms

Patients experience and report a vague pain around the umbilicus (navel), but it may also be generalised. In most patients, the pain lasts around 1–3 hours, with pain-free periods between episodes.

The patient might double up wincing and clutching the abdomen. Nausea, dizziness, headache, pallor, excessive sweating and slightly raised temperature (99–100°F) are often present along with the pain.

There is no relation between the pain and food, activity or bowel habits. Usually, this pain does not radiate to other parts.

Although the pain often causes difficulty sleeping at night, almost never does it cause the patient to wake up from sleep.

Necessary investigations

In functional RAP, it is necessary not to go overboard with excessive tests and investigations. Such panicky response would only cause more stress to parents and patient and possibly worsen the pain episodes.

When the clinical pattern is suggestive of functional RAP and the physical examination is normal, only basic investigations are needed. These include complete blood count, ESR (erythrocyte sedimentation rate), urine analysis with culture and a detailed stool examination to rule out occult blood and parasites.

Danger signals

Abdominal pain may have serious underlying causes. The danger signals of such causes are:

- Pain awakening the child from sleep
- Location of pain away from umbilicus
- Weight loss or growth slowdown
- Sleepiness following attacks
- Associated symptoms (fever, vomiting, change in bowel habits, blood in stools, skin rashes or joint pains)
- Positive family history of peptic ulcer or inflammatory bowel disease

If any of these signs are found, a more detailed investigative work-up is necessary to find the cause.

Treatment

Demystification of the situation is the first step in treating the condition. It should be explained to the parents and the child in simple words that, though the pain is real, it is self-limiting and not dangerous. The transient nature of the condition should be emphasised.

Modification of the environment helps. Parents should try to note which events—or stressful stimuli—precipitate the painful episodes. Then they should try to remove the stimuli if possible.

Parents, and even school authorities, should promote normal activity as far as possible even during pain episodes instead of indulging in overprotective, anxious behaviour.

Regularisation of the child's sleep and food timings is helpful.

Some **diet modifications** help. However, high-fibre diets do not ease the pain and, in fact, might worsen it. Avoiding excess lactose (milk products), fructose (fizzy drinks), starches (potatoes, corn, wheat, oats) and sorbitol (gums and candies) might offer some relief.

Medicines are usually not needed on a long term basis. Local massage and warmth, besides occasional symptomatic medicines, are helpful.

Prognosis

Almost half of the cases of functional RAP improve within 2–6 weeks of diagnosis and with better understanding of the condition. But the other half may continue to have episodes, which may continue even in adulthood.

Final word of advice

Functional recurrent abdominal pain is the commonest type of abdominal pain in the age group of 5–15 years; 10–15% children in that age group suffer from it.

It is not dangerous and is mostly self-limiting. Reducing stress, encouraging normal activity, regular food and sleep timings, slight modification of the diet and occasional anti-spasmodic medicines usually suffice as treatment.

Myth	Reality
Recurrent abdominal pain in children is usually faked.	Recurrent abdominal pain in children is usually genuine.
Such pain needs detailed investigations in most patients.	Detailed investigations are needed in only a few patients.
Such pain requires regular medications.	Medications are only occasionally needed in such pain.

10

Worms

Scenario

For the last few days, Akshata has been noticing that her 3-year-old son Manish is constantly scratching around his anus. His sleep has also been disturbed by this itching. She cannot see any dryness or skin rash around the anus.

When she calls her doctor, he asks her if Manish has been having any other symptoms. Akshata recalls that he has also often been complaining about abdominal pain and that his appetite has also decreased a little.

After listening to the history, the doctor tells her not to worry, "I guess he has got worms. I will prescribe a medicine, which should hopefully fix it."

Discussion

Roundworm, hookworm, pinworm, whipworm, tapeworm ... the mere mention of these names makes one feel queasy. Worms are perfect parasites, using someone's body as their residence, and doing nothing useful but feeding off the system of their gracious though unwitting host and harming the host's health in the process.

The number of human cases infested by different types of worms runs into millions if not billions. Exact estimates are not available for lack of studies, which is probably because of the common but not deadly nature of the problem. Children between 1–6 years are most commonly affected.

Roundworms, hookworms, pinworms, whipworms, strongyloides and tapeworms are common worm infestations.

Ingesting food or water contaminated with the eggs or larvae (motile immature forms) of worms is the commonest route of infection. When infected people void stools or dumping their sewage on open land, these eggs or larvae pass into the soil and water.

The larvae of tapeworms enter the human body through ingestion of raw and undercooked meat like beef, pork and fresh water fish. The larvae of some worms (hookworm and strongyloides) penetrate through the skin.

Symptoms

Among common general symptoms are:

- Itching around the anus
- Vague abdominal pain
- Mild abdominal distension
- Bloated stomach sensation
- Diarrhoea
- Appetite changes (decreased as well as increased appetite)

Some symptoms are popularly attributed to worms but have not been medically proven to be related. Among these are:

- Teeth grinding at night
- Eating more sweet foods
- White spots on the cheeks
- Pica (eating inedible things like mud and clay)

Severe symptoms and complications of worm infestation are:

- Severe night-time itching around the anus leading to sleeplessness
- Iron deficiency anaemia due to chronic blood loss
- Decreased absorption of proteins and vitamins (A and B12)
- Intestinal obstruction
- Skin rashes
- Allergic cough or pneumonia

Diagnosis

The presence of the symptoms mentioned above indicates worm infestation. Certain tests confirm it.

Stool examination for the presence of worms, their eggs or larvae is not a foolproof test and can miss the evidence in some samples. Ideally, stool samples should be checked on three consecutive days.

Tapeworms, which grow to astonishing lengths of 4–10 metres, usually give a clue to their presence when their segments are expelled along with stools.

Sometimes the allergy-indicator white blood cells (eosinophils) are increased in number. This usually happens when the infective larvae are migrating through the tissues.

Treatment

Routine broad-spectrum medicines against worms (like mebendazole or albendazole) are quite safe. Their courses are usually of short duration (1 to 3 days). Some specific worm types may need different kind of medicines. Consult your doctor before starting the treatment.

The following are some good preventive measures:

- Avoiding unhygienic habits like passing stools or dumping sewage in the open
- Strict washing of hands before preparing or eating food and after every toilet visit
- Trimming the nails of the hands short
- Careful cleaning of vegetables and meat
- Drinking clean boiled water
- Eating well-cooked food

Using a broad-spectrum anti-worm medicine regularly at the intervals of 6 months is sometimes advised for children living in areas with poor sanitation. But to be really effective for the entire community, the medicine has to be administered as a mass treatment.

11

Growing Pains

Scenario

"She is an active child. She keeps running and jumping all day long. But at bedtime, she starts complaining of pain in her legs. Sometimes she even wakes up from sleep with the same complaint. Then we give a little massage and she feels better."

This is 6-year-old Aarti Desai's problem, and it is shared by many children in her age group. The doctor has examined her and reassured her parents that it is nothing serious, just 'growing pains'.

Discussion

Growing pains are recurring but essentially harmless leg pains, which usually affect children of 5–12 years of age. Typically, the pains occur in the evening or in the night after hectic daytime activity.

Growing pains occur around and behind the knees and in the calves, the thighs and sometimes in the shins. Sometimes they can occur in upper limbs.

They do not cause limping but can sometimes disturb sleep.

Causes and outcome

The exact cause for the occurrence of growing pains is not known but is thought to be a mild repetitive stress injury to growing bones. These pains are often recurrent and may even occur over months or years. The main thing to remember is that they are harmless and the child eventually outgrows them.

Diagnosis

The following help differentiate the benign growing pains from other limb pains with serious causes:

- Total relief by the following morning
- No signs of inflammation like swelling, redness or warmth
- No other symptoms or signs

- Normal growth and development
- Normal investigation results (CBC, ESR, x-rays etc, though usually unnecessary)

Management

These pains are easily managed at home by locally applying warmth, rubbing the affected areas, using analgesics like paracetamol and doing thigh and leg muscle stretching exercises.

12

Diaper (Nappy) Rash

Scenario

Rekha's 9-months-old baby has been fussy and cranky for the last two days. While changing her diaper, Rekha notices that the baby's bottom is red and slightly swollen. Over the last few days, she had observed some redness there, but now it is looking much more severe. It also seems to be sore.

Rekha calls up her doctor, who tells her that the baby is most probably suffering from a diaper rash or nappy rash, which may have got infected.

Discussion

Diaper rash or nappy rash is a very common skin condition affecting babies and toddlers who are not yet toilet trained and who require multiple nappy changes through the day. It is especially common between 9 and 12 months of age.

Note that not all rashes in the diaper area are diaper rashes. Sometimes the diaper area may have other rashes such as seborrheic dermatitis. But usually those rashes are not limited to only the diaper area and are more generalised. That means, even if such rashes first appear in the diaper area, they will soon appear on other areas of the body. Diaper rash is typically localised to the area covered by the diaper.

Causes

The simple diaper rash happens when the skin becomes irritated and inflamed from being in contact with a wet or soiled diaper for a long time. The irritation is caused by moisture, friction and the chemicals in urine, stools or the diaper. The inflamed skin loses its 'protective barrier' function, giving a chance to secondary infections by bacteria or yeasts (like candida) to invade the body.

Infrequent changing of diapers (especially at nights) and frequent stools (because of gastrointestinal infection or antibiotic use) are the common factors leading to diaper rash.

Both cotton nappies and readymade diapers can cause nappy rash. Neither is found to be superior. The key is to change nappies frequently and to avoid leaving wet or soiled nappy on the baby for a long time.

Cotton by itself is well-tolerated clothing, but the baby's skin may react to the detergents, bleach or fabric-softeners used for washing these reusable nappies.

Among readymade, disposable diapers, even the so-called super-re-absorbent types cannot totally avoid moisture or nappy rash. Sometimes the baby may show sensitivity to the plastic covering or the gel used in such diapers.

Appearance

The simple diaper rash is typically seen in the area covered by the nappy. It is a red, raised, scaly rash on the genitals, groins, buttocks and the skin coming in contact with the outer edges of the diaper.

When the rash is infected with a fungus (yeast) like candida, it becomes bright red, itchy and produces a burning sensation. Such a rash shows small red spots (satellite lesions) near but outside the main rash area. This type is especially common when the baby is on antibiotics.

When diaper rash is infected with bacteria, it becomes bright red, warm, swollen and tender.

Management

Keep the affected area open as much as possible. The exposure of skin to air will keep it dry and help it heal faster.

Change diapers frequently, that is, every 2–3 hours.

Clean the soiled diaper area with cotton dipped in lukewarm water. Use mild baby soap if necessary. Avoid using marketed readymade baby-wipes as their frequent use often irritates the skin further.

After cleaning, pat dry the affected area. Don't rub it. Apply a light layer of a specifically formulated diaper-rash cream to the diaper area at every change.

Depending on the severity and type of diaper rash, the doctor may prescribe a plain barrier cream (with zinc oxide or petroleum jelly), an antibiotic cream, an anti-fungal cream or an anti-inflammatory steroid cream.

Prevention

Don't use too tight diapers, too much barrier cream or any talcum powder. All these factors reduce aeration of the skin and facilitate diaper rash formation.

If you use cotton nappies, make sure that they are washed with mild detergents and rinse well so that no trace of cleaning material remains in them. Avoid using bleach or fabric softeners.

Frequent changing of diapers; good cleaning of the soiled nappy area with cotton, lukewarm water and mild baby soap; avoiding regular use of readymade baby-wipes, patting the wet skin dry and applying simple barrier cream (zinc-based protective cream) are as effective measures in prevention as they are in the treatment of diaper rash.

13

Atopic Eczema

Scenario

From his 2nd month onwards, Shailesh started showing a dry reddish itchy rash on his cheeks and forehead. Later, a similar rash also appeared on the outer surfaces of his elbows and knees. The red, round, rough patches of the rash sometimes would disappear completely but then would flare-up again.

Shailesh's parents sought medical opinion and were told that it is a condition called atopic eczema. They were also told that they would have to be patient about handling this rash as it is likely to bother Shailesh for a few years. They were given a regular skin-care schedule and told how to manage this rash.

Shailesh is 6 years old now and mostly free of this rash. But his mother still takes care to follow his skin-care schedule.

Discussion

Atopic eczema, also known as atopic dermatitis or allergic eczema, is a very common skin condition that affects almost 5% of children.

The condition usually begins in early infancy; 60% of atopic eczema cases begin in the 1st year and almost 90% by 5 years.

Disturbingly, this problem is becoming more common in urban populations.

Causes

Like most complex illnesses we are stumped for an exact answer. But here are some factors:

- Genes play a major role judging from the fact that there is a strong family history of allergic conditions in affected individuals.
- The environment also plays a role. Often, a genetically prone individual starts showing the manifestations after moving from

a rural to an urban area or from an area of high humidity to one of low humidity.
- Allergy (hypersensitivity due to disturbed immune mechanisms) is the main culprit.

Manifestations

Some characteristic features of atopic eczema rashes are:
- Itching
- Redness
- Papules (small raised skin spots)
- Varying skin colour in different parts of the body
- Lichenification (dry, thickened, darkened skin areas with increased crisscrossing texture)
- Some degree of skin dryness
- Chronic and recurrent nature of the rash
- Strong family history of allergic disorders (asthma, allergic rhinitis or atopic eczema)

Types of atopic eczema

According to the age at which it begins, there are three types of atopic eczema—infantile eczema (2 months–5 years), childhood eczema (5–12 years) and adulthood eczema.

Infantile atopic eczema starts on the face, mainly on the cheeks, and later spreads to the outer surfaces of limbs, sparing the diaper area. This is the commonest type of allergic eczema and usually subsides by school age if managed well.

Childhood atopic eczema involves the neck and the inner surfaces of limbs. Most of these cases subside by adolescence.

Adulthood eczema has a distribution pattern similar to the childhood variety but is more widespread and has more lichenification.

Itch-scratch cycle

The eczema rash is very itchy. Scratching the skin to relieve the itch breaks open the already dry, damaged skin and makes it more prone to infections, mainly to the staphylococci bacteria. Some other bacteria and viruses are also likely to invade and infect such broken skin.

Any such infection then makes the rash worse. Infected eczema suddenly becomes more red and crusty. It starts oozing and shows pus-filled boils and blisters.

Management

The management of atopic eczema is based on following principles: 1. Avoid the triggers for flare-ups. 2. Break the itch-scratch cycle through good moisturisation of the skin and use of anti-itching (anti-allergic) medicines. 3. Use adequate appropriate anti-inflammatory topical steroid treatment.

The trigger factors to avoid are:

- Dust-mite exposure (thick carpets, curtains, or blankets; stuffed toys; feathered pillows)
- Extremes of temperature and humidity
- Stress
- Infections
- Woollen or synthetic clothes
- Harsh soaps and detergents
- Fabric softeners and bleach
- Skin-care products containing alcohol
- Swimming or bathing in chlorinated water

Although in some infants and pre-school children, foods like cow's milk, fish, eggs or soya can act as triggers, it is unwise to eliminate these foods without a detailed medical evaluation to find out whether your child is allergic to the food. Avoiding specific foods without a proven allergy is usually not helpful and it is more likely to cause nutritional deficiencies. Only in very severe and resistant cases is the role of food allergy evaluated medically through 'food challenge' and allergy tests.

The prime aim in management is to **break the vicious itch-scratch cycle**. This can be done in various ways, but scolding the child not to scratch is not a solution.

Gentle rubbing of the skin and applying cool water-soaked cloth gives some relief from the itching sensation.

Trimming the nails short daily and wearing cotton mittens (gloves) are useful to minimise harm from scratching.

Moisturising creams and lotions are of central importance in reducing dryness and itching.

Sedative anti-histaminic (anti-allergic) medicines are useful to control itching and also help the child get enough sleep.

Moisturisers or emollients

Dryness of the skin is a factor in eczema and needs to be controlled. That is where moisturisers help. They control skin dryness by putting an oily layer on the skin that reduces the evaporation of water through the skin pores and thus improves hydration of the skin.

White soft paraffin, petroleum jelly and glycerine-based emollients can usually be used safely and effectively as ointments, creams or baths. Special bath oils, mineral oil, and coconut, olive or almond oil are also commonly used to reduce skin dryness.

The best way of applying any emollient is immediately after the bath on the still-moist skin to trap the moisture inside the skin.

Bathing

Bathing strategy for eczema varies from patient to patient. Some children do well with multiple (up to 4 per day) short baths or showers followed by emollient application. Others are better off avoiding baths and having an occasional shower.

Glycerine soaps, emollient soaps, emollient liquids, oil baths—with so many choices available, one tends to get confused. But no one product can be endorsed as the best. It is more a matter of trial and error to find the product best suited to a particular patient.

Most patients should do well with the following bathing tips:

- Keep the bathing time short (5–10 minutes).
- Use lukewarm or warm water and avoid hot water.
- Use mild non-perfumed moisturising soaps, shampoos and bath oils, preferably after consulting your doctor.
- After the bath, lightly dab the skin dry but do not rub it hard.
- On the slightly moist after-bath skin, immediately apply the moisturiser cream or lotion.
- Avoid harsh soaps and shampoos and skin-care products containing alcohol.

Topical steroids

Topical steroids (ointments, creams, lotions) reduce the itching, redness and inflammation. Oral steroids are usually unnecessary in atopic eczema.

When proper potency of the preparation is chosen, topical steroids are quite safe and very effective in controlling flare-ups. They are used in the lowest possible potency and for short periods of 2–3 weeks to avoid side effects like skin atrophy and other complications of steroid therapy.

There is a tendency among parents to minimise the use of steroid applications on their own judgement. This is mostly done out of fear of steroid side effects. But when used as per the doctor's instructions, these applications are useful as well as safe. Not using them adequately is perhaps the most common cause of unsatisfactory control of atopic dermatitis.

Only in suspected secondary bacterial infections are topical or oral antibiotics used. A complicated herpes virus infection of eczema needs antiviral medicines.

Outcome

Like many chronic illnesses (asthma, diabetes, essential hypertension), atopic eczema cannot be 'cured' by medicines but rather needs to be 'controlled'. It has a waxing-waning (up-and-down) course in which there are periodic flare-ups alternating with relatively quiet periods.

Fortunately, it has a very good outcome and tends to be self-limited in most patients who experience remission by 3–5 years of age. As many as 75% of patients outgrow this problem by adolescence.

Final word of advice

Atopic eczema has an up-and-down course. It is a self-limited disease and has an excellent prognosis.

Breaking the itch-scratch cycle by improving skin hydration (moisturisers) and using anti-allergic medicines, along with adequate anti-inflammatory measures (topical steroids), is the mainstay of treatment.

Diet changes are usually unnecessary.

14

Asthma

Scenario

Prathamesh is a week away from his second birthday. In these 12 months, he has suffered from four episodes of severe breathlessness, which were without fever but had a peculiar whistling sound from the chest. All these episodes needed hospitalisation.

Sandra is a fifth standard school student. She has a long-standing dry cough, which particularly bothers her at night or sometimes in the early morning. This cough also bothers her whenever she exerts herself or plays in the playground. Even when she doesn't have a cough, she feels tired and sometimes complains that her chest feels tight.

In both cases, after all the check-ups, the doctors have arrived at the same diagnosis. Both Prathamesh and Sandra are suffering from asthma.

Discussion

Seeing your child struggle for breath, looking all sweaty and doubling up with terrible cough and noisy breathing is not a pleasant experience. To see this happen repeatedly is even worse. Asthma does precisely this, and that's why it is one of the most feared illnesses. On top of that, it is a prolonged illness with no permanent cure. But, with proper precautions and treatment, asthma can be controlled quite well.

As the worldwide incidence of asthma increases at an alarming rate, it is wise to get some information about this important medical condition.

Asthma

When we breathe, the air is inhaled through the nose and passes through the windpipe into a set of branching airways, called the bronchi and bronchioles, which traverse through lung tissue and carry it to the small sacs in the lungs called alveoli. In the alveoli, the oxygen in the air is used to purify the blood.

In asthma, the small airways inside the lungs are hypersensitive. They react excessively to some triggers and become inflamed. They then become narrow and are filled up with mucus (phlegm). As less air can pass through the narrowed and congested airways, the patient experiences difficulty in breathing. The body tries to clear the mucus, which causes cough. There is wheezing, a whistling breezy sound from the chest, which is caused by air passing through the obstructed airways.

These symptoms fluctuate. They suddenly flare up and then subside. Between the symptom-free periods and the flare-ups, there are nagging symptoms such as night or early morning cough, tiredness, tightness of the chest and cough after exertion.

Danger signals

A prompt visit to hospital is needed in asthma attacks with the following danger signals:

- Increased wheezing sound
- Rapid breathing
- Increasing distress while breathing (flaring of nostrils or sucking in of chest or abdomen)
- Lips or nails turning blue or black
- Difficulty in talking or walking
- Disappearance of wheezing sound with continuing breathing difficulty, which usually indicates very severe airway blockage.

(It may seem contradictory that greater wheezing and no wheezing are both danger signals. Here's why. The wheezing sound indicates obstruction in the airway. Greater obstruction means greater wheezing. However, the obstruction may increase to a point where even a little air cannot pass through. Disappearance of wheezing is a good sign only if the breathing is easier.)

Characteristics of asthma

Asthma is a **lifelong condition**. The lung airway sensitivity in an asthma patient is likely to last throughout life. But it often shows dramatic improvement by adolescence and may remain dormant for many years. But it can reappear when patient enters the 30s or 40s.

With proper understanding, strategy and treatment, we can control asthma almost completely. Patients with well-controlled asthma can lead perfectly normal lives.

Wheezing is different from asthma though it is an important diagnostic feature of asthma. Wheezing can also be heard in some lung infections and with some congenital anatomic abnormalities of airways.

Often, there is an unfortunate tendency among doctors to convey the diagnosis of asthma as a 'wheezing tendency' because that somehow seems to be more acceptable to parents and patients who find the diagnosis of asthma too overwhelming.

Practically speaking, repeated wheezing episodes without any accompanying fever usually indicate the presence of asthma.

Asthma is often an **inherited condition**. The likelihood of asthma is higher in a child whose parents, siblings or close relatives have asthma or other allergic disorders. But not all cases have a positive family history.

Unfortunately, no age is exempt from asthma and it **can even start in infancy**.

Triggers

The following factors often trigger asthma flare-ups:

- Viral infections like influenza
- Exercise
- Allergies (to dust mites, pollens, grasses, moulds, cockroaches, animal dander, medicines and foods)
- Smoke
- Air pollutants
- Fog or smog
- Changes in weather
- Cold air exposure
- Strong smells (paints, perfumes and deodorants)

Role of allergy

Even though the triggers for asthma attacks differ, allergy plays a role in a majority of them. Often, asthma patients have other allergic illnesses.

Allergy is a hypersensitive, exaggerated response from body's immune system to factors outside or inside the body. The simplest analogy is that of a highly sensitive and irritable person. Most people would tolerate a casual remark with good humour, but the same remark can make an irritable man have a fit of anger. The same thing happens in allergy, and even a minor irritant triggers a severe reaction.

Diagnosis

A detailed history and physical examination, especially during an attack, reveal the possibility of asthma. These are more important than lab investigations in diagnosis.

A complete blood count and a chest x-ray are a part of initial evaluation.

Special lung function tests help to judge lung performance and detect airway obstruction. Allergy tests are sometimes needed in suspected cases of asthma.

Peak-flow meter is a simple diagnostic device, which can be used even at home to monitor the severity of asthma and the progress of treatment. It is a tubular instrument into which the patient blows after full inhalation. The reading shows the level of air-flow to give an idea about airway obstruction that is otherwise not obvious.

Treatment

It is important to understand that asthma is a long-term chronic problem with a waxing-waning pattern. Currently, there is no permanent cure for it. But with a proper treatment strategy, it can be controlled very well. So the aim of treatment is to ensure good control of symptoms and prevention of flare-ups.

The steps to effective asthma treatment are:

1. Identifying and eliminating asthma triggers
2. Prompt treatment of acute attacks
3. Planning long-term strategy to control symptoms and prevent flare-ups

Different patients may need different medicines according to the frequency and severity of their symptoms. Some medicines are used for short-term and for immediate relief. Some are used for long- term control and prevention. Some of these medicines are given orally and some are given through inhalers or nebulisers.

Nebulisers and inhalers

Nebulisers and metered dose inhalers (MDIs) used in the treatment of asthma deliver anti-asthmatic medicines directly to the lungs bringing instant relief from symptoms. MDIs can even be carried on the person, which allows flexible and timely treatment according to the patient's need. That's why modern treatment of asthma relies a lot on them.

Because asthma is a chronic and recurrent condition, these inhalations may be needed repeatedly. But that does not mean that patients become dependent on them.

Don't be afraid to use these 'new' treatments like nebulisers or MDIs if they are prescribed by a doctor. They are quite safe and effective.

Spacers and masks with MDIs

Using MDIs directly requires a certain control and coordination of breathing in and out. Most children lack such control and coordination. A spacer and an airway mask are used for children to make sure that the medicine from the inhaler is fully and properly going into the patient's lungs.

The MDI is attached at one end of the spacer, which is a cylindrical holding chamber. At the other end, an airway mask is attached. The medicine dose puffed out of the MDI enters the spacer, which holds it so that the child can normally inhale it from the mask placed on his mouth and nose.

Steroids

The main problem in asthma is the chronic inflammation of small airways in lungs. Steroids are potent anti-inflammatory medicines and hence, very useful in the treatment of moderate or severe asthma cases.

Steroid inhalers, injections and oral preparations are sometimes needed in asthma treatment. If used as per medical advice, they are safe and invaluable in treating severe asthma cases and achieving long-term control.

General helpful measures

If your child is diagnosed with asthma, discuss the condition and treatment in detail with your doctor. Clear your misconceptions and misapprehensions.

Follow the treatment plan correctly, using medicines in proper doses and for proper duration. Learn the correct use of MDIs and spacers.

Get your child the yearly flu (influenza) vaccination as flu is one of the triggers.

Protect your child against dust mite exposure. Minimise or preferably avoid carpets, curtains, thick clothed sofas, thick blankets and stuffed toys, all of which accumulate dust and dust-mites. To keep clean the items you must use, regularly vacuum the house including carpets, curtains, and sofas; use dust-mite-proof covers for mattresses and pillows; and wash blankets, bedsheets and pillow covers weekly in hot (120°F) water.

Avoid irritants such as smoke (including cigarette smoke), strong smells (paints, perfumes, deodorants, hair sprays), and pollution. Avoid exposure to pets. Reduce exposure to pollen. Keep the doors and windows closed in pollen season. Have the child take a bath and change clothes after any activity outside the home.

Fried foods, excessively spicy foods, excessively cold foods (juices, colas or ice creams) and foods with artificial flavours or colours should be avoided.

Avoid going out in extreme weathers and in foggy conditions.

Myth	Reality
Asthma cannot be treated.	Asthma does not have a permanent cure but can be fully controlled with proper treatment measures.
Asthma severely limits growth, activity and life in general.	Patients with well-controlled asthma lead perfectly normal, happy and productive lives.
Inhalers (MDIs) are to be avoided as they make the patient dependent.	Inhalers (MDIs) are very safe and effective in the treatment of asthma. They don't cause dependence.
Steroids are harmful medicines which should be avoided at all costs.	Steroids are very effective and, at times, life-saving medicines. They can be safely taken under a doctor's guidance.

15

Croup or Barking Cough

Scenario

Winter has set in. It's four o'clock in the morning. The sound of a strange heavy, hoarse, barking cough rattles through the house. Both parents awake up to find their toddler sitting up and producing those horrible coughing sounds. To their horror, they also hear him inhale with a rasping, grating sound. At this, they feel at the end of their wits and become panicky.

That's how 'croup' usually announces its arrival.

Discussion

Croup is not a single illness but a term collectively used for a group of illnesses, all of which are caused by inflammation and obstruction of the air passage at the level of the larynx (voice box). All these illnesses lead to varying degrees of hoarseness, cough and a grating sound when inhaling called inspiratory stridor.

Types of croup

Viral croup, which is caused by parainfluenza and influenza viruses, is the commonest variety. It mainly strikes in winter. The age group susceptible to this type is 3 months to 3 years.

This type of croup usually starts as common cold and, over 2–3 days, shows its true character with barking cough, hoarseness and stridor. Often, a family member may have a minor upper respiratory infection at the same time. The fever is mild or even absent.

Most of these cases are mild and can be managed at home. Some severe cases need hospitalisation.

Allergic croup has manifestations almost the same as viral croup, but they tend to be recurrent in nature. The episodes usually occur at night and don't start with upper respiratory infection.

An allergy in addition to viral infection is a simplified scientific explanation for this type.

Although individual episodes of this condition tend to be mild and self-limited, many cases tend to progress to asthma.

Bacterial croup may be caused by H. influenzae type-b (Hib) bacteria and inflammation of the epiglottis, which is the opening of the voice box. This 'epiglottitis' is a medical emergency and needs urgent expert management in a hospital as the obstruction of this area can progress very rapidly and block the airway completely.

The age group likely to suffer this type is 2–6 years.

Sick look, painful sore throat, drooling of saliva and high fever are clues to the presence of this condition. The characteristic barking cough is not seen in this condition and stridor is much softer in this type compared to viral or allergic variety.

An affected child often sits leaning forward with extended neck, open mouth and protruding tongue.

Management at home

Viral and allergic croup can be managed at home by following some simple instructions.

Hold the baby upright or make her sit in your lap. Older children are usually better off sitting independently and leaning forward.

Don't panic. Reassure the young patient that everything is going to be fine. Try to distract her by telling a story. Agitation or crying only makes croup worse, so try and avoid that.

Exposure to humidified outside air for 15–20 minutes often gives dramatic relief. An easy way of humidifying the air in your home is to open the hot water tap in the bathroom and let it run for few minutes. The bathroom air will be humidified with warm mist. Stand there with the patient for 15–20 minutes. Humidifiers delivering cool or warm mist are the best apparatuses for this purpose. Remember that warm mist must be given at a safe distance to avoid scalds and burns.

Avoid over-the-counter cough syrups as they are useless and can even prove harmful.

Vaccinations against influenza and Hib infections are useful as preventive measures.

Watch for the following danger signals and never delay taking a medical opinion if in doubt.

- Laboured, distressed and rapid breathing
- Increasingly severe or continuous stridor
- Loss of voice
- High fever
- Drooling of saliva
- Difficulty in swallowing
- Excessive lethargy or agitation
- Sick look
- Lips turning blue or pale

Treatment in hospital

Severe cases of viral and allergic croup and all cases of bacterial croup should be treated in a hospital. The doctor will first rule out similar illnesses and then decide the treatment.

Humidified oxygen, nebulizers, antibiotics and other medicines are used according to the type of croup. In very severe cases, respiratory support is needed in the ICU set-up.

Final word of advice

Croup is a common condition in early childhood and, although frightening, requires only patience, reassurance and mist inhalation in most cases. Remaining alert to danger signals and seeking medical help unhesitatingly are the ways to avoid any unpleasant complications.

16

Nosebleed

Scenario

When 5-year-old Akshay wakes up, he sees fresh blood on his pillow. He also feels as if his nose is very sticky and wet. As he runs to his mother to share his discovery, she screams, "What happened to you? Why is your nose bleeding?"

Discussion

Nosebleed, also known as epistaxis, is a rather common and frightening but mostly harmless occurrence. It is more common in children from 3 to 10 years of age but can happen at any age. It is more common in winters and in dry, cold climates.

Causes

The commonest conditions for nosebleeds are when a person has a cold or a nasal discharge as a result of an infection or an allergy. The inner lining of the nose is inflamed. Frequently and forcefully blowing or wiping the nose easily injures that inflamed nasal lining and weakens the small blood vessels there.

Cold medicines (decongestants and antihistamines) and dry, cold air can dry the nasal secretions and lead to formation of crusts on the inner nasal lining. The lining is injured when these crusts are forcibly removed by picking the nose (putting a finger in the nose).

These minor injuries to the nasal lining (through blowing, wiping and nose-picking) ultimately cause bleeding from the weakened small blood vessels situated in the front part of the nose.

There are a few other causes of nosebleeds.

External injury to nose can happen as a result of accidental bumps in infants or toddlers who are yet to master walking and running. In older children, it can happen during cycling, contact sports or fights.

In accidental insertion of foreign body into nose—when an object gets into the child's nose—the bleeding usually happens from one nostril, often with foul smelling nasal discharge.

In bleeding disorders or cancers the nosebleeds are frequent and usually associated with easy bruising.

Congenitally malformed nasal blood vessels are another possible cause. Medicines that interfere with blood clotting can also cause nosebleeds.

High blood pressure is an uncommon cause of nosebleeds in children and never causes nosebleeds alone.

Management at home

Make the child sit leaning forwards, on a chair or preferably held in your lap. Do not make the child lie down or lean backwards. This allows the blood to trickle down the throat. Because the blood is sticky and bitter, it often induces coughing, vomiting or choking.

Keep the child relaxed by talking to him or making him watch television. Do not panic yourself. Most of the nosebleeds are ultimately harmless.

Firmly pinch the lower, softer part of the nose, the part just below the bony ridge. This will exert pressure on bleeding blood vessels and eventually stop the bleeding. Do not release the pressure to see if the bleeding has stopped. Maintain firm pressure continuously for 10 minutes. Time it using a watch or a clock.

You can use a tissue or a soft cloth while pinching. There is no need to use an icepack. It is not useful.

If the bleeding has not stopped after 10 minutes of firm pressure, take the child to the doctor. But continue the firm pressure on the nose while on the way.

If the bleeding stops, then discourage the child from nose-picking. Do not allow rough physical play for a day or two.

Prevention

In case of frequent nosebleeds, get a thorough medical check-up and investigations done to rule out the more serious causes of nosebleeds.

If the nosebleed is happening because of crusting, keep the nasal cavity moist and clean through saline nasal drops or low-pressure saline sprays. Soften the inner nasal lining by lubricating it with petroleum jelly. Keep the child's nails trimmed.

Use appropriate protective gear for sports where nose injury is likely.

If a weakened blood vessel is repeatedly bleeding, the doctor may seal it by cauterising it. If a foreign body is detected in the nose, a specialist doctor should remove it.

Final word of advice

Even though nosebleeds look terrifying, most of them are ultimately harmless and can be managed just by exerting firm pressure on the lower soft part of the nose.

Frequent nosebleeds need to be thoroughly investigated to rule out more serious causes.

17

Tonsils and Adenoids

Scenario

Nisha's mother is worried. The doctor has suggested a tonsil and adenoid surgery for Nisha, who is 9 years old and has suffered from recurring severe throat infections and continuous mouth-breathing for the last 3 years.

Her mother is unsure about the surgery. She wants to know more about these problems.

Discussion

Tonsils and adenoids are made up of lymphatic tissue that produces antibodies. They act like guards protecting the respiratory tract. They filter the inhaled air by trapping foreign particles, including bacteria, and eliminate them through the action of the antibodies.

Tonsils are situated at the back of the throat and if they are enlarged, we can see them there as soon as the patient opens his mouth. Adenoids are situated behind the nose and above the throat. They are covered by the soft palate and are not seen easily.

Enlarged tonsils and adenoids

Abnormal enlargement (hypertrophy) of tonsils and adenoids occurs when their lymphoid tissue starts working overtime as a result of a chronic infection or an allergy. Once enlarged, they lose their protective role and instead become easy targets for infections. They also start blocking the respiratory passage. Enlarged tonsils also block the passage of food. This results in the following symptoms:

- Difficulty in swallowing solid foods (in severe tonsil enlargement)
- Snoring
- Mouth breathing
- Sleep disturbances

- Increased risk of throat, sinus and ear infections
- Sleep apnoea, or intermittent stoppages of breathing during sleep, leading to slowing of the heart rate and decreased oxygenation of blood (In the long run, sleep apnoea causes overwork, strain and even enlargement of the right side of heart.)

Tonsillitis and surgery

Acute tonsillitis, which is an acute infection of tonsils, causes them to become enlarged, severely congested and red. Sometimes we may see pus spots on them. Throat pain, fever, difficulty in swallowing and enlarged neck glands are other common symptoms.

Usually this infection is caused by a specific group of bacteria called Group B Streptococci. With appropriate antibiotics, the infection subsides and the size of the tonsils returns to normal.

If the tonsils were already hypertrophied before the infection, when the infection is treated the size of the tonsils remains enlarged but the congestion subsides.

Significant, recurrent tonsillitis is an indication for tonsil surgery, or tonsillectomy. Significant and recurrent here means seven episodes in 1 year or five episodes every year for 2 successive years or three episodes every year for 3 successive years.

Among other indications are:

- 'Kissing tonsils', which are severely enlarged tonsils that touch each other at the midline and block the airway
- Continuous mouth breathing and snoring with enlarged tonsils
- Episodes of sleep apnoea with enlarged tonsils
- Enlarged tonsils that have become chronic 'carriers' of Group B streptococci in spite of medical treatment with antibiotics
- Tonsil abscess, bleeding or tumour (in rare cases)

Enlarged adenoids

We suspect enlarged adenoids in the following conditions:

- Repeated upper respiratory tract infections involving the nose, the throat, the sinuses and the ears
- Persistent thick pus-like nasal discharge, bad breath, mouth breathing or snoring
- Nasal-sounding voice
- Recurrent sleep apnoea

These are indicators that enlarged, and sometimes infected, adenoids might be present, especially if the tonsils are normal in size. Even when tonsils are enlarged, simultaneous adenoid enlargement is possible and should be ruled out by a doctor.

Management

Humidification of air (cold mist humidifier), nasal drops, decongestants, anti-allergic medicines and antibiotics are used with varying degree of success to treat adenoid problems.

The failure of medical treatment and significant symptoms, together with x-rays showing enlargement of adenoids, necessitates adenoidectomy, which is surgical removal of adenoids.

Removal of adenoids and tonsils

The removal of adenoids and tonsils **does not hamper immunity or growth**. There is no negative effect on immunity or growth of the individual whose tonsils and/or adenoids are removed. In fact, many operated patients may show improved growth as their recurrent infections are reduced, leading to better food intake.

If symptoms or complications are significant and severe, these operations can be performed **at any age** according to the surgeon's decision. The operations are fairly common, not too time-consuming and usually without major complications.

In moderate cases, a **wait-and-watch policy** is adopted up to the age of 6 or 7 years. This is done because the lymphatic tissues naturally become less active after that age, which may result in spontaneous shrinking of enlarged tonsils and adenoids.

18

Middle Ear Infection

Scenario

Pratik is a 2-year-old is in the doctor's office, clutching at his right ear and crying loudly. Almost shouting to make herself heard over the wailing, the mother recounts the ordeal.

"Doctor, at night, he was lying down in his crib as usual and having his bottle-feed. But then suddenly he started crying loudly and kept pulling at his right ear. He wouldn't even allow us to touch that ear. I put some warm oil into the ear but the pain did not ease."

The doctor examines the boy's right ear with an otoscope and says, "It seems that your child is suffering from a middle-ear infection."

Discussion

Middle-ear infection, or otitis media (OM), is the second most common childhood disease. Two-thirds of all children suffer from at least one ear infection by their second birthday. Almost 80% of these cases are caused by bacteria and the rest by viruses. Such infections show a strong tendency to recur, and their complications may have long-term effects on hearing, speech and mental development. Otitis media can be acute or chronic.

Risk factors for OM

OM is more common in winter and spring months. It affects children between 6 months and 6 years of age. More boys than girls suffer the condition.

Congenital anatomic problems like cleft palate and weakened immunity are risk factors for OM. Bottle-feeding, particularly in a lying-down position, worsens the risk as does barotrauma, which is pressure injury to the eardrum because of diving or flying in an airplane. Parental smoking is also a risk factor.

Symptoms of AOM

Acute otitis media (AOM) usually starts after about a week after a bout of cold. Fever, ear fullness or pain, decreased hearing and sometimes ear discharge (pus-like or bloody) are the usual symptoms.

In infants and toddlers, the important, and sometimes the only, clues are irritability, excessive crying, refusal to feed and pulling at the ears.

The pain of AOM is worst when the pus is accumulating behind the eardrum, causing it to bulge outwards. When the eardrum ruptures and the pus flows out, the pain subsides. The tear in the eardrum usually heals within a week or two.

Treatment

A **wait-and-watch policy** is advised if the ear infection seems to be viral or is mild in nature.

Prompt, appropriate and adequate **oral antibiotic therapy** is needed in moderate to severe bacterial infections. The duration is 7–10 days, but single high-dose, appropriate antibiotic injections also work well.

Analgesics and antipyretics, which are medicines like paracetamol or ibuprofen, are used to control pain and fever.

Avoid over-the-counter **cough and cold syrups** for a child below the age of 6 years. Instead, just keep the nose clear by frequent use of **saline nose drops or saline nose sprays**.

Antibiotic eardrops alone are not sufficient to treat AOM and are useful only to keep external ear canal free of bacteria when the eardrum has perforated and pus is oozing. **Pain-relieving eardrops** are sometimes useful in cases of severe pain prior to perforation.

Surgical removal of pus is done by puncturing the eardrum with a needle and sucking out the pus into the attached syringe. It is necessary when AOM is unresponsive to antibiotics after 24–48 hours or for very young or immune deficient patients. The removal of pus not only helps to relieve the pressure and pain but also to identify the type of bacteria and choose the right antibiotic.

Middle ear fluid collection (Glue ear)

In many middle ear infections, there is some degree of fluid collection (effusion) behind the eardrum. This condition is called otitis media with effusion or chronic otitis media or glue ear. The condition is quite common and, up to 3 weeks after the middle ear infection, fluid can be seen in almost 50% of cases. But in 9 out of 10 such cases, the fluid disappears within three months even without any treatment.

Tube inserted in the ear

In some cases, the ENT surgeon places a small ventilating ear-tube (a grommet) in the ear by making a small cut in the eardrum. Such an ear-tube is made up of metal or plastic. It helps to ventilate and drain the middle ear space and significantly reduces the recurrence of middle ear infection. Such a tube stays in the ear for a period of 6 months to 3 years. Then as the eardrum starts to heal, the tube is slowly pushed out and usually falls out on its own.

Ear-tube insertion is advised in the following cases:

- Fluid in both middle ears for more than 3 months
- Fluid in one middle ear for more than 6 months
- Frequent recurrences of middle ear infection (more than three in the previous 6 months or more than five in the previous 12 months)

Complications

The following are some serious complications in untreated acute middle ear infection, but they are rare:

- Hearing loss
- Permanent hole in the eardrum
- Long-term fluid collection in the middle ear
- Chronic middle ear infection with ear discharge
- Cholestatoma (a cyst like growth)
- Infection of skull bones (petrositis and mastoiditis)

Investigations

A routine AOM episode usually does not warrant any investigation. Only in recurrent AOM are investigations done to rule out underlying causes like respiratory allergy, immune deficiency, hidden cleft palate or enlarged adenoids. Two important tests are tympanometry to check middle ear pressures and audiometry to check hearing.

Final word of advice

Never take any ear infection lightly or treat it yourself. Always get medical opinion and follow the advice thoroughly.

19

Hearing Loss or Deafness

Scenario

Rahim is 3 years old. Since infancy, he has suffered from recurrent colds and middle ear infections. He started speaking late. Now his parents have observed that Rahim does not respond when they call him. He is not startled even at a loud sound such as an alarm clock ringing.

After examining him, the doctor says that Rahim is suffering from hearing loss and needs immediate detailed evaluation and treatment.

Rahim was found have a moderate to severe degree of hearing loss, which was partially corrected after treatment of his middle ear problem. He was then prescribed hearing aids for both ears. After using them, both his hearing and speech have improved dramatically.

Discussion

Hearing is a complex process. Sound waves enter the ear through the outer ear. They travel across the membrane called the eardrum. The eardrum and three small interconnected middle ear bones (ossicles) vibrate when sound waves pass through. These vibrations amplify (strengthen) the sound waves. The amplified sound waves reach the inner ear, where a snail-shaped organ called the cochlea further amplifies these waves and then converts them into electrical nerve signals. The nerve signals are carried by the auditory nerve to the brain's auditory (hearing) area, where they are decoded and interpreted as meaningful sounds.

Hearing loss takes place when this hearing process is hampered at any part of this pathway. As hearing is so important in any individual's speech, language, social, emotional and educational development, even mild hearing loss in a child can cause serious problems. That is why it needs to be detected and treated at the earliest.

According to the World Health Organisation fact sheet, 5% of the global population, which is about 360 million people, suffer from hearing loss severe enough to be considered a disability. Out of those sufferers, 32 million are children.

Symptoms

In **infants**, lack of response to speech or other sounds suggests hearing loss. The normal responses are being startled at a sudden or loud sound, being soothed by the mother's voice and turning the head to see the source of the sound.

Because speech is imitative, children who cannot hear do not learn to speak. A child not speaking two-syllable words such as 'mama' and 'dada' by the age of 1 year may have hearing loss.

In **older children**, delayed or unclear speech signals hearing loss. Such children may have observable difficulty in hearing at home or in the nursery or school. A clue is that the child turns up the volume of the radio, television, or music player too loud.

A child not responding to his or her name called out. A child with hearing loss takes long to understand a story, a joke or a lesson and often asks for it to be repeated. Because the child cannot hear the teacher well, he or she is usually not doing well at school.

Types of hearing loss

If the hearing loss is present at birth, it is called **congenital** hearing loss. If it develops later, it is called **acquired** hearing loss.

According to the place where hearing is hampered, hearing loss is classified as **conductive** (problem in the outer or middle ear), **sensorineural** (problem in the inner ear, the auditory nerve or the brain) or **mixed**.

Conductive hearing loss is usually **temporary**, whereas sensorineural hearing loss (also called nerve deafness) is **permanent**.

According to severity, hearing loss is classified into **mild, moderate, severe** and **profound** types.

Causes

Among the causes of **congenital hearing loss** are:

- Birth problems such as prematurity, low birth weight, stay in neonatal intensive care unit, birth hypoxia, severe newborn jaundice and unusual shape of the face, the head or the ears

- Genetic syndromes such as Down's syndrome
- Problems passed from mother such as infections (e. g., toxoplasmosis, rubella, cytomegalovirus and herpes) and use of some ototoxic or ear-damaging medicines
- Brain or central nervous system problems such as injury, infections, tumours and malformations
- Family history of congenital hearing loss
- Unknown causes in 25% of cases

Among the causes of **acquired hearing loss** are:

- Middle ear problems such as infection, hole in the eardrum, fluid behind the eardrum and middle ear bone problems
- Obstruction of outer ear by wax, a foreign body or other matter
- Damage caused by excessive noise or excessive air-pressure
- Problems of the brain or the central nervous system such as injury, infections, tumours
- Other serious infections such as measles and mumps
- Use of ototoxic medicines in the child

Treatment

The treatment depends on the underlying cause and the severity of hearing loss.

The treatment of **correctable cause** includes the following. Earwax blocking the outer ear is treated with wax-softening eardrops and wax removal. A foreign body blocking the outer ear is removed. The fluid behind the eardrum is treated with medicines or, at times, with an ear tube (grommet) insertion to drain the fluid.

Hearing aids are devices that amplify sounds and improve hearing in mild to moderate cases. They are commonly worn externally, but occasionally they are surgically fitted inside the ear.

Cochlear implants are used in severe cases where hearing aids are not helpful. These implants are special devices that are surgically fitted into the inner ear. They convert sound waves into electrochemical nerve signals.

Supportive techniques such as lip-reading, sign language and subtitled captions (for videos) are helpful when hearing loss is not adequately treatable.

Prevention

Preventive measures against hearing loss include:

- Good care of the mother and baby during pregnancy, delivery and the newborn period
- Avoiding ototoxic medicines
- Being alert to early warning signals in daily activities
- Avoiding exposure to loud noises
- Conducting hearing screening tests

Hearing tests

Hearing screening tests are done to identify individuals at risk for hearing loss. The ones found to be at high risk undergo further hearing evaluation tests that are done in much more detail. Because very small children cannot respond to questions, there are separate tests for newborn babies and for older children.

In newborns, hearing screening is done through a specialised test like the **auditory brainstem response (ABR)**, in which electrodes are placed over the head to record the electrical activity of the brain in response to sound. This test classifies the results as pass or fail, without providing details.

Oto-acoustic emission (OAE) is another newborn hearing screening test. Here, a probe is placed in the baby's ear canal, which measures the echo of the inner ear noise produced in response to sound. It provides more details about problems in the outer, middle or inner ear.

Both these tests are quick (10–15 minutes long), simple and painless. They can be done even in a sleeping baby.

In older infants, children and adults, sounds of different loudness and frequencies heard by each ear are plotted on a graph through a specialised test called **audiometry**, which is performed through various techniques, either by using pure sound tones or speech sounds.

Ideally, to do this test, the child should wear headphones and indicate that he heard a particular sound by making a gesture or by clicking a switch. In uncooperative patients, audiometry is done by making them listen to speakers in a sound booth. But in this format, it is not possible to separately detect problems of each ear.

In the 6 months to 2 years age group, audiometry is done by observing the baby's visual response to sound and in the 2–5 year age group by observing the child's play activity in response to sound.

The **recommended timing** for hearing screening test is routine screening in the newborn period (before discharge from hospital) and at school entry and at any age if there is suspicion of hearing problem.

Final word of advice

Hearing problems are very common and often are missed. Delayed speech is often associated with hearing loss.

Screening tests are very important in early identification of hearing loss. Apart from treating the underlying cause, hearing loss can be managed by using hearing aids, special implants and supportive techniques such as lip reading, sign language and subtitle captioning for videos.

20

Swimmer's Ear or (Otitis Externa)

Scenario

Sujit is a 10-year-old boy who is usually chirpy and bubbly. But today he sits quietly in front of the doctor, looking miserable and in pain. He is gingerly covering his left ear with his hand. His worried mother starts describing his problem.

"Doctor, since yesterday, Sujit's left ear is aching very badly. It hurts even more when he speaks or eats. For the last 2 weeks, since his summer vacation began, he has joined a club for swimming lessons. He complained of fullness in the left ear for the last 3–4 days, but we thought it must be normal after swimming. I even tried cleaning his ear with the earbud and kept putting drops of oil to relieve the ear block. But it did not help and now, since yesterday, he has had this unbearable pain."

The doctor examines the affected ear. Even from the outside, the ear looks red and swollen. It is very tender to the touch. Turning to Sujit's mother, the doctor declares, "This is a typical case of swimmer's ear or otitis externa. In simple words, it is an infection of the outer ear."

Discussion

Otitis externa, or swimmer's ear, is an infection of the skin of the ear canal or the outer ear or both. It usually happens after swimming or other activities that cause water to enter the ears. The resultant moisture softens the skin and facilitates the growth of bacteria (and sometimes even fungus), leading to a painful infection.

In mild cases, itchiness of the ear and a blocked ear sensation are the initial symptoms. Then, the affected ear becomes slightly red, swollen and tender.

In severe cases, the redness, swelling and pain of the outer ear are much more pronounced. The ear canal opening may close because of swelling, and we may see discharge (pus or cheesy substance) oozing out. The patient may hear less through the affected ear, but this hearing deficit is temporary and lasts only as long as the infection.

Risk factors

Summer months are the time for this infection. Activities such as swimming, diving, water sports, tub baths and prolonged showers increase the risk. The use of ear buds is a risk factor as is the frequent use of oil as ear drops. Eczema or seborrheic dermatitis can also lead to the infection.

Treatment

Antibiotic (and sometimes anti-fungal and anti-inflammatory) eardrops for 5–7 days is the treatment to clear the infection. Anti-inflammatory and analgesic medicines (like paracetamol and ibuprofen) may be given to relieve earache. Oral antibiotics are given if the infection is severe.

Administering eardrops

Have the child lie on the side with the affected ear up. Instil the eardrops so that they trickle down along the side of the ear canal. Let the child remain in the same position for a few minutes to ensure that the drops reach the deepest parts of the ear canal and do not run out.

If the ear canal opening is too narrow because of the swelling, the doctor may insert a wick of cotton or a special dressing material soaked in the medicated eardrops. The medicine seeps through the material and reaches the inner ear. In such a case, it may be necessary to put the eardrops every 3–4 hours to keep the wick wet with medicines.

Cleaning the ears

Most people are overzealous when it comes to cleaning the ears. Ear buds are the popular tools for removing water or wax from the ears. Some people even try using their fingers or sharp metal objects for this 'cleaning'.

But using a ear bud (or any pointed object) is almost a sure way of scratching and damaging the skin of the ear canal. Remember, the ear wax is not 'dirt' accumulating in the ears. It is a natural body secretion with a purpose; it is necessary to protect the inner ear from moisture, bacteria and even from accidental entry of small insects and objects. Only when ear wax is too hard or causes hearing deficit does it need to be removed and that, too, only by a trained doctor who would syringe it out after softening it with eardrops.

In daily situations, the wet ear canal needs to be cleared of excess water only with a gentle shake of the head and by inserting the corner of a cloth. A blow-dryer on a very low setting may be used but should be held at a safe distance from the ear.

Regular use of oil

Many families traditionally use warm oil (usually coconut or olive oil) as regular or emergency eardrops. It is a useless habit that carries unnecessary risks. It can lead to blockage of the skin glands or an allergic skin reaction followed by an infection. In case of an already established infection, it can worsen the situation.

Prevention

In children who get swimmer's ear frequently, the following preventive measures are useful:

- Limit stays in the water to less than 1 hour.
- Use earplugs and a bathing cap.
- Do not use ear buds or any pointed object to clean the ears.
- Acetic acid ear-drops are sometimes prescribed, which are to be used in the morning, after each swim and at bedtime.

Myth	Reality
It is necessary to regularly clean the ear with ear buds.	Ear-buds or any pointed objects are not to be used for cleaning the ears as they can cause injury and infection.
The wax in the ears is useless and dirty. It needs to be removed.	The wax in the ears is a natural and necessary body secretion which protects the inner ear.
It is good to regularly put oil into the ears.	It is a potentially dangerous habit.

21

Delayed Speech

Scenario

Akanksha is almost 3 years old. Her mother feels that she is not speaking as much as other children of her age.

"Doctor, I feel that she understands most things and follows simple instructions. She speaks around 10–15 common words but doesn't form sentences. She uses a lot of gestures and many words that we don't understand. I think she is more interested in just playing and too lazy to speak. My mother said that I too started speaking late. I guess she has taken after me. Am I right?"

The doctor says, "Yes, it is quite possible that she is just a 'late bloomer' in terms of speech. But I think before arriving at that conclusion, we have to rule out certain common problems … because, if we find out any underlying problem, then we can intervene early to improve her speech and language."

Discussion

Human beings pride themselves on their ability to think, understand and meaningfully communicate. Language represents all forms of meaningful communication, whether through spoken or written words or simply through gestures. Speech is the spoken (verbal) form of language.

Any delay or other problem of speech or language development can seriously hamper a child's daily life, learning and overall ability to reach his or her full potential.

Normal speech and language developmental milestones

Going from a vigorously crying newborn baby to a toddler who hesitantly identifies body parts to the preschooler singing nursery rhymes is a wondrous process of speech and language development which has many milestones. There are wide variations in these milestones, which are discussed in detail earlier in the Growth and Development section.

Here is a quick overview. Vocabulary begins with one-syllable words at 6 months; two or three bisyllable words at 1 year; steadily increases to around 50 words at 2 years; explodes to 500 words by 3 years and reaches up to 2,000 words at 6 years. From 2 to 6 years, the child's ability to form sentences goes from two-word sentences to five-six-word sentences. By 4 years, the child's speech is usually fully understandable.

Common reasons for delayed speech

Natural delay (late bloomer): In this condition, the child's language and understanding are appropriate for the age, but the spoken language lags. The child may use many expressive gestures. At least a slow, gradual development of speech and language (new words as well as better usage) is apparent. There are no other abnormal findings. There may be a family history of delayed speech. With proper intervention, the child will acquire speech normally.

Family factors: Parental neglect, exposure to multiple languages, poor family communication or excessive early exposure to television and gadgets can significantly delay speech development.

Hearing deficit or deafness: This reason should always be ruled out early. Even mild hearing deficit can cause a significant delay in speech and language development. Repeated middle ear infection is one major risk factor.

Auditory processing disorder: In this condition, the child has normal hearing but the brain cannot process the information received correctly. This leads to faulty understanding and expression of language. The problem is especially evident in noisy surrounding, where the person cannot make out subtle differences of sounds in words.

Developmental speech and language disorder: It is a learning disorder in which speech and understanding are both lagging, abnormal and disorderly. These children are at risk for specific learning problems such as dyslexia.

Brain functioning: Any severe problem affecting brain functioning—such as severe prematurity, mental impairment, autism, brain trauma and cerebral palsy—can lead to delayed speech.

Speech production: Any severe problem affecting speech production such as cleft lip, cleft palate, vocal cord paralysis (in muscular dystrophies) hampers speech development.

The chid being tongue-tied or lazy, or the parent doing everything and not giving the child the chance to talk are never reasons for delayed speech.

Signs

Simple guidelines for suspecting delayed speech and seek intervention are to look for the baby's ability to make sounds, respond to sounds and imitate sounds and actions in the 1st year. Later, the child's ability to speak spontaneously, follow commands and acquire new words, concepts and sentence-making skills are things to watch. Observe if the child's speech is progressively becoming clear and understandable not only to caregivers but also to outsiders.

A simple 1-2-3 guideline is that the baby should speak at least one word by 1 year, two-word sentences by 2 years and three-word sentences by 3 years.

Another simple guideline is that 50% of the speech is understandable by 2 years, 75% by 3 years and fully understandable by 4 years.

Warning signals

- In infancy, no cooing or babbling sounds and no response to caregiver's speech
- At 1 year, no two-syllable words and no gestures (bye-bye, pointing at an object)
- At 1½ years, not saying at least one meaningful word, not understanding simple commands, preference for gestures over words and sounds and not imitating words and actions
- At 2 years, only producing a few repetitive and imitative sounds, words and actions; no spontaneous speech; unusual tone of voice (raspy or nasal) and inability to make two-word sentences
- At later ages, vocabulary, sentence-formation, clarity, understandability and conceptual understanding lagging severely behind norms for the age

Management

Parents are best advised to seek medical opinion at the first suspicious sign. The doctor will do a thorough clinical examination, check overall physical and mental development and assess family factors.

Hearing assessment, with specialised tests like audiometry, may be conducted. An audiologist or speech and language pathologist will do detailed specialist assessment of the speech mechanism and development.

After evaluations, correctable factors will be treated, including with speech therapy.

Prevention

Here are some tips for parents to prevent these problems.

- Be aware of your baby's or child's speech and language development milestones.
- Talk to your baby, right from the time she is born.
- Respond to her coos and babbles. Later, when she starts speaking those first short words and sentences, listen attentively and do not interrupt.
- Sing to and play with your baby. Involve her in imitative play activities in which she imitates your words or actions.
- Read books to her. Choose books according to her age and liking. Illustrated books, especially pop-up picture-books, are good choices for early development. Rather than using the popular 'sing-along' books or 'talking' books, read or sing the text to the baby yourself.
- Learn the art of small talk with your child. Talk about everyday activities and never use 'baby talk'. Talk normally using simple words and give the baby enough time to grasp and respond.
- Avoid television, computer and gadget exposure before 3 years of age.

22

Stammering

Scenario

Deepak's mother is ecstatic; his father is surprised. For the last few months, the father has seen his wife anxious or irritable over Deepak's stammering. By the way, Deepak is just 4 years old.

"What happened, dear?" The father asks nervously. There is a hint of a stammer in his speech, too.

"Darling, I just read my heartthrob Hrithik Roshan's interview. He said that he used to suffer badly from stammering. But look, how he has overcome his problem to become Bollywood's superstar! He also said that most stammering patients would improve with proper care. I am sure Deepak will also be perfectly fine!"

Discussion

Stammering or stuttering affects the fluency of speech and is a common childhood problem. Having the right ideas about the child's speech development and knowing the triggers for stammering will help you if your child has the problem.

Stammering

Stammering, which is the same as stuttering, is a defective speech pattern in which the flow of speech is interrupted with unintended stoppages, with repetition, prolongation and non-production of words or syllables. The speech sounds jerky and hesitant. The condition often worsens at certain words and in certain situations.

It is estimated that 1% of people worldwide suffer from stammering. If we only talk of children, 5% of children below the age of 5 years stammer at some point of their life. As many as 80% sufferers are males.

Causes

No one knows the exact cause of stammering. Speech is a complex task, needing an intricate coordination of multiple physical and mental processes. The brain seems to falter at times in stammerers, judging by the fact that their brain scans show significant differences compared to normal individuals.

The strong family history of stammering in sufferers shows that genes must be playing some role.

Some **triggers** for stammering are:

- Stress and anxiety
- Tiredness
- Change of environment
- Parental neglect or excessive expectations, scolding, criticism or controlling attitude
- Speaking in front of audience or authority
- Speaking complex words
- Trying to speak rapidly

Management

Parents should be aware that stammering is common in early development of the child's speech. Speak slowly to your child. Listen to him and don't interrupt while he is speaking or attempting to speak.

Don't set perfect speech as your goal. Accept the occasional stammer and mistake without jumping in to correct or point it out.

Keep the family conversations and atmosphere relaxed. Encourage every positive step and do not make derogatory remarks when the child makes mistakes.

Seek early medical guidance if you think that the stammering is becoming troublesome. There are modern speech therapies which will help control the problem.

23

Headache in Children

Scenario

"But he is only a child. How could he get headaches?" Sanjeev's mother asks exasperatedly. Her 6-year-old son has been complaining of regular headaches, and that is baffling her.

The doctor looks at her with understanding and starts to explain.

Discussion

Many people think that headaches are an exclusively adult problem. In reality, headaches are quite common in children, and any significant headache in a child warrants much more serious evaluation compared to adults.

The main problem in young children is their inability to articulate the exact nature of the headache and associated symptoms. A toddler who is cranky, irritable, prefers the dark and often rubs the eyes or head is likely to be suffering from a headache. Older children are usually able to describe their symptoms.

Causes

Do you know that **migraine** is the most common cause of frequent headaches in children? Migraine in adults has received more than its fair share of publicity, but very few parents are aware of its existence in children.

Tension headache (also called stress headache or psychogenic headache) is another common cause.

Illnesses such as the flu, colds, throat infections, sinusitis, ear infections, eye problems (e. g., refractive errors and squint), dental problems or **depression** are comparatively rare causes.

In children, there is a high possibility of **organic** headaches. These headaches are caused by some serious underlying disorders, often directly linked to brain.

Migraine in children

Migraine has been reported in a child as young as 1 year and as many as 4% of school-age children suffer from it. Below 10 years, it is more common in boys, but later girls are the more likely sufferers.

No one knows the exact cause of migraine. Personality traits, hormonal changes, food allergies and exposure to bright lights or loud sounds have all been blamed.

Migraine is thought to be resulting from an abnormal electrical discharge pattern in some brain cells, which leads to an abnormal blood-flow pattern in some brain areas.

The features of migraine in children are:

- Episodic nature of the headache
- Severe, debilitating, throbbing or pounding pain
- Located in the forehead or temples
- One-sided or two-sided
- Worsened by physical activity
- Associated with nausea, vomiting or abdominal pain
- Hypersensitivity to light or sound (photophobia or phonophobia)
- Duration of 30 minutes to 48 hours

In many cases, the headache is preceded by aura. Aura is a state of unusual immediate premonitory symptoms giving a warning of a coming attack. Aura can be in the form of disturbances of vision (blurring, bright flashes, dark spots or distorted images of objects or own body), vertigo or sensations of tingling or numbness. It usually happens a few minutes before the onset of headache.

Some symptoms such as hyperactivity, increased or decreased appetite, mood changes and sleep disturbances start almost 24 hours before the actual attack. These are called prodromal symptoms meaning prolonged preceding symptoms.

Treatment and prevention

Treating migraine involves controlling acute attacks and also preventing them. Most acute attacks can be managed with common analgesics. Anti-vomiting medicines or specific anti-migraine medicines are needed in some cases.

Prevention involves **avoidance of irritating triggers** that precipitate migraine attacks. Foods like chocolates, nuts, colas, hotdogs and monosodium glutamate (MSG or ajinomoto) in Chinese food; bright lights; loud noises; sun exposure; overexertion; hunger and motion sickness are known to aggravate the condition and should be avoided. In adolescents, care should be taken to avoid alcohol, smoking and oral contraceptives.

Behavioural modification in the form of bio-feedback and self-hypnosis often gives good results.

Preventive medicines are sometimes used when the attacks are too frequent and severe and disrupt routine activities.

Tension headaches

These headaches are caused by involuntary tightening of the muscles of the jaw, the forehead and the back in response to stress and anxiety related to studies, family or friends. They typically occur in older, school-going children. The headaches are neither throbbing nor associated with nausea or vomiting. They are not worsened by exertion. A common description is a feeling of a tight constricting band around the forehead or sometimes the top or the back of the head. A waxing and waning pattern is common in these headaches.

Reassurance, removal of the cause of stress and analgesics are enough to manage most cases of tension headaches. Sedatives and anti-depressants are rarely required.

Organic headaches

Headaches can sometimes be caused by serious underlying conditions, often directly linked to the brain or associated with an abnormal rise in intracranial pressure (the pressure in the skull cavity). Some of these conditions are brain tumours; brain infections; hydrocephalus (abnormal enlargement of brain cavities); internal bleeding, blood clots or malformed blood vessels in the brain; high blood pressure and pseudotumour cerebri (a condition of raised intracranial pressure due to various causes).

Organic headaches are dull, diffuse, generalised, worse in early morning, worsened by coughing, sneezing, straining for stools but improved on standing. They are often associated with early morning vomiting but usually without any nausea. Vomiting often relieves the pain.

Treatment obviously is directed towards correcting the causative disorder.

Guidelines for parents

Never take any headaches in your child lightly. A thorough evaluation by a doctor is a must for narrowing down the list of probable causes, ruling out serious underlying disorders and, if necessary, referrals to other specialists (e. g., ophthalmologist, ENT or dentist).

In certain situations, it is necessary to do detailed investigations like CT (computerised tomography) or MRI (magnetic resonance imaging) of the brain.

The following situations usually merit urgent detailed evaluation:

- Any child of less than 6 years old whose main complaint is a headache
- Increasing frequency or severity of headaches
- Abnormal neurological findings
- Recent or progressive associated symptoms such as fever, drowsiness, neck stiffness, seizures, speech disturbances, visual disturbances, limb weakness or losing balance while walking
- Headache awakening the child from sleep
- Early morning headaches with vomiting
- Recent deterioration in school performance or changes in behaviour or personality
- Growth failure associated with headaches

Myth	Reality
Children do not get headaches.	Headaches are common in children and can happen even at very young age.
Migraine is an adult problem.	Migraine is the commonest cause of headache in children.
Just treat the headache with analgesics and do not bother any further.	Headaches in children need detailed evaluation, much more so than in adults, because some serious causes need to be ruled out.

24

Urinary Tract Infections

Scenario

For the last 2 days, Nandini, a preschooler, has been complaining of pain below her navel. She has been frequently going to the loo and says that whenever she passes urine, it hurts and burns.

Nandini's mother is familiar with these symptoms. She suspects a urinary infection in her daughter and tells her to get ready to see the doctor.

Discussion

The urinary tract consists of kidneys (which form the urine), the ureters (the tubes that carry urine from the kidney to the bladder), urinary bladder (a sac which holds urine for some time) and the urethra (another tube that finally excretes urine outside the body). Infection of any of these parts constitutes a urinary tract infection (UTI).

At least one newborn out of every one thousand suffers from a symptomatic UTI. In infancy, it is more common in boys (particularly those who have not been circumcised) but later more common in girls. By the age of 5 years, 1–2% boys and 8% girls have suffered at least one UTI.

Causes

Most UTIs are caused by bacteria, especially E.coli, a type of germ that normally resides in the intestines. Some UTIs are caused by viruses, fungi and parasites.

Almost 90% of UTI are acquired by the ascending route, that is, they enter from below through the urethra and rise upwards towards the bladder and the kidneys. The rest take the descending route, reaching the urinary tract from some other organ through the bloodstream. Rarely do infections go directly to the urinary tract through a penetrating injury.

Signs and symptoms

In older children, it is easy to guess the presence of UTI when they complain of urinary symptoms like increased frequency or urgency of urination or pain or burning sensation while passing urine. Bed-wetting in a previously 'dry' child, foul smelling urine and abdominal pain are some other pointers.

In infants, it is more difficult to diagnose UTI. They may have vague symptoms like unexplained fever, failure to gain weight, irritability, poor feeding, nausea, vomiting or loose motions.

Types of UTI

UTI could mainly affect the lower urinary tract (bladder and urethra) or the upper urinary tract (kidneys).

Cystitis (bladder infection) is the most common UTI. Urethritis (urethra infection) can occur alone or along with cystitis. Pyelonephritis is an infection involving kidneys, which is less common but much more serious.

Symptoms directly related to urination (frequency, urgency and burning) and lower abdominal pain are more common in cystitis. Systemic symptoms like high fever, chills, vomiting and pain in flanks are seen more in pyelonephritis.

Dangers of pyelonephritis

Acute pyelonephritis can lead to the collection of pus in the kidneys. It could cause life-threatening sepsis. Even after treatment, it could leave behind scars and chronic pyelonephritis which, in rare cases, could even lead to renal failure.

High blood pressure is the most common long-term complication of recurrent or chronic pyelonephritis.

Risk factors for recurrent UTIs are:

- Congenital anatomic problems (of the urinary tract and the spine)
- Chronic constipation causing incomplete emptying of the bladder
- Using bubble baths and strong soaps
- Faulty wiping ('back to front') of urogenital area after using the toilet
- Holding off urine for long periods of time
- Inadequate water or fluid intake

VUR

Due to a valve mechanism, the urine can only pass from above downwards, that is, from the ureters to the bladder and not in the opposite direction. This is the normal process. When the valve mechanism fails, urine can go back from the bladder to the ureters and reach the kidneys. This abnormal backflow is called vesicoureteric reflux (VUR). It is a common risk factor in recurrence of UTIs.

VUR exposes the kidneys to the high pressures generated in the bladder during voiding and also leads to backward passage of the bacteria in the urine.

This is usually a self-limiting condition, but in severe cases it needs surgical correction.

Investigations

In any suspected case of UTI, the most important investigations are lab tests of the urine and blood and certain scans.

The urine is sent to the lab for routine examination and also for a culture and sensitivity test to find the infective organism and determine the antibiotic that will be most effective against it. Blood cultures are taken in febrile or sick UTI patients. Ultrasonography, specialised x-rays and scans are sometimes needed to rule out any congenital anomaly or suspected complication.

Treatment

Any UTI needs prompt and correct antibiotic treatment. Antibiotics are commonly used for a course of 7–10 days in a case of cystitis. For acute pyelonephritis, oral or sometimes intravenous (IV) antibiotics are used for a longer course.

There are certain **precautions** to take after UTI. UTI differs from most other acute infections of childhood in one respect, which is the need for regular follow-up. A repeat urine culture test a week after completing therapy and every 1–2 months for the next 1–2 years is ideal. This is because UTIs tend to recur even in absence of any risk factor. When a risk factor like VUR is present, long-term preventive low dose antibiotic treatment is sometimes needed.

Here are some simple **preventive measures** against UTIs:

- Adequate water or fluid intake
- Regular bladder and bowel voiding habits

- Correct wiping technique (front to back) after using the toilet
- Frequent change of diapers
- Avoiding tight or synthetic underpants
- Avoiding bubble baths and strong soaps
- Check-up at the slightest suspicion

Final word of advice

UTIs are common. They tend to recur. They are often difficult to identify, particularly in infants and small children.

UTIs are sometimes caused by congenital problems. They can lead to serious complications or long-term problems. That is why they need thorough investigations and careful follow-up.

25

Limping in Children

Scenario

Rahul is 3 years old. His father is surprised to see him walk with a limp. Rahul was absolutely fine in the morning, running and jumping all over the house. After getting up from his afternoon nap, he is walking hesitantly. His steps are uneven and unsteady. He is favouring his right leg and dragging his left leg. But outwardly there is no sign of injury or inflammation.

The doctor examines Rahul and says, "Yes, he is definitely limping. Do not worry. Most probably he has hurt his leg without realising it and should be fine after a dose or two of a painkiller. But if he continues to limp, we may need to do a few tests to rule out other causes."

Discussion

Limp is a term used for an uneven and unsteady walking pattern, which is different from the usual walking pattern expected for the age. A child starts walking by 12–15 months and reaches the adult level of proficiency by 3 years. The causes of limping in children vary from minor to serious.

Causes

A child's limp may be a result of pain, unequal length of legs or faulty function or coordination of the nerves and muscles. It is commonly associated with problems of the back, hips, thighs, knees, legs or feet. But sometimes the cause may be a problem in the abdomen or the genitals.

The most common cause for sudden unexpected limping in a small child is an unidentified minor injury. A blister, a splinter or overexertion are among common causes. Usually, such cases produce a sudden painful limp, which is easily treated with a painkiller and by correcting the underlying problem.

Prolonged painful limps with a localised swelling or tenderness in the bones, joints or abdomen need careful evaluation to rule out causes such as internal injury (fracture), infection (osteomyelitis, septic arthritis, toxic synovitis), inflammation (juvenile rheumatoid arthritis) or cancer (leukaemia, lymphoma, bone tumours).

Gradually developing painless limps are often seen with developmental problems of the bones and joints or with some problems of the brain, nerves and muscles.

Tests

If the doctor is unsure of the diagnosis after examination, or suspects a serious cause in a limping child, she will order some common and some specialised blood tests (CBC, ESR, CRP, rheumatoid factor, blood culture, sickle cell test, etc.) and some plain x-rays and some specialised scans (such as ultrasound, bone scan, CT scan or MRI).

Final word of advice

The sudden development of a limp in a small child is often related to a minor, non-apparent injury and responds well to treatment with a painkiller. Careful medical evaluation is needed in case of a limp with a localised swelling or tenderness or a prolonged limp with or without pain. In such cases, we may need to do investigations such as blood tests, x-rays and special radiological scans.

26

Eye Problems

Scenario

Satish is a very inquisitive 7-year-old. His father is an eye specialist.

One day, Satish comes home all excited and says, "Papa, a doctor came to our school today. He was also an eye specialist. He checked the eyes of all the students in my class. He told us that we should get our eyes checked regularly. He also found that some of my classmates are suffering from some eye problems. He was talking about things like lazy eye, pink eye, white eye, near vision, far vision ... Some of my friends are going to use glasses. Papa, you must be doing the same things in your clinic, right? Why don't you tell me things like these?"

Satish's mom saw an opportunity to make her usually quiet husband talk and said, "Dear, look how interested our son is in knowing more about the eyes. Why don't you tell us some things about eyes and their problems?"

The doctor is always happy to talk about these things and wastes no time in delivering a detailed lecture. Whether or not his son and wife understood it, you can learn many interesting things from the lecture. Here is a concise account of this 'family talk'.

Discussion

Regular eye check-ups

Regular eye check-ups are a must to detect and treat eye problems in the early stages, as many eye disorders become irreversible over a period, leading to decreased or lost vision. For a child, eye check-ups should be done as follows:

- Before discharge from the newborn nursery
- At 6 months
- At 3 years

- At 5–6 years before school entry
- At the first sign or suspicion of any problem related to eyes or vision

Methods of eye check-up

In the newborn period and infancy, the doctor checks the eyes for things like infection, cataract, congenital abnormalities and squint. In later visits, the doctor checks for additional problems such as refractive errors and lazy eye.

The examination is carried out in a dark room with a retinoscope or fundoscope, which is an instrument with a light source and a lens that enables the doctor to see whether the light rays are properly focusing on the retina.

To carry out the examination properly, the baby or child may need to be sedated or even anesthetised. This is done to ensure that the child doesn't struggle and remains still to allow a thorough examination. Eye drops may be administered to widen the pupils and relax the eye muscles to allow the doctor to see inside.

At older ages, besides retinoscopy, the near and distant vision charts are used to assess vision.

Development of vision

The newborn baby's vision is weaker compared to normal adult vision. Gradually, vision improves and approaches mature levels. Here is a chart to understand that development.

Age	Vision
Birth to 3 months	Blurry far vision Can see light, shapes and detect movement Not yet learned to use both eyes together, so they may move independently
3 months	Focuses on faces and nearby objects Follows a moving object with eyes Random eye movements are reduced
4 months	Detects nearby objects and reaches out to grasp them
6 months	Visually identifies and distinguishes between objects
2 years	20/60 vision Sees at 20 feet what a normal mature eye can see at 60 feet
2 to 3 years	Progressive improvement to 20/25 vision Sees at 20 feet what a normal mature eye can see at 25 feet

3 to 4 years	Reaches adult visual level of 20/20 Sees at 20 feet what a normal mature eye can see at 20 feet

Squint

Squint or strabismus is a condition in which imbalance in eye muscles causes faulty alignment of the eyes. It could be present at birth (congenital type) or develop later (acquired type). As many as four out of a hundred children have squint.

The eyes of all newborns show 'wandering' or random movements, which is natural and normal. By 3–4 months, these wandering eyes stabilise to move together in one direction. After that age, if the baby's eyes continue to move in different directions (up, down, inward or outward), **congenital squint** is suspected.

The treatment of such squint cases depends on their severity and involves glasses, eye drops or even surgery. The surgery needs to be done early (between 6 and 18 months) in order to let the binocular vision or 'vision through both eyes', develop normally. Even after surgery, glasses may be needed for some period.

Acquired or late-age squints may develop because of an eye injury or any severe visual impairment in conditions such as cataracts or refractive errors. Central nervous system infections and tumours are rare but more serious causes. Any late-age sudden or gradual squints need immediate medical attention and investigations. The treatment depends on the underlying cause.

Pseudosquint is a condition in which the eyes give a false impression of being misaligned, because of a wide nose bridge, epicanthic skin folds or facial asymmetry. Here formal testing does not reveal squint and so no treatment is needed.

Lazy eye

Lazy eye, or amblyopia, is a unique condition seen in about 2% children. The vision from one eye progressively deteriorates because the brain keeps ignoring its images and relies entirely on the other eye for visual information. This happens when the affected eye has a problem such as squint, refractive error, injury or ptosis (droopy eyelid) and the other eye has better vision.

In such a case, the brain receives a clearer image from the better eye and a blurry one from the weaker one, leading to double vision. In order to avoid double vision, the brain starts to ignore the weaker eye's images and uses only the stronger eye's visual information. Over time, the weaker eye stops working actively and becomes 'lazy'. This leads to even further reduction in its visual ability.

The problem needs to be detected before 3 years of age in order to restore normal vision in the weak eye by 6 years. If the problem persists too long (past 7 to 9 years of age), it may lead to total blindness in the weak eye.

The treatment is to make the lazy eye work more and this is done by blocking the vision from the stronger eye, either by covering it with an eyepatch or putting specific eye drops or ointments in it to blur its images. This treatment may be needed over weeks or months and sometimes even for some years.

Red eye

If the whites of the eyes and the insides of the eyelids start looking red, take the child for a check-up. The doctor will consider the following common conditions to determine the cause and prescribe treatment.

Condition	Comments	Treatment
Conjunctivitis (pinkeye)	Commonest cause of red eye Caused by viral or bacterial infections, allergy, chemicals or dryness Typical infective conjunctivitis lasts 7–10 days	Periodic eyewashes with cool water. Eye drops or ointment if necessary. In newborns, treatment must be started urgently as the underlying infection may be serious. To prevent the spread of infection to other family members, frequently wash the hands and avoid direct contact with the patient's eyes.
Eye injury	Caused by penetration, blunt impact or irritation by foreign body	Urgent check-up and treatment by the specialist

Glaucoma	Increased pressure in the eyes as a result of overproduction or inadequate drainage of internal eye fluid.	Urgent check-up and treatment by the specialist Surgery is needed.
Inflammation of important eye structures	Serious conditions such as keratitis, iriditis, cyclitis, iridocyclitis and panophthalmitis Involves inflammation of cornea, iris, ciliary muscles or eyeball as a result of an infection, injury or both	Urgent check-up and treatment by the specialist

The **danger signals** in a red eye are:

- Excessive redness of the eye, swelling, crusting or discharge
- Excessive production of tears
- Severe eye pain
- Reduced vision
- Excessive sensitivity to light (photosensitivity)
- Single eye involvement
- History of eye injury or chemical exposure
- Unequal-sized pupils
- Persistent red eye beyond 1 week
- Hazy or cloudy cornea

White eye

White eye is a white reflection at the centre of the pupils, which is visible directly or in a photograph.

Condition	**Comments**	**Treatment**
Cataract	Commonest cause of white eye Cataract is clouding of the lens, which is the transparent tissue inside the eye that helps to focus light rays on the retina. This condition may be caused by viral infections, metabolic disorders or injury.	Removal of affected lens. Glasses or corrective lenses (first external and then intraocular) along with eyepatch therapy until the eyes are fully mature at about 10 years of age

Reflection of optic nerve head	Light of the camera flash entering the eye at a peculiar angle may cause this white eye which is seen only in some photographs.	No treatment needed as this is just an optical phenomenon.
Vitreous humour conditions	Vitreous humour is a gel-like substance inside the eye. Its faulty embryologic development or bleeding inside it could cause white eye.	Specialised treatment
Eye tumours	Retinoblastoma is a tumour arising in the retina and is a relatively rare but serious cause of white eye.	Specialised treatment
Retinopathy of prematurity	A retinal disorder seen in babies born prematurely	Specialised treatment

Refractive errors of the eyes

Myopia (near-sightedness): This is the commonest vision problem in children in which the parallel rays of light focus in front of the retina. It is often inherited from parents. Contrary to popular belief it is not caused by poor nutrition or excessive reading or television viewing or watching the television at very close distances. The condition is caused by a longer eyeball, forward displacement of the lens or greater than normal refractive power of the cornea or lens.

The symptoms are:

- Blurred distant vision
- Holding books or objects too close
- Preferring to sit near the blackboard in the school

Using concave lenses (spectacles or contact lenses) of sufficient power to provide clear and comfortable vision is the treatment. Since myopia tends to increase in growing years, regular check-ups and corrections are necessary.

Hyperopia (hypermetropia or far-sightedness): The parallel rays of light focus behind the retina. This is caused by smaller eyeball, backward displacement of the lens or less than normal refractive power of the cornea or lens.

In mild cases, the condition is asymptomatic. Eye strain, headache, fatigue, rubbing the eye, eyelid inflammation, indifference to reading matter are typical symptoms. In mild cases, the condition is asymptomatic.

Using convex lenses (spectacles or contact lenses) of sufficient power to provide clear and comfortable vision is the treatment.

Astigmatism: There is irregular refractive power in different planes of the eye as a result of corneal or lens irregularity or an irregularly shaped eyeball.

Mild cases are asymptomatic. Eye strain, headache, fatigue, rubbing the eye, eyelid inflammation, indifference to reading matter, holding books too close are some symptoms.

Using cylindrical lenses of the correct power is the treatment.

Glasses or contact lenses

Glasses with prescription lenses are most commonly used in the treatment of refractive errors. Unbreakable plastic is the preferred material for the frames and lenses of spectacles for small children.

With advanced technology, contact lenses are becoming popular even among children. Contact lenses fit the eye better and offer better optics and hence better vision, especially better peripheral (side) vision. By getting rid of the traditional glasses, they offer a definite cosmetic benefit with a boost in self-image.

Doctors prefer prescribing contact lenses to children over the age of 8 years, who show good motivation and maturity to follow instructions for proper daily wear and maintenance of the lenses.

The decision to use either spectacles or contact lenses should be taken only after a detailed discussion with the doctor, in which the participation and understanding of the young patient is very important.

IX

Something Informal

1

Hand that Rocked the Cradle

Fears confirmed

The laptop monitor flashes. It's taking a long time to download the message.

'That must be the one!' I mutter to myself.

After about 10 minutes, I get the message: 'Three new mails in your inbox.' I look at the name of the sender. It's the one I am expecting. I open the first mail. There are three video attachments. I click the first and a short video clip plays, sending a cold shiver down my spine. My worst fears have been confirmed. A diagnosis has been reached in a baffling case.

A strange case

I won't forget those few moments when I went through all those videos. The sender was the father of one of my patients, and the patient was a cuddly toddler just about to complete two. As her paediatrician, I had been seeing her since she was a 6-month-old baby—a sweet, healthy baby who mostly came to me for routine, 'well baby' vaccination visits. The parents were nice, easy going and friendly, the types with whom you easily lapse into idle chatter about life in general.

The parents' smiling faces had been growing clouded with worry over the last 2 months. Over that period, their visits to the clinic had become alarmingly frequent. The reason was some strange marks that kept appearing and disappearing on baby's skin. Her cherubic face looked strangely puffy. Dark circles appeared below her eyes. The ears were swollen. There were some scratch marks on her chest and fingers. The pattern of the skin rash did not fit any particular allergy or infection. It was like clusters of small superficial bruises. Sometimes they would be on her face, sometimes on the thighs, sometimes on the arms, sometimes on the buttocks and sometimes on the abdomen. One site would clear, and another site would develop the rash. This cycle went on and on in spite of medicines. Laboratory tests had revealed no particular abnormality. I was getting worried, too. Was it a hidden malignancy or some rare skin disease? I pored over reference books and Internet sites to find a clue. After the child's every visit, I would go home and discuss the findings with my wife, who is a dermatologist. But despite all efforts, the diagnosis eluded me. There was one dark possibility, 'child abuse'.

Unearthing the mystery

If someone at home was physically hurting this baby in some way, the strange findings could be explained. Knowing the parents as well as I did, I would have defended them if someone had accused them of child abuse. But both of them were working in offices, and the baby was in the care of a maid. By their second or third visit, I had asked the parents about possible beatings by the maid, but both vouched for her sincerity and efficiency. The only thing they had noticed until then was that the moment the parents arrived home, the baby would cling to them and would just refuse to go to the maid. There wasn't much to read into that observation. Or was there?

I got the child x-rayed to see if I could get any evidence of a bone injury, which is a very common finding in cases of severe physical abuse. All x-rays turned out to be normal, ruling out that method of getting confirmation of my suspicion.

It was decided that we should try and do some surveillance on the housemaid's activities. But it was to be done only after informing her that her activities in their absence were going to be monitored. There was a webcam attached to the computer kept in their hall and that could capture short video clips at regular intervals.

Caught in the act

Two weeks of surveillance bore no fruit, or so the parents thought. There were a number of clips on the computer but none showing anything suspicious on initial viewing. Just before deleting them all, the father decided to go through each clip thoroughly, and there it was. The evidence was staring him in the face. A hideous, horrific slideshow of torture and torment inflicted by a treacherous and vicious adult on a helpless, defenceless child, revealed by the gadget that most people use for sending fun photos and doing live chatting!

The grainy images captured by the webcam showed the housemaid handling the child as if she was a rag doll, rubbing the child's face with a towel so hard that her entire body jerked backwards, pulling her hair tightly, pushing the feeding spoon down her throat, repeatedly hitting her face with a plastic toy. It was a terrorising graphic tale of a savage human being who was entrusted with care of a baby but had instead chosen to harm and hurt her without feeling any pangs of conscience. Once in a while, the maid took care to hide her actions by covering the field of the camera with her back, but on a number of clips she had been caught off guard, which showed that her cruelty had often got the better of her cunning. Only the fact that the child was too young to articulate had saved the maid.

Now everything was clear. The baby's puffiness of face and black eye were a result of repeated facial blows and pushes. The ear swellings were because of pulling and twisting the ear. The scratch marks were made by servant's long nails. The other bruises were all results of various bodily injuries.

The maid was sacked immediately, and her relatives were instructed to repatriate her to her country. The decision was not accepted without a fight, but they had no choice after the parents showed them the evidence, the black deeds captured by webcam.

It was a story that ended happily in the sense that it did not leave any lasting damage in its wake. Just imagine how many more such stories go untold and, worse still, unearthed.

The physical bruises of the child have healed long since. About the bruises on her little mind, we can only hope that they would heal soon. Broken trust about humanity and kindness is hard to mend!

Discussion

Child Abuse

Child abuse is physical or mental injury, sexual abuse, neglect or maltreatment of a child by a person responsible for the child's welfare. The child is defined as anyone under the age of 18 years.

Here are some disturbing global figures from the international body UNICEF.

- On an average, about 6 in 10 children (almost 1 billion in all) between the ages of 2 and 14 are subjected to physical (corporal) punishment by their caregivers on a regular basis.
- Slightly more than 1 in 10 (around 120 million) girls have experienced sexual abuse at some point in their lives.

Likely aggressors

There is no particular profile for a potential child abuser. Anyone who comes into contact with children could be that dangerous, dreadful person.

In 90% cases, the aggressor is a family member, relative or other member of the household; and in around 5% cases, domestic servants or babysitters are involved.

Factors like poverty, unemployment, psychiatric disturbances, drug abuse, marital discord and having suffered childhood abuse themselves makes adults more likely aggressors.

Likely victims

Any child is a potential target for abusers. But handicapped, developmentally challenged, hyperactive, difficult and foster children are more likely sufferers.

Common situations

One of the commonest situations where child abuse can happen is at home where parents commit the crime behind closed doors. But there are a few situations when abuse by other people may happen at the child's home or outside:

- Child left alone with a care-giver for a long time (The care-giver may often be a close relative.)
- Child going for personal tuitions or coaching
- Child staying overnight with a relative or a friend
- Child entering a lift or a public lavatory alone
- Child entering or exiting school-premises or school-bus alone, when other children are not present
- Child lured by gifts, offerings or favours
- Child lured over the Internet chats or social networks

Warning signs

A child who suffers abuse of any form almost always develops psychological problems such as anxiety, depression, aggression, risky behaviour or poor peer or family relationships. So, these may be indications of abuse. Some physical indications are specific to types of abuse as follows:

- ***Physical abuse:*** Unexplained injuries, bruises, fractures, scalds, burns, frequent hospital visits for so-called accidents
- ***Sexual abuse:*** Signs of frank sexual violation, bite marks, genital warts, sexually transmitted diseases, presence of pornographic material, teen pregnancy
- ***Neglect:*** Failure to thrive; smoking, drugs or alcohol abuse

Management

Ideally, cases of child abuse should be managed by adopting a team approach, with the presence and co-operation of paediatricians, psychologists, psychiatrists, social welfare agencies and government authorities.

Always being watchful in regard to this problem, early identification and reporting, immediate withdrawal from the dangerous environment, physical and psychological rehabilitation of the victim and strong legal action against abusers are the steps to manage this menace.

Here are some things socially responsible persons and concerned parents can do to prevent child abuse:

- Be aware that such a problem exists and that it could happen to any child.
- Be alert to detect early warning signs.
- If you suspect such thing happening to your child or any other child, report it to the authorities.
- Teach your children the following basic preventive measures against abuse.
    - Not to let anyone shout at them or use bad language in their presence
    - Not to let anyone physically hurt them
    - Not to let anyone touch their private parts
    - Not to let anyone embrace, fondle, kiss or undress them

- ♦ Not to let anyone share any lewd sexual jokes, images or videos with them
- ♦ Not to let anyone undress in front of them
- ♦ Not to be too friendly with strangers
- ♦ Not to accept any gifts, offerings or favours from strangers
- ♦ Not to accept any online invitations to meet someone outside
- ♦ Not to enter a lift, lavatory or any closed room in the presence of a single stranger if alone

- Teach your child to immediately share any uncomfortable experience with you.
- Form an active group of parents to ensure that the school and residence premises are under tight security surveillance.
- Ensure that a senior teacher (preferably a female) is always present in the school-bus when the children are transported to and from the school.
- Try to create public awareness and pressure groups to ensure that strong legal measures and social support structures are established to address this problem.

Myth	**Reality**
Child abuse is rare.	Child abuse is very common and is happening to millions of children every day.
Child abuse cannot be happening in the homes of good families.	The homes of the outwardly good families are often the very places where such abuse is happening behind closed doors.
Child abuse is mostly a handiwork of an outsider or a stranger.	The majority of child abuse takes place at the hands of a known person, who may even be a parent or a close relative.

2

Saluting the Special Ones

Scenario

"How are you, Jigisha?" I asked.

"I am fine, doctor." The bespectacled girl answered shyly. The words came out hesitantly. The eyes barely made contact.

"So now you are going to school, huh? Do you like your teacher?" I continued.

She nodded.

"What's her name?"

"Amy ma'am."

Her parents looked on beaming with pride. It was a moment to savour for them. Their daughter had grown big. She was engaging in a meaningful conversation with her doctor.

Jigisha is 12 years old. She is now in her second year at a special needs school.

Discussion

As I looked at Jigisha, my mind went back to the past. I remembered the day Jigisha was born. She was a premature baby, born with a crooked backbone and an ill-formed right lung and had been rushed to the hospital in a helicopter to be kept on a ventilator in the NICU (newborn intensive care unit). It was my first time of accompanying a sick patient in a helicopter transfer.

I remembered her stay in NICU—the weeks spent in treatments and tests, the weeks spent hooked to machines and monitors, the weeks spent with tubes and needles stuck into the tiny body, the weeks spent in warding off complications and just keeping her alive.

I remembered the years that followed. The first sad realisation was that Jigisha would always lag behind in terms of physical and mental development. There would always be a series of hospitalisations, a constant stream of complex investigations, futile attempts at finding a valid medical diagnosis, the unfortunate detection of additional physical deformities, serial surgeries to correct those deformities and prolonged recovery phases, physiotherapy sessions, speech therapy sessions and occupational therapy sessions. Trying to find a good special needs school and then trying to fit into it would be challenging.

Jigisha had braved all these challenges. And now, there she was. Sitting in front of me, talking to me one on one. She was a winner.

Then, I look at her parents. Looking at their proud happy faces now, one would not have known what they had gone through over all those years. Anger ... frustration ... despair ... financial troubles ... marital stress ... public humiliation. Nature had dealt them a cruel hand. Modern medicine had not really offered them any diagnosis or cure. But they had fought all these demons and finally triumphed against all odds. The one thing that had kept them going was their unflinching and uncompromising love for their child. It was their tenacity and will that had made Jigisha a winner.

In my mind, I saluted them and millions of other parents of children with special needs. That term covers children with physical, mental or sensory impairments such as cerebral palsy; Down's syndrome; speech, hearing or vision deficits; learning problems; autism and similar conditions. Without the tireless efforts of these selfless, loving souls, their children would never reach their full potential.

Parenting of special needs children is a highly skilled and specialised job. On the surface, it is tiring, frustrating and unrewarding. But believe in my practice, when it comes to special needs children, I have only seen parents who give every ounce of their love, affection and energy to help their children improve and to prepare them to take on the world. They keep doing it day after day, year after year, in some cases even knowing fully well that even minor improvement may be impossible leave alone full recovery. These parents' positive attitudes, uncomplaining acceptance and untiring efforts centred on their special needs child—and most of all their priceless smiles—have never ceased to amaze me.

For me, the parents are special ones. They are the parents who truly teach us what parenting is all about. It is about giving unconditional love and lifelong care to children.

Fact File

The term 'special needs children' is used for children who have any physical, sensory or mental (intellectual or psychological) impairments significant enough to hamper them from achieving their full individual potential.

Terms like disabled or handicapped are often used to describe such children or adults, but such terms are best avoided because they are discriminatory and excluding in nature. Instead, such persons are now referred to as children with special challenges or as differently abled children.

A 2009 UNESCO report had these facts:

- Worldwide, there are about 650 million people with disabilities.
- This represents 10% of the global population and more than 20% of the world's poorest population.
- Children with disabilities experience stigma from birth and are more prone to exclusion, concealment, abandonment, institutionalisation and abuse.
- Mortality rate amongst such children is 80%.
- 98% of such children in developing countries never attend school.

Some common causes of disabilities are:

- Cerebral palsy
- Mental retardation
- Congenital deformities of bones or organs
- Down's syndrome and other conditions with chromosomal or genetic abnormalities
- Problems of speech, hearing or vision
- Any major chronic illness requiring prolonged care
- Learning problems such as dyslexia
- Social problems such as parental neglect, child abuse or extreme poverty
- Autism
- Psychological or behavioural problems such as anxiety, depression, attention deficit hyperactivity disorder

Challenges for parents

Parents of special needs children experience emotional and psychological burden. They experience feelings such as: Why me? How will I manage? I can't cope with it! I can't accept my child!

There are financial burden due to the cost of medicines, hospitalisations, special therapies and special education.

Sibling rivalry can become complicated because the normal child may feel jealous of the extra attention showered on the special needs child.

The family may experience social alienation if they stay away from friends, relatives and other people out of embarrassment or the bitter realisation that no one really cares!

A child's difficulties put a strain on the relationship between parents. There may be marital discord due to the constant stress, lack of personal space and time and different perspectives on how to deal with the child's problem.

Strategies

Here are a few strategies to improve the current situation of special needs children and their parents:

- Making specialised care easily available and affordable
- Support groups that bring together parents of various special needs children
- Correcting the underlying social, environmental or economic factors
- Compassionate involvement of government and society in general
- Co-operation among international bodies tackling these issues

3

Parental Fights and Children

Recently I received a phone call. The woman journalist at the other end wanted to know my opinion on parental fights and their effect on children. Her question set off a chain of thoughts in my mind about this all-important issue in parenting. Here are some of those thoughts.

Parental Fights

Why parents fight is relatively easy to understand. The modern lifestyle, where both parents are busy working outside the home, is often the main culprit. With both parents spending long hours in commuting to work and actually at work, it is but natural that tending to children becomes a chore. The division of labour—who does what—becomes the main flash point of fights.

When both parents are not working, there is often the tendency of one parent to dominate the other in matters of how the children should be reared and how the workload should be shared. In the long term, this behaviour spawns resentment in the other parent, leading to arguments and fights.

Among other causes of parental fights are financial problems, disputes over in-laws and relatives, alcohol or drug abuse, health problems, intellectual or physical incompatibility, infidelity and emotional immaturity.

What form parental fights take—sullen silences, noisy quarrels, or violent beatings—depends on the social, cultural and mental make-up of the parents.

Effect on children

A secure, happy and loving home environment is the protective cocoon in which children grow up to be positive and productive adults. Parental fights, if frequent and severe, break this protective cocoon and that seriously affects children's well-being.

Children end up being neglected and feel insecure. They are often forced to take sides, which leaves them confused. The mental scars of serious parental fights often stay with children for a long time well into their adulthood.

Anxiety, depression, suspicion, paranoia, inability to positively interact and bond with people may be found in such children.

Solution

There is no one-size-fits-all solution to the problem of parental fights and their ill effects on children. Every family's situation needs to be tackled on an individual basis. Each case is different and should be handled differently.

Parents should know that trust and love is the bond binding the family together, and they should make sure that their interaction sends the right signals to their children.

It is natural to have a few skirmishes between parents in daily life's stress, but parents should make sure that, as far as possible, they should have their fights in private, away from children's inquisitive eyes and ears.

Raised voices and raised hands are not the right tools to raise children!

4

Parental Stress

Anger and anxiety. Doubts and despair. Fears and frustrations. Stresses and strains. Has life become too complicated for today's parents? If what I see in my routine practice as a paediatrician is any indication of a social trend, the answer has to be a very disturbing 'yes'.

Parenting in today's fast-paced world presents unique problems, and although their solutions are not easy to find, it is important to identify these problem areas to devise a strategy to tackle them. What I am going to discuss here is not based on any social study reports but is just a personal reflection.

Time factor

The traditional roles of parents—the father as the provider and the mother as the nurturer—have become obsolete. Both parents working outside the home is now a rule rather than an exception in an urban household. Although this has made for more economic freedom for the family, the time together has been a casualty.

Television has already taken up a big chunk of family time and now computers, mobile phones and other gadgets have brought office work into the home, further reducing family interaction.

This time constraint is so severe that parents often find themselves struggling to balance career and child-rearing, with little or no time for pursuing their own interests and hobbies that are so important for self-development.

Lack of support

Disintegration of the joint family structure has taken away the role of elder relatives like grandparents in child care and development. Young, inexperienced parents find themselves unsupported and lonely in this respect. Even handling minor illnesses or other problems in the family often induces a panic that could have been calmed by a soothing word from an older family member.

Relying on housemaids or unqualified day-care providers (babysitters) is an accepted norm for working parents. Practically none of these carers have the capability to offer quality care. The time the child spends with these caregivers usually proves unproductive developmentally as emotional attachment is often lacking.

Economic considerations

House rents, utility bills, school fees, medical care costs ... The amount of money required nowadays just for subsistence of a family is substantial, and I am excluding savings and the occasional indulgences. Meeting these demands often means working more and devoting less time to oneself and one's family. It also means that both parents will have to work.

Educational load

Take a look at the number of textbooks and notebooks, or heft your child's heavy school bag, to understand the woeful tale of today's education system. The seemingly impossible load of information today's school kids are expected to cram into their brains gives the parents a headache. Teaching unfamiliar subjects to kids, helping with their homework and preparing them for exams are testing tasks for any parent.

Faulty health concepts

I see most of today's parents as obsessively health conscious as regards their children's health. It may be a direct result of the small family phenomenon. Parents are bothered by the slightest variation from the normal routine and often worry about non-existent health problems. Even in this age of information-explosion, their medical knowledge is inadequate. Most of their medical concepts are half-baked amalgamations of their own ideas and those of their equally ill-informed relatives and friends.

Most parents expect medicines for every possible complaint and are skeptical of the importance of preventive measures. Web searches have become their main sources of health education, but they often fall prey to false or incomplete information.

Attitude problems

Day by day, more and more importance is being placed on the materialistic aspect of life. 'Success at any cost' and 'wealth is health' seem to be the mottos of the new age. Parents are pushing their children to go faster, higher and longer right from the word 'go'. Improbable goals are set and immeasurable pressures are put on oneself and the child.

Looking on the lighter side of life has almost become a thing of the past. A too serious outlook on life has become commonplace. The fact that people need laughter clubs to laugh is an indication of this unhealthy outlook.

Solution

Life has become one big pressure cooker with a dysfunctional safety valve for all people, but more so for parents who have to think of their children's future. I don't really think I have the authority or the experience to offer a solution to such a complex and global social problem. But as a socially conscious individual in the medical field, seeing stress taking its toll mentally as well as physically on families, I feel it my duty to at least point out the problem areas. Each family has its own set of problems that will have to be dealt with judiciously through a concerted effort by all family members. What kind of role model we choose to be for our children today will decide the shape of things to come tomorrow.

5

Good Manners

'Sorry', 'excuse me', 'please', 'thank you'—are these words going out of the dictionary? Is politeness going away for good? Are good manners on the road to extinction?

Looking at contemporary behavioural patterns of children and adults, I have often wondered about these questions. I haven't been to the rural areas for quite a while and so don't know much about the current social trends there. But my city life has certainly showed me one thing clearly: Slowly but surely, today's urban people are forgetting or sometimes even actively rejecting good manners.

Surf the Internet for an hour, and you will find thousands of rude, arrogant and obnoxious comments on major websites. Most of the people writing them are hidden behind the cloak of anonymity, though. They write as ABC25 or XYZ72. Even in real life, people are often displaying the rude side of their personality without any regret or remorse. Shouting at the top of the voice at a restaurant waiter for spilling water or giving a dressing down to an employee in front of his fellow workers are considered signs of being aggressive, which is seen as being in tune with the changing times. A simple social smile is becoming an obsolete trend! Being polite, being nice is being perceived as being weak and meek, and today nobody wants to be in that category.

The rot begins right at the top, and parents are often responsible for passing on these behavioural patterns to their children. Far too much importance is placed on reaching the top, even if by shamelessly pushing and pulling those ahead in the queue. This success-at-any-cost attitude may very well propel a person to the top, but it will also leave the person quite lonely up there. After all, not everything in life can be measured in money.

From my personal experience, I can definitely claim that 'nice people finish last' is just another myth. You can be nice and still develop the firm resolve and mental toughness necessary to succeed in life. Politeness, a smiling face and good manners often open unexpected doors and windows of opportunities. Using foul, aggressive language doesn't make you an achiever; it just makes you a loser, one who loses out on potential friendships and fruitful relationships.

6

Terrorism and Us

With a silent prayer in my heart, I read the front page news report about yet another bomb blast ripping apart dozens of people. The accompanying gruesome images were difficult to forget. An inconsolable mother wailing at the loss of her young daughter, a wounded man looking helplessly at the mangled body of his dead friend, a restaurant hall destroyed beyond recognition. It seemed as if the ugly reality of terrorism was looking me square in the face with a wicked smile.

From Mumbai to New York and from London to Hyderabad, international terrorist acts have become far more frequent and far more destructive over the last few years. The so-called war on terror has not only miserably failed to contain the menace of terrorism but, in fact, has served to escalate it to unimaginable proportions. No country and no city can be considered safe from this threat today. That is why it is imperative that today's parents and care-givers try to make the young ones understand this complex worldwide phenomenon.

There might be different political, ideological and economic conflicts at the surface, but on careful scrutiny, it becomes clear that religious strife has been the single common denominator of global terrorism. Advances in technology have shrunk the world. Television, the Internet and mobile phones have made it easy to disseminate information (and also misinformation) to any corner of the world. This technological advancement has played into the terrorists' hands. Spreading hatred and malice through misrepresentation of facts has been an age-old technique in covert wars, and it has now become easier with the speed and reach of modern information technology. By portraying terrorists as 'religious warriors' and terrorist acts as 'religious duties,' these misinformation campaigners have managed to cleverly manipulate modern media to perpetrate their 'ideology of violence' into immature, malleable minds.

As geographical and political boundaries become increasingly obsolete in this world of globalisation, it is important for all of us to understand that building walls and fences between people in the name of religion has been a typical terrorist ploy. The purpose of any religion is to build bridges between people, not to create obstructions. Every religion has been built on principles of the innate goodness of human beings. Fraternity, compassion and empathy are the cornerstones of all religions and sects. Those preaching or practicing violence in the name of religion can never be considered as true followers or believers of any religion.

It is very natural for any individual and any community to feel proud of their racial, regional or religious characteristics. But while maintaining that pride, every individual and every community must also understand, accept and respect the diversity of human cultures. This broad-minded attitude of tolerance and respect towards differences in ethnic background, ideological viewpoint and cultural practices should be instilled in the minds of young children by the parents and teachers right from the beginning.

Mahatma Gandhi once said, "An eye for an eye would turn the whole world blind." That remains true today. Unless the concept of universal brotherhood is inculcated in the minds of the young, we run the risk of making monsters out of our own children and creating a new generation of terrorists in our homes. After all, terrorists are not an alien species; they too were born as human beings but then turned into heartless, inhumane creatures for want of the right kind of guidance in their formative years.

Race, region and religion have always been important facets of our mental make-up. Now let's add 'reason' to that list.

7

Teaching Good Values

As a parent, one has the responsibility of instilling the right values in one's children. With the world becoming an increasingly complex place professionally, morally and ethically, it is a real challenge to find good values that would be relevant in contemporary times.

The outlook on life is bound to be different in different families, and that would obviously reflect in their values. But still, the basic core values remain the same across countries and cultures.

Here are a few tips from me.

Identity

Our family lineage, community, language and traditions give us a sociocultural identity. What we achieve in our lives gives us an individual identity. Both these identities are important and should be nurtured carefully.

We should do everything we can to preserve our sociocultural identity. Changing times and practices may make us look at it in a different light, which may be unfavourable at times. But in the heart of our hearts, we should be proud of this identity. We should always bear in mind that, because of these roots, we are what we are today.

Relationships

We human beings are social animals, and our relationships with family, friends, workmates and others form the very basis of our lives. Each relationship offers us something different. Together, all of them greatly contribute towards our success and sense of fulfilment. One simple rule for making any relationship work is to value it regardless of the power, position or possessions of the other person. Relationships formed on the basis of such petty materialistic considerations never last long.

That is why you should always teach your children to understand and appreciate the value of each and every relationship in life.

Respect

People usually get it right when it comes to respecting their own cultural, linguistic or religious identity. They also get it right when it comes to respecting their own individuality and individual rights. But they err in equating that self-respect to an arrogant intolerance of anything that does not conform to their own views.

Respecting our own self and respecting others are not contradictory values; they are complementary to each other. Just because we feel it is right to do something in one particular way, it doesn't mean that others are wrong in doing it in some other way. There are going to be multiple perspectives, and we should respect them even when we do not agree with them.

We gain respect when we give respect.

Care

The word 'care' has many meanings. If it means showing concern, it also means attending to someone or something. Both these meanings should be taught when teaching about 'care'.

Caring for people, work or causes gives our life meaning, and taking care to understand, plan and execute a project ensures that we increase our chances of success.

Compassion

Compassion is a unique human trait that makes us understand people's sufferings and prompts us to do our bit to help them. Unfortunately, many of us are becoming so engrossed in our selfish pursuits in life that we are becoming desensitised to other people's pains and misfortunes. This can change only if we teach our kids to rise above our selfish motives and be kind and sensitive to others.

Courage

We are going to face adverse situations in life when we would need to stand up for what is right. The situation may be personal or social. We should have enough courage to stand up for what is right. Courage has nothing to do with physical or economic strength. It just needs mental strength and a strong belief in the rightness of your cause.

Dream

Encourage your children to dream. Tell them: 'No dreamer is ever too small and no dream is ever too big! Unless you imagine it, you can't do it. Dreams are ideas waiting to happen.' But also make it clear to them that just dreaming is not enough. One has to work in the real world to turn dreams into reality.

Effort

The famous inventor Thomas Alva Edison once said, "Genius is one percent inspiration, ninety-nine percent perspiration." What he meant was simple. Just a brilliant idea is not enough. It needs a lot of hard work to make things happen.

No effort is too much if we really want to achieve something, and we should be prepared to put it that effort to attain our goal.

Passion

Passion is to feel strongly about something. It is the spark that fires up our lives. Without passion, life becomes dull and dreary. Passion about any worthy cause provides the drive and energy to achieve great things in life.

Patience

What we want or aim for will not happen overnight. Dreams and desires take time to develop into realities. Patience is the ability to wait during that time. Impatience makes you do rash things and leads to defeats and disasters.

Perseverance

Sometimes, when we are not getting a project right in the first attempt, we should be prepared to work on the same things over and over until everything falls into place. We should not lose heart and drop the project midway. This is the quality of perseverance and is an amalgamation of patience, commitment and determination.

Integrity

All our dreams, passion, patience, perseverance and efforts would mean little if we don't have the integrity to follow our ideals and stand up for them. Underhand dealings and unfair practices have become the norms in contemporary public life and are often touted as the easy ways to success. But we don't have to follow those corrupt ways to reach the top. Success does come our way if we are honest to ourselves, our work and our society, and such success is always cherished more.

Final word of advice

As I said earlier, depending on your own background, there could be many other values which you would want to inculcate in your children, but these particular values, to me, represent the core values in every individual's mental make-up.

If I have to summarise this advice, I will say:

Teach your children to spread their wings and fly to great heights, but ensure that they never lose their roots in the soil!